Journal of a Tamed Bureaucrat

NILS A. OLSEN AND THE BAE, 1925–1935

edited by RICHARD LOWITT

THE IOWA STATE UNIVERSITY PRESS, *Ames*

JOURNAL OF A

Tamed Bureaucrat

NILS A. OLSEN AND THE BAE, 1925–1935

To the memory of
ALLAN NEVINS *and* HOWARD K. BEALE,
mentor and friend who also edited diaries

Richard Lowitt is professor and chairman, Department of History, Iowa State University. Besides this book, he is author of the three-volume biography of Nebraska Senator George W. Norris, and of other publications in the field of history.

Frontispiece: NILS A. OLSEN. *Courtesy, Iowa State University Library. Special Collections Department.*

Composed and printed by The Iowa State University Press, Ames, Iowa 50010

First edition, 1980

Library of Congress Cataloging in Publication Data

Olsen, Nils Andreas, 1886–
    Journal of a tamed bureaucrat.

    Bibliography: p
    Includes index.

    1. Agriculture and state—United States—History. 2. United States. Bureau of Agricultural Economics. 3. Olsen, Nils Andreas, 1886–   I. Lowitt, Richard, 1922–
II. Title.
HD1765 1925.044   353.008′233′0924 [B]   79-20342
ISBN 0–8138–0930–4

C O N T E N T S

FOREWORD

Nils A. Olsen was a man of action, full of energy and competitive. As head of an outstanding federal bureau in the late 1920s and early 1930s he was in the center of one of the most important policy battles of this country—government aid to agriculture. It was Olsen with his high-caliber group of farm economists who urged Agriculture Secretary Hyde to persuade President Hoover to cut the farm surplus by taking marginal farmland out of production. Then after 1932 it was a beleaguered Olsen who tried to persuade Agriculture Secretary Henry A. Wallace into a less radical farm program. In this Diary we see how Olsen reported his ups and downs as he played his role in the making of farm policy during the turbulent years 1925–1935.

Olsen was a scrapper, a fighter for his Bureau and his ideas. Of this I can testify from actual experience because I worked for him; he hired me as an assistant agricultural economist in the fall of 1926. My assignment was to study the financial problems of the livestock ranchers of Montana. Many of these ranchers were complaining bitterly to their congressmen that the Federal Intermediate Credit Bank of Spokane, established in 1923 to help farmers and ranchers, had failed to aid them. Olsen received the complaints from the congressmen and in his typical method of seeking evidence took me to Montana, introduced me to the leading banker in Miles City, the center of the complaints, got the banker to open his loan files, and told me to go to work. Nine months later, after working in the banks, interviewing ranchers, and working with the officials at the Spokane Credit Bank I sent my report to Nils Olsen. The report indicated that most of the complaining ranchers were either hopelessly broke or beyond rescue unless their debts could be scaled down. But the study also showed that the Spokane Credit Bank was unduly tight in making only "gilt-edge" loans. Olsen wanted my report released but was unable to get the Treasury Department's Farm Loan Board which supervised the Intermediate Credit Banks to agree. He put up a good fight but couldn't budge Andrew Mellon's Farm Loan Board. I resigned at the end of a year to take a position at Iowa State College, admiring the energetic, personable Olsen but despairing of the frustrations in a career in a government bureau.

The Diary is exciting and revealing. You can put yourself in Olsen's shoes as he gets a call from Secretary of Agriculture Arthur Hyde to get material ready in an hour for him to use at a hastily called cabinet meeting by President Hoover. Or you will find yourself listening to Olsen and Oeveste Granducci (of the Kiplinger staff) in a confidential chat in which Granducci is pumping Olsen for tidbits to use in the Kiplinger Agricultural Letter.

Best of all you can get in on those intimate morning chats between Olsen and Secretary Wallace as they walked from Wallace's residence at the Wardman Park to their offices at the Department of Agriculture several miles away. These morning walks, initiated by Wallace in March 1933 as Olsen reports, "he (Wallace) said 'how would you like to meet me at the Wardman Park Hotel about 7:15 and walk down to the department?' " Olsen reports on these walks with pithy comments on Wallace until early 1934 when the walks ended. Why did Wallace continue for almost a year these morning walks with Olsen who did not share his policy views? Was it because he wanted to test his views against those of Olsen? Was it to get Olsen's ideas on the day-to-day running of the department? Or was it because he liked Olsen's fighting spirit or wanted a continuation of a friendship which began when Olsen, a close friend of his father, Henry C. Wallace, had worked with him in completing his father's book manuscript after his death, *Our Debt and Duty to the Farmer?* Your reading of the Diary may supply a clue to the answer.

Readers of these Diary excerpts need to be forewarned. This is not a continuous story from 1925 to 1935 and it is definitely one-sided. You will have to read elsewhere to fill in the gaps in the formation of governmental farm policy. You will find yourself caught up by Olsen's comments on the struggles with the Department of Commerce and President Hoover over the Foreign Agricultural Service but you do not find the outcome of the battle in the Diary. Actually it was won by Olsen, for in 1930 Congress finally established the FAS in the Bureau of Agricultural Economics.

However, Olsen's Diary does give you an intimate view of inside power struggles on farm policy, insights not to be had elsewhere. But the reader must remember that the views expressed are those of Nils A. Olsen and no one else. You are getting only one side of what in many instances, is a many-sided, fascinating story.

The original Olsen Diary notes were a long way from final printer's copy. Richard Lowitt's familiarity with the congressional scene gained from years of researching and writing for his definitive books on Senator George W. Norris placed him in an excellent position for the hard task of judging and selecting the pertinent passages to be included. The footnotes identify the large number of individuals referred to and in the background statement Lowitt sets the stage for the Diary.

A final note on how the Olsen diary became available is in order. Back in 1965 I received a telephone call from Nils's sister, Anna, asking my advice about some papers of her brother that had been given to her after his death. My suggestion after looking at the papers and finding that they included a diary was to have them deposited in the Iowa State University Library for safe keeping, which was done. At the time, I recognized the historical value of the Diary but then with the pressure of other events I forgot all about them until Lowitt, a newcomer to Iowa State, uncovered them in searching the files of the library's Special Collections.

WILLIAM G. MURRAY

Iowa State University
Ames, Iowa
March 1, 1979

DIARY

INTRODUCTION

Agriculture in the 1920s and 1930s was a central issue in American history, primarily because the collapse of the American economy in the 1930s was foreshadowed by declining farm prices and rural depression in the 1920s. Farm spokesmen and concerned officials during this decade devoted much of their time and effort to grappling with the dilemma of overproduction and declining prices and to finding ways and means of placing the rural sectors of the nation on a more nearly equal basis with the industrial and urban areas which, with some notable exceptions, were experiencing greater prosperity. The Department of Agriculture, the House Committee on Agriculture, and the Senate Committee on Agriculture and Forestry were the main groups in government focusing on the plight of agriculture; and the Department of Commerce under Herbert Hoover quickly involved itself. Later in the decade, Hoover, as president, offered his own solution to the farm problem.

Crucial questions cast within the parameters of the plight of agriculture were raised in this period. As the farm depression became more acute and melded at the end of the decade into a general depression affecting the entire economy, suggestions became more extreme because of desperation and the realization that more drastic solutions seeking better balance in relation to the American economy were necessary to set the rural sectors of the nation on the road to recovery. The questions revolved around the role of government in facilitating the agrarian economy: Should government make credit more easily available? Should it encourage cooperation and assist in marketing crops both at home and abroad? Should it encourage better land use by further closing the public domain and exhorting farmers to diversify their production? Should it take further and more drastic steps to curb production and reduce the surplus in an effort to increase prices? Questions such as these were crucial in that they challenged prevailing views regarding the role of government in the operation of the economy. Most Americans by this time were willing to accept government interference to curb "the malefactors of great wealth" (Theodore Roosevelt's phrase); to limit the concentration of wealth; or to regulate abusive conditions affecting some natural resources, public health, safety, and welfare. But thus far government had shown little inclination to interfere with or to guide and encourage particular practices within an industry to raise prices and avoid social deterioration. In the past these problems were left to private sectors to resolve in ways that corporate managers, powerful bankers, and their allies in the political structure found satisfactory. Now, however, the national government recognized a critical situation affecting American agriculture and sought to remedy the situation. A fundamental change in outlook had occurred. What had to be worked out within this new context was an approach that would begin to alleviate rural depression.

In 1920 the Department of Agriculture, created during the Civil War and granted cabinet status in 1889, was an effective and efficient organization devoted to improving production and to scientific research. By the time of the First World War, according to a recent study, the department was "the world's outstanding scientific research institution."[1] During the tenure of Henry C. Wallace, Warren G. Harding's secretary of agriculture, the department was led by a man keenly aware that new approaches were necessary to cope effectively with the increasingly distressing farm situation which quickly became evident as wartime agricultural prosperity faded. Farmers, as their contribution to the war effort, had increased production to provide food and fiber for enhanced military and civilian needs both at home and abroad. Although their profits were low compared to other sectors of the American economy and were circumscribed by price regulations, farmers had met

1. Wayne D. Rasmussen and Gladys L. Baker, *The Department of Agriculture* (New York, 1972), p. 12.

3

all the demands imposed on them. Now with the loss of overseas and military markets and saddled with debts incurred in expanding their production, they found that domestic demand—owing to improved technology, dieting, and a more sedentary existence for increasing numbers of urban dwellers—was also declining.

As secretary of agriculture, Henry C. Wallace was aware of and sympathetic to increasing calls for action to meet the farm crisis. In addition, Herbert Hoover, as secretary of commerce, was vitally interested in the farm problem. He had headed the Food Administration during the war period and was in charge of overseas war relief. His primary responsibility was with distribution, and he carried this concern with him into the Department of Commerce where he became the leading opponent of Wallace's growing concern for federal aid for agriculture. Moreover, the American Farm Bureau Federation created in 1919 and fashioned from local groups, many of which had been established by county agents in the course of their extension work, was calling for federal assistance and found congressional support among representatives and senators from the rural regions. Some agricultural measures were enacted—extending further controls over meat packers, regulating the trade in grain futures, eliminating cooperatives from the provisions of the antitrust laws—but none came to grips with the dilemma of the surplus. And those that were introduced met continual presidential opposition. The most notable was expressed in the McNary-Haugen bills, designed to provide equality for agriculture by providing parity through the overseas sale of surplus production. The complicated two-price mechanism—a competitive price at home and a lower price abroad— found support in the Department of Agriculture among economists in the Bureau of Agricultural Economics established in 1922 by Secretary Wallace, who brought able young researchers and economists into the department. The domestic allotment plan, which proposed to pay producers to limit crop production, was formulated in the department and found some support in the bureau. It was further developed and advocated as an alternative to the McNary-Haugen proposals by a small but able group of agricultural economists, chiefly academicians. Since no secretary endorsed the allotment plan, proponents within the department could not openly champion it without risking their careers.

Secretary Wallace, interested in possible programs involving broader federal intervention in the interest of agriculture, called a national conference in 1922 to explore ways and means of dealing with the farm crisis. But the balance he provided against the more moderate approach of Hoover, who stressed federal encouragement of cooperative marketing, disappeared with his death late in 1924, and Hoover's views predominated for the rest of the decade. Calvin Coolidge's secretary of agriculture, William Jardine, allied himself with Hoover in encouraging cooperatives and opposing any involvement of government with the price mechanism. And when Hoover became president, Congress translated his views into what he considered an effective solution. The Federal Farm Board, through a program of loans to cooperatives, would promote the orderly marketing of farm products. To control the surplus, loans would be made to cotton and wheat stabilization corporations organized by the cooperatives. Hoover's secretary of agriculture, Arthur M. Hyde, loyally supported the Federal Farm Board even though it created difficulties within his department. The Federal Farm Board, like the Agricultural Adjustment Administration which followed it, was concerned with immediate pressing problems and staffed in many instances with key personnel from bureaus within the department, which played a more passive role in the shadow of the action agency.

This situation, involving in effect a second Department of Agriculture, became more pronounced with the advent of the New Deal when the necessity for federal action to raise prices was almost self-evident, owing to the dismal failure of President Hoover's approach to seriously affect the desperate plight of agriculture within the context of a general depression affecting all sectors of the American economy. Within his first one hundred days in office President Franklin D. Roosevelt signed the Agricultural Adjustment Act "to relieve the existing national economic emergency" by the then drastic step of seeking to support prices by having farmers adjust production to demand. Among other things it created an action agency, the Agricultural Adjustment Administration (AAA) within the department. The secretary of agriculture, to restore farm puchasing power, gained the authority to secure voluntary acreage reduction by paying farmers to limit production of basic crops. He also secured authority to regulate marketing through voluntary agreements and to license processors and others servicing agricultural commodities for the purpose of eliminating unfair prices and practices. In this connection he could also determine the rate of processing taxes which would help meet the cost of the program.

Henry A. Wallace thus helped bring into being what his father and others were suggesting in the 1920s: namely, that production must be limited if price levels were to be raised and that government must play a role in this process. The approach championed by Herbert Hoover—that prices are the result of conditions affecting supply and demand and that the best way to secure fair prices was through individually adjusted production and expanding markets—was now markedly modified if not reversed. This shift in viewpoint caused most of the individuals engaged in research and educational and service work in the field of agriculture to modify their views to keep abreast of the New Deal as it affected American agriculture. Those who could not adjust their thinking to this shift in outlook became dissatisfied, critical, and even hostile.

As Franklin D. Roosevelt's secretary of agriculture, Henry A. Wallace had to hurriedly organize and staff an agency to meet situations demanding immediate and drastic action. Because the Agricultural Adjustment Act was approved after the 1933 crop planting season had begun, it was not until 1934 that the AAA and its various programs began to fully affect American agriculture. By that time the agency and the entire Department of Agriculture abounded in tension and confusion. Once again old-time bureau chiefs complained about loss of personnel to the new action agency, which in effect, like the Federal Farm Board, functioned as a second department of agriculture. Whereas Hyde had reservations about the Federal Farm Board and sympathized with both the criticisms and plight of his bureau chiefs, Wallace endorsed the AAA and then sought to fashion it so that it reflected his own views and those of his closest advisers. During the early New Deal the Department of Agriculture was an exciting, challenging, and confusing place in which to work. It housed spokesmen for a wide range of views, touching all points on the political spectrum, on how to cope with agricultural problems in their broadest manifestations. Individuals with little practical farm experience now occupied important posts, and Wallace listened and often accepted their views. Old-line bureau chiefs, many of whom served under Henry C. Wallace, at first were delighted when his son became secretary of agriculture. Many quickly became disillusioned and then hostile as the secretary ignored them while focusing his concerns on the AAA. Such a bureaucrat was Nils A. Olsen, chief of the Bureau of Agricultural Economics.

This bureau came into operation on July 1, 1922, by combining the Bureau of Markets and Crop Estimates and the Office of Farm Management and Farm Economics. It became the economic research bureau of the department—conducting investigations in the costs of production and marketing, farm organization, farm financial relations, farm labor, agricultural geography and history, land economics, and the problems of rural life. The bureau also acquired and disseminated information concerning marketing and distribution of farm and nonmanufactured food products, and it was a storehouse for the collection and dissemination of statistical data relating to agricultural production. A publication program was inaugurated, making the results of its research easily available. In addition, information was also secured and published pertaining to the supply of and demand for agricultural products in foreign countries. Weekly summaries and analyses embodying current statistics on acreage, yield, condition and production of crops, numbers of livestock, and value of farm products were required along with a weekly review of weather conditions. The bureau continually sought to improve methods of data gathering, reporting, and forecasting.

The Bureau of Agricultural Economics provided staff for a market inspection service at many of the principal producing and receiving centers throughout the country. It also conducted the regulatory work performed in connection with the enforcement and administration of several such pieces of legislation as the Cotton Futures Act, the Warehouse Act, and the Grain Standards Act. With its varied responsibilities, it became the largest and most important bureau within the Department of Agriculture.

In 1925 Olsen became assistant chief of the Bureau of Agricultural Economics. He was promoted in 1928 and he resigned in 1935. During Olsen's tenure, as the entries indicate, some of its functions were modified and reduced; in one important area—the Foreign Agricultural Service—it expanded, despite Herbert Hoover's intense opposition. Basically, however, its functions focused in three areas—production, marketing, and general service—designed to assist farmers, consumers, and others in their production and marketing plans.

Olsen's tenure covered a critical period in the history of American agriculture and he was involved in agricultural politics during an equally critical transitional period in American history. He was the fourth chief of the bureau first headed by Henry C. Taylor, author of the first American textbook of agricultural economics and the first professor of the subject at a land-grant institution. Taylor pioneered the field at the University of Wisconsin and brought his pioneering enthusiasm to his new role. Entering the Department of Agriculture in 1919 as chief of the Office of Farm Management, Taylor encouraged the consolidation of economic work in the department. Along with Secretary Henry C. Wallace he endorsed the McNary-Haugen bill; after Wallace's death, which left no member of the administration supporting this measure, Taylor resigned. The ferment of ideas within the department, encouraged and stimulated by Wallace, quickly dampened with the arrival of Wallace's successors in the era of Republican ascendancy. Thus Olsen's association with the Bureau of Agricultural Economics began during a period when the expression of new approaches and ideas was not encouraged. It ended when such views were championed by new recruits brought into the department by Henry C. Wallace's son and Franklin D. Roosevelt's secretary of agriculture, Henry A. Wallace.

Nils A. Olsen was born near Herscher in Kankakee County, Illinois, on August 31, 1886. His father, Andreas Christian Olsen, a native of Norway, served as a Lutheran minister while earning his livelihood as a farmer. His mother, Anna Risetter Olsen, was born in the United States of Norwegian parents. Nils was one of five children, three of whom besides himself had distinguished careers. One brother, Holden, became president of Bethany College in Mankato, Minnesota; another, Martin, was a respected physician in Des Moines, Iowa. His sister Anna received the master of science degree in 1931 from Iowa State College, where she served also on the faculty of the food and nutrition department. From 1932 to 1940 she lived in New York and was editor of *America's Cook Book* and *Young America's Cook Book,* published by the *New York Herald Tribune.* His older sister, Mrs. Gertrude Dahl, resided in Chicago.

Prior to entering government service, Nils Olsen was a university instructor and farmer. He attended high school in Chicago and was graduated from Luther College in Decorah, Iowa, in 1907. As a graduate student in history and economics he attended Johns Hopkins University in 1907–1908 and transferred to the University of Wisconsin where he received the M.A. degree in 1909. He then taught for a year as an instructor in history and economics at Muhlenberg College in Allentown, Pennsylvania, before proceeding to Harvard University for further graduate work. For reasons not clear but probably concerned with family finances, he dropped out of graduate school and spent the years 1912–1919 managing the family farm in Kankakee County, Illinois.

In the fall of 1919 he entered the Department of Agriculture as an assistant agricultural economist in the Office of Farm Management to assist with research work in agricultural history. In 1922 he engaged in the administration of seed loan funds in the Northwest and soon was placed in complete charge of this work with headquarters at Grand Forks, North Dakota.

Olsen returned to Washington in July 1923 as an agricultural economist in the Division of Statistical and Historical Research, Bureau of Agricultural Economics. He became executive secretary of the committee which prepared a report on the wheat situation submitted to the president by Secretary Henry C. Wallace in the fall of that year. In November 1924 he became chief of the Division of Agricultural Finance in the Bureau of Agricultural Economics. Here Olsen conducted studies relating to farm taxation, credit, and insurance. In addition he was cooperating with Secretary Wallace in preparing a volume surveying the agricultural depression and its remedies. When Wallace went to the hospital on October 15, 1924, nine of the eleven chapters had been approved. Olsen, working in conjunction with Henry A. Wallace, revised and completed the manuscript by adding another chapter. The volume, *Our Debt and Duty to the Farmer,* was published in 1925 when Olsen was appointed assistant chief of the Bureau of Agricultural Economics.

Secretary William M. Jardine, Wallace's successor, was impressed with Olsen's abilities and promptly approved in April 1925 the recommendation of Henry C. Taylor, chief of the Bureau of Agricultural Economics, that Olsen be promoted to assistant chief in charge of its research program. In this position Olsen was responsible for coordinating the research work of the bureau, developing new research programs, and disseminating data analyzed and compiled as a result of research done in the bureau. In addition Olsen continued to direct the activities of the Division of Agricultural Finance. On July 16, 1928, Olsen became chief of the Bureau, succeeding Lloyd S. Tenny who had resigned to take an executive position with the Associated California Fruit Industries, Inc. He held the position for almost seven years, one of the longest terms in the history of the bureau.

Secretary Jardine, in announcing his appointment, said that Olsen "has a sympathetic grasp of the economic problems facing American agriculture and with his background will be able to mobilize the resources of the bureau in their solution."[2] But solutions to the problems afflicting American agriculture did not fall within Olsen's purview. He could only assist the secretary, members of Congress, and other senior officials as they prepared legislation or formulated programs. Secretary Jardine did neither. Following the lead of Secretary of Commerce Herbert Hoover, he stressed cooperative marketing. Jardine's successor, Arthur Hyde, had little choice but to accept President Hoover's approach to the problems of agriculture centering around the Federal Farm Board, which usurped some of the personnel and functions of bureaus—particularly the Bureau of Agricultural Economics—in the Department of Agriculture. Olsen and Hyde soon became intimates; as Hyde became increasingly dubious of Hoover's approach, he came to rely on Olsen's advice and judgment, though as a loyal party man he never openly expressed his criticisms. Throughout the Hoover years Secretary Hyde sympathized with and supported the Deparment of Agriculture in its opposition, if not hostility, to the Federal Farm Board. When it became clear, as it did by 1930, that Hoover's approach was not going to resolve even partially the plight of American agriculture, Olsen, who had been critical from the outset, was strengthened in his long-held views that stabilization corporations and effective marketing procedures by themselves were not the way to proceed. The spirit of Henry C. Wallace lingered throughout the department. Thanks to Olsen's prodding and his own compromised position in presiding over a department that was overshadowed by an independent agency, Secretary Hyde defended the department and at times presented Olsen's views to the President. He also suggested that Hoover appoint Olsen as one of the official delegates to the International Conference on Wheat at London, England, in May 1931 and to the International Dairy Congress at Copenhagen, Denmark, in July 1931.

With the advent of the New Deal and the appointment of Henry A. Wallace as secretary of agriculture, Olsen had every reason to believe that his advice and the work of the Bureau of Agricultural Economics would find a receptive audience. He knew the secretary, having completed with him the book his father was preparing at the time of his

2. Department of Agriculture Press Release: June 26, 1928; copy in Nils A. Olsen Papers, Box 3, Folder 11, Special Collections, Iowa State University Library.

death. And both men had been critical of the Hoover program for American agriculture. But Olsen's disappointments were to become increasingly numerous and embarrassing as he quickly found that Henry A. Wallace had little use for his advice and bypassed his bureau except to raid it of personnel for the Agricultural Adjustment Administration, which, unlike the Federal Farm Board, was within the Department of Agriculture.

The department was rife with tensions and controversies, most of which Olsen learned about second- or third-hand. He had frequent contact with the secretary, but Wallace relied on other advisers who were new appointees, or, like Mordecai Ezekiel and Louis H. Bean, former subordinates in the Bureau of Agricultural Economics. And as the Agricultural Adjustment Administration developed its own research divisions and became the central bureau within the department, Olsen became increasingly embittered and disillusioned. In April 1935 he resigned to accept a position as manager of the farm investment department of the Equitable Life Assurance Society in New York. He was succeeded as chief of the Bureau of Agricultural Economics by Albert G. Black, director of the Livestock and Feed Grains Division of the Agricultural Adjustment Administration, who had entered the department in 1933.

Moving to New York Olsen made his home at Bronxville and commuted to his office in New York City. After a year as manager of the Farm Mortgage Department he became a second vice-president in charge of the department and continued in that capacity until his death on July 28, 1940, from a streptococcic infection.

He never married and was survived by his two brothers and two sisters.

Olsen's diary, containing 500 entries, commences in 1925 when he became assistant chief of the Bureau of Agricultural Economics and ends with his departure from the bureau a decade later. This edition contains less than a third of the entries.

Olsen apparently dictated entries to his secretary and then rarely, if ever, reviewed them. Occasionally clippings, letters, or other relevant documents were attached to particular entries. In editing the diary I have tried to select those entries in which Olsen was dealing with individuals on a similar or higher level of government service and with top officials of various farm and other organizations in order to focus on the politics, policies, and programs of these critical years for American agriculture. Entries wherein Olsen records his dealings with lesser officials deal largely with technical or specific topics of less than national concern or are reflected and repeated in other entries in a broader context. However, at times, particularly during the New Deal years, I have departed from this guideline because discussions with lesser officials reflected the tensions, controversies, and gossip rampant in the Department of Agriculture.

With regard to the entries herein presented, I have eliminated redundancies and material comparable to that in the entries already included. In addition, since the journal is not an item of literary significance, I have corrected misspellings (they occur most frequently with the names of individuals) and obvious grammatical errors (including punctuation) made either by Olsen in dictating or by his secretary in hurriedly typing the entries. In most instances the entry itself provides enough information for the reader to follow the matter under discussion. I have added footnotes when necessary to provide background or additional information. Most often, however, footnotes are used to identify individuals. While I have been able to identify most individuals mentioned in the diary, some, despite persistent searching, have eluded me.

For help beyond the call of duty in identifying elusive individuals I want to particularly express my gratitude to Wayne Rasmussen, chief of the Agricultural History Branch of the Economic Research Service in the Department of Agriculture, and to Robert Wood, assistant director of the Herbert Hoover Presidential Library at West Branch, Iowa. Stanley Yates, Becky Seim Owings, and Ivan Hanthorn in the Special Collections Department of the Iowa State University Library merit a special note of thanks for cheerfully responding to numerous queries and assisting my work in other ways. Susan Ulrickson did a splendid job in deciphering my scrawl and typing the manuscript.

1 9 2 5

May 11, 1925

Mr. [D. D.] Borodin[1] called at my office, May 5, and requested that the Department express itself in regard to the placing of an Agricultural Commissioner at Petrograd. He pointed out that our Department had extended every courtesy to the representatives of the Soviet Government during the last three or four years, that they had appreciated very greatly the accommodations extended and they deemed it only fair that like accommodations should be extended to us on the part of the Russian Government.

He had two specific propositions in mind. In the first place he indicated that the Russian Government contemplates taking a census in 1926 as preliminary to the census of 1930 and that in the connection he had conferred with Mr. [Leon E.] Truesdell of the Bureau of the Census and that they have indicated their willingness to cooperate with the Russian Government in laying out and putting across this preliminary census. Mr. Borodin expressed the thought that an agricultural commissioner would be of service in connection with this census, but what he had in mind, particularly, was the stationing in Russia of a Department representative who could help the Russian Government whip its annual agricultural statistics into shape and report back to us whether the kind of information that we would find there would be particularly helpful to our agriculture. He went on to state that he had taken the matter up with Mr. [Ernest C.] Ropes[2] of the Department of Commerce, that the Department of Commerce was deeply interested in the suggestion and that they were disposed to take such steps as might result in the placing of a Department of Commerce man in Russia. I stated that while we were very much interested in the proposition that he proposed, never-

1. President of the Russian Agricultural Agency in America located in New York City.
2. Chief of the Central European Section, Western European Division of the Bureau of Foreign and Domestic Commerce.

theless that it was a matter that we were not free to act upon, certainly not without the full consent and approval of the Department of State; that I, of course, knew about their refusal to date to recognize the present Russian Government and that I did not know how they would stand with reference to an agreement between our Department of Agriculture and that of Russia.

Mr. Borodin stated that he had interviewed the Secretary of Agriculture and while he had not expressed himself definitely and finally on the subject, he gathered that the Secretary was interested in the proposal. I advised Mr. Borodin that I would be glad to take the matter up with the Secretary and, if it seemed desirable, make inquiries at the State Department to ascertain their position.

The same day I arranged to see the Secretary with reference to Mr. [Lloyd V.] Steere's Berlin appointment. The Secretary expressed the thought that he wishes the differences between the two departments adjusted before we made any further moves in the foreign field, that it was virtually waving the red flag to send new men to Europe at this time, even though the men were merely replacing those already stationed there and that he wished to make no moves whatever in the foreign field until the two departments had an opportunity to canvass their differences and to arrive at some working arrangement. He went further and expressed the wish that we should, in these conferences, present in the most effect-[ive] way possible the position of the Department of Agriculture in these conflicts between the two departments.

With reference to the Russian situation, the Secretary indicated that at this time it would be clearly out of the question to consider the appointment of a commissioner, in part because of his general policy of not expanding in the foreign field at this particular time and, in part, because it did not and would not have the approval of the Department of State.

The following morning Mr. Ropes, of the Department of Commerce, called me by telephone and advised that he had conferred with Mr. [Evan E.] Young of the Eastern European Division, State Department; that Mr. Young had expressed approval of the proposition and that he could see no good reason why the appointment should not be made. Mr. Ropes suggested that I get in touch with Mr. Young and get his reaction with reference to an agricultural commissioner. Accordingly, I arranged for a conference with Mr. Young for 10 o'clock Saturday morning, May 9. In arranging this conference Mr. Young stated specifically that his opinion was, of course, merely a personal one and that in a matter of this kind the last analysis would have to be decided by Secretary [Frank B.] Kellogg, but nevertheless he would be glad to discuss the matter with me.

On further consideration, I took the whole matter up with Mr. [F. M.] Russell[3] and decided that it would not be politic to take the mat-

3. Assistant to the Secretary of Agriculture.

ter up with the State Department at this particular juncture and I, accordingly, cancelled my appointment with Mr. Young, stating, in so doing, that the Secretary had expressly taken the position that the time was not opportune for sending a representative to Europe and, in view of the Secretary's position, there would be nothing gained by discussing the matter with the State Department. Mr. Russell agreed with me that there is something rather unusual in the whole situation—the fact that the State Department should have indicated to Commerce their approval of the proposition and that, on the other hand, the Secretary of Agriculture had advised me that the State Department was not friendly to the proposition. I was also impressed by the fact that Mr. Ropes, of Commerce, seemed rather anxious that I should get in touch with Mr. Young; whether or not any significance attaches to his attitude in the matter, I am unable to say. Mr. Russell felt quite sure, however, that the State Department could not very well approve of sending a Commerce man to Europe and not also approve of a Department of Agriculture man.

Saturday afternoon (May 9) Mr. Borodin called by telephone from New York City to ascertain what conclusions had been arrived at in the matter. I told him in a general way the Secretary's position and also added that we had not as yet taken the matter up with the State Department. I found it rather difficult to understand him over the telephone and the conversation wound up with the statement by Borodin that he would be here Monday to see me.

Monday, May 11, Mr. Ropes of Commerce called me just before 11 o'clock and asked for my decision in the matter of Mr. Borodin. I stated that the Department was not in a position at this time to go into the matter. Mr. Ropes stated that, of course, until the matter was put up formally to the Department of State a decision could not be given but that, inasmuch as Mr. Borodin was to call him at 11 o'clock, he wanted to know the Department's decision. When I said that the Department could not see its way clear to go into the matter at this time, Mr. Ropes said that he agreed with the decision and that it was the one that he felt would be arrived at. I advised him that Mr. Borodin had called me from New York on Saturday by telephone and said he would be down to see me today. Mr. Ropes was not aware of this and when I asked him if he wished to have me mention to Mr. Borodin that he would like to see him, Mr. Ropes said it was not necessary as Borodin would get in touch with him anyway. Before finishing the conversation I told Mr. Ropes that it was my hope that we would have an opportunity to become acquainted with each other and he expressed a similar hope.

May 21, 1925.

In a conversation with Mr. [Wells A.] Sherman of the Division of Fruits and Vegetables last night (May 20) he brought out some of the very significant background of our controversy—Agriculture-Commerce.

Back in the War days the Department of Agriculture was requested to draw up the Food Control Act and practically all of the work on this measure was performed by Mr. [Charles J.] Brand, assisted by Mr. Sherman and others here in the Department. In preparing this measure for introduction in Congress, Mr. Brand was of course working on the assumption that the administration of the Act would be placed here in the Department. It so developed, however, and perhaps fortunately so, that President Wilson decided to create a special unit to administer the Act. This was conceded, on the advice of Secretary [David F.] Houston who thought that criticisms which the Food Administration could not very well escape, might permanently handicap the work of the Department of Agriculture. The decision to create a separate body to administer the Act was probably wise. However, this was a great disappointment in Mr. Brand's life, since of course he had put his heart and soul into the formulation of the Act and he was about to lose all contact with its administration.

Shortly after the passage of the Act, President Wilson had [Herbert] Hoover return from Europe. On his arrival here, Mr. Hoover [then head of the Commission for Relief in Belgium] called up Mr. Brand and asked if he would not come over and discuss some matters relative to the Food Control measure. Mr. Brand told him he was working in an official capacity here, that he had his office and that he would be available to anyone who wanted to see him at any time. Parenthetically, Mr. Sherman added that Mr. Brand was working on the theory that Mr. Hoover was still a private citizen like anyone else and that he would have to expect to take his place, in order, in seeing him. This, of course, offended Hoover and he brought it to the attention of the President.

At the same time Mr. Hoover proceeded to establish a contact with G. Harold Powell and had him take charge of the Fruits and Vegetables Division of the Food Administration work. Mr. Powell was then a member of the Department and it was thought that close cooperation could be established between the Department of Agriculture and the Food Administration in the handling of this Act. Sometime later on Mr. Hoover made a special request to Mr. Brand that he give him the services of Mr. Sherman and one or two other men in handling the work. To this Mr. Brand replied that he had his work to perform here, that he could not disorganize his staff to meet the needs of another Department of the Government and that he could not see his way to comply with the request. This merely added fuel and the feeling between Hoover and Brand became increasingly strained. Mr. Sherman did not know all the points of friction that had arisen since then, but he felt that they had been very numerous indeed.

Out of this situation grew Mr. Hoover's feeling that it was essential to transfer the Bureau of Markets to the Department of Commerce. On every move he had made to obtain cooperation from the Department of Agriculture he had been balked.

When [Warren G.] Harding was elected, the opportunity to effect this transfer seemed unusually good. Mr. Harding was in Florida and requested Hoover to call on him there with reference to the Commerce portfolio.

On one of his trips to North Dakota Mr. Sherman met an individual, whose name he did not give, at the College and the whole subject of the transfer of the Bureau of Markets to Commerce came up for consideration. In a conversation which followed, this individual referred to an agreement which was said to have been drawn up between Harding and Hoover in Florida, to the effect that Hoover stipulated that the Bureau of Markets should be transferred and that Harding virtually consented to this transfer. Unfortunately for Hoover's plans, the announcement of his selection to the Cabinet was made from New York instead of Florida and the hue and cry went up that the financial interests had virtually dictated the appointment of Hoover and that they had succeeded in getting a committal to the transfer of the Bureau. This agreement was supposed to have contained, further, a list of other government units that were to be transferred to Commerce as a consideration for his accepting the portfolio. Mr. Sherman, of course, does not know to what extent an agreement of that kind was drawn, but he felt that there was probably good ground for believing that there was at least an understanding between the two along the lines indicated.

Shortly after [Henry C.] Wallace came to the Department, Mr. Sherman's story of this agreement was brought to Wallace's attention. The Secretary smiled in a rather knowing way, to indicate that he had expected as much and he expressed his gratification that he had men in the Department who had their eyes and ears open and were bringing to his attention matters that were of vital importance. Naturally, Wallace was placed in a position where he had to watch every move that Hoover made and the supposed existence of this agreement perhaps had some influence upon the personal relations between Wallace and Hoover from then on.

I called Mr. Sherman's attention to the fact that the personal feeling between Hoover and Wallace dated back to the Food Control days, when Wallace took serious issue with Hoover on the question of a corn-hog ratio. (Through reliable channels I have been advised that Hoover was about to ask for the suppression of "Wallace's Farmer" as a result of this controversy.)

Mr. Sherman feels that the difficulties between the two departments have been very much intensified because of personalities involved in the controversy. He believes that there was an opportunity to make con-

siderable headway in getting together when Brand was removed from the
headship of the Bureau [of Markets], but he realizes that there were real
difficulties to overcome since Hoover is anxious to expand the field of
his department's activity, just as we might very well have the same
desire. As far as he can see, however, there should be a way of getting
together and limiting the field in which each should work. He thought
that anyone who attempted to iron out the difficulties should have
clearly in mind the background, such as he narrated it to me.

May 21, 1925 [a second entry].

Since Saturday, May 16, the Secretary has been giving the major
part of his time to the consideration of the Grain Marketing Company of
Chicago.

The suggestion was made by Secretary Hoover that a conference be
called of men representing the cooperatives, representing the Grain
Marketing Company and representing men in the trade such as [Bernard
M.] Baruch and others. When this suggestion came to the Secretary's Office it was modified in a manner whereby the Secretary of Agriculture arranged to call a separate conference between him and the three men
representing the cooperative, namely, Carl Williams,[4] [Clifford V.]
Gregory of the "Prairie Farmer" and Dan Wallace.[5]

Saturday, May 16, these men met with the Secretary, canvassed the
situation very carefully and gave it as their opinion that the Cooperative
Marketing Company was non-cooperative, was launched by business
men to protect their own business, was an effort to unload depreciated
properties at inflated values and that it could not be saved in the interests
of the farmer. Mr. [Gray] Silver[6] called up Saturday to find out when
and where this meeting would be held if it was called and [F. M.] Russell
advised him that the Secretary had arranged to call a special meeting
with the three men and after he was through with the conference with
them, they would enter into the larger conference in which Silver and
Baruch and others would be represented.

Later on, the afternoon of Saturday, May 16, the larger conference
was called, at which Hoover, Silver and others were present. The
Secretary in the meanwhile had obtained a clear view as to the position
taken by the representatives of the cooperatives on the subject and took
an attitude of open-mindedness. In this discussion matters were not
minced. It was clearly brought out that the bankers were interested in

4. Editor of the *Oklahoma Farmer-Stockman,* prominent in agricultural affairs, and a
former president of the American Cotton Growers Exchange.

5. A Minnesota farm editor.

6. A former director and Washington representative of the American Farm Bureau and
an officer in the Grain Marketing Company.

saving this company, by reason of the heavy loans that they had made to the individuals prior to the consolidation and, in general, it was made perfectly clear that there were real difficulties in the way of presenting this as a cooperative movement and saving it as such.

Sunday, May 17, Secretary Hoover entertained at dinner Gregory, Dan Wallace and Carl Williams. Russell was unable to give me the details of the conversation, but the motive underlying this function, on the part of Hoover, apparently was to sound out a little more fully if something could not be done to save the Grain Marketing Company and if favorable support could not be obtained from the representatives of the cooperatives. In this he received no encouragement from this group.

Monday, May 18, 1925, Russell was called to the Washington Hotel to sit in conference with the three men just mentioned. They stated that they wished to draw up a statement which would set forth the position that they have taken, as a matter of protection. At the same time, Russell indicated that the Secretary would be very glad to have such a statement drawn up in order to protect him in the matter. Accordingly, a memorandum to the Secretary was drawn up by the group, in which was pointed out, very specifically, the facts bearing on the Grain Marketing Company and the reasons why they did not think it could be saved. A copy of the memorandum was shown to me last night (May 20) by Mr. Russell and will be made available to me in the course of a day or so. In order to make doubly sure that the position taken by these three could not be used as a basis for a Marketing Company, it was specifically stated at the conclusion of the memorandum that they deemed it essential that the resignation of all officials of the Grain Marketing Company be placed in the hands of the Secretary of Agriculture for such action as he saw fit to take before anything could be done in the matter of reorganization. This matter from the Secretary's point of view will serve two purposes. In the first place, it is concrete evidence that he has wrestled honestly with the problem of the Grain Marketing Company, that he has conferred with representatives of the cooperatives who are most vitally interested and that it cannot be said of him that he in any way flirted with members of the grain trade or the Grain Marketing Company, without working closely and fully with representatives of the cooperatives.

One of the three cooperative representatives got in touch with [Judson C.] Welliver of the White House and let him know that they were in town. Welliver came over at once and expressed a desire to know what it was all about. They frankly told him that they were in to consider the future of the Grain Marketing Company and he expressed a keen interest in their mission and indicated that the President, also, would be very much interested in what they were doing. He said the President would be very glad to meet them. They arranged to go over and shake hands with the President, at which time an invitation was extended by the President to take lunch with him. This is significant, because it indicates that the President appreciates that he must reckon with the cooperatives, that he cannot force down their throats a Grain Marketing Company which is non-cooperative and which stands good chances of going on the rocks, and that he is going to p[l]ay the game with Jardine in good fashion. Jardine, of course, was delighted to know that the people whom he had called in to consider, with him, the Grain Marketing Company had also been taken into camp by the President. In this connection, the political angles of the whole situation may well be noted.

The Grain Marketing Company is, of course, a pet of Mr. Hoover's, as well as of the President. They do not like to have it "go by the board" because of the political reactions that may result after its failure. That accounts for Mr. Hoover's heroic efforts to save it. On the other hand, Mr. Coolidge apparently begins to understand that there is little to be gained by saving a defunct body, furthermore that his political interests will lie with the farmers and farm groups rather than with the interest represented by Mr. Hoover. This is not meant to convey the idea that he is not still thoroughly industrially-minded, but that he appreciates that as far as this particular cooperative movement is concerned, he has to reckon very seriously with the stand taken by the farm representatives and by the Secretary of Agriculture. In fact, the change which Secretary Jardine's thinking has been undergoing on this subject is exceedingly gratifying, since it is apparent that he realize, more and more, that his interests lie with the farmer group and that in the last analysis he probably is going to fortify his position with the President by standing squarely on the proposition and not permitting himself to be influenced unduly by Hoover's position. On the other hand, it is worthy of note, too, that Hoover is approaching these problems with an open mind and is going to be willing to make concessions that will have far reaching significance. . . .

The Secretary's attitude on the Cooperative Marketing Board is undergoing very wholesome and encouraging changes. We have battered away at him for the last several weeks and a meeting, such as he just held with Dan Wallace and others, has no doubt been very helpful in shaping his thinking. This is particularly true of the conference which Chester Davis[7] had with him and in which this matter was gone into in some detail. As a matter of fact the Secretary will be willing, I think, to have no reference made to the Marketing Board in his western speeches. . . .

Chester Davis and I canvassed, rather fully, the situation in the Middle West relative to Jardine. Davis stated that there was hostility to

7. At this time working for a Chicago firm, Agricultural Service, providing research, information, and representation for agricultural organizations; also commissioner of agriculture for the state of Montana and editor of *The Montana Farmer*.

begin with and that organizations were card-indexing the Secretary very carefully. For example, they had taken his famous McNary-Haugen speech and paralleled it with speeches made by the United States Chamber of Commerce and found it difficult to arrive at any other conclusion than that his speech had been written by United States Chamber of Commerce people, but that the organizations were now adopting a policy of watchful waiting. They were willing to give the Secretary an opportunity to reveal his position and thought he had been very fortunate in the move he had made with reference to Russell and myself. That had been looked upon as an assurance that he is not violently breaking with Wallace and with Department policies for which Wallace stood. They have the belief that he is, of course, very close to Hoover, that he represents the business man's viewpoint of agriculture, etc.

I assured Chester that the position which he, personally, had taken in this matter was fine and absolutely sound and that I felt convinced that if they would only bide their time, they would find Jardine absolutely 100 per cent for agriculture and that he would be found working with the agricultural leaders in the finest spirit possible. We discussed in some detail the position which the Secretary must take with reference to the surplus problem during his speaking campaign in the West. I told Chester something about the conversations I had had with the Secretary on the subject and indicated that the Secretary had shifted his position very materially, that he was not at all unmindful of the surplus problem, that as a matter of fact he wanted us to find some practical solution for it. Chester thought that it would be well for the Secretary to make clear that he recognized the problem and that he was seeking a solution to it.

1926

August 14, 1926.

Under date of August 9 Dr. [O. C.] Stine[1] and I called on Mr. [James B.] Aswell[2] at the Capitol in connection with his trip to Europe. He indicated over the phone, in advance of our meeting with him, that the primary purpose of his European trip was to obtain data that would be helpful in defeating all price control measures now advocated in Congress. We, accordingly, brought together a certain amount of material which we thought would be useful, but counted on being of greatest help to him in our personal conference.

Mr. Aswell was in a very happy frame of mind and jollied a good deal about various phases of the problem that he wanted to study. He, jokingly, said that he was not altogether sure he called up the right man when he got in touch with me—the name "Olsen" sounding rather suspicious in connection with any proposition that Mr. [Gilbert N.] Haugen[3] had been advocating. I assured him that while perhaps we were of the same racial stock, there very clearly was no relationship between his thinking and mine. From this he went on to comment upon the general temper of Congress. He stated that at the present time Congress, to his mind, was running very strongly to Bolshevic theories. He stated that you would be surprised to know the number of men who were strongly advocating what he deemed very radical measures. His purpose in making the trip was to obtain information that would help him this fall to offset the activities of these so-called Bolshevists.

Mr. Aswell also expressed considerable disappointment in tht support received from Secretary Jardine. He believe[d] Jardine was sound in his thinking and in the position he had taken, but he said he had not

1. An agricultural economist in charge of the Division of Statistical and Historical Research in the Bureau of Agricultural Economics.
2. A congressman from Louisiana and a bitter opponent of the McNary-Haugen bill.
3. An Iowa congressman who was the leading agricultural spokesman in the House of Representatives in his capacity as chairman of the Committee on Agriculture.

the moral courage to stand up for his proposition; in fact, he considered him a moral coward. That was the phrase he used. He, jokingly, said I might tell the Secretary that if I felt inclined. I assured him that I did not think that would be in good order and thought it might be in better taste for him to convey that message to the Secretary direct, if he was so inclined. In this connection I asked him, in regard to the Tincher-Fess[4] measure, to what extent he deemed it sound and had supported it. His reply was that he had given it a tremendous amount of attention, in fact had remained up nights until midnight and later in order to devise ways and means of defeating what he considered a sham piece of legislation. He considered the Tincher bill not only unsound but put forth as a proposition to defeat the other measures. . . .

August 14, 1926 [a second entry].

During Thursday and Friday, (August 12 and 13) I held rather lengthy conferences with Mr. Russell relative to an article which he and Mr. [Albert B.] Genung[5] recently prepared on the tariff for the farmer and also another article on the Agricultural Problem, prepared for the Secretary's signature and to appear in the "Saturday Evening Post."

A careful analysis of the article on the tariff clearly showed that it is very largely propaganda. Mr. Russell, at the outset, felt that he had built up a very strong argument for the tariff and its benefits to the farmer. Apparently he was rather anxious to have my approval of his general treatment. This, of course, I could not give. In fact the article is so open to attack that I felt it would be a serious mistake if the Secretary or any one connected with the Department issued it under his own name. After a lengthy discussion Mr. Russell was finally convinced that the article did have very serious weaknesses and he admitted that, after all, his object in putting it out was to offset propaganda against propaganda. From that point of view the article would be looked upon as good, since it of course would fool a lot of people into believing that the tariff had been extremely effective in elevating farm prices.

The article prepared for the "Saturday Evening Post" is based almost entirely upon statements and speeches issued by the Secretary from time to time during the last year. The treatment of the material to my mind, however, was extremely unfortunate in many places. There was a disposition throughout the article to throw out slurs and nasty insinuations that would, in my opinion, prove real boomerangs. I convinced Mr. Russell that the Secretary had absolutely nothing to gain by directly and

4. The Tincher bill was an administration-sponsored bill calling for a farm marketing commission with a revolving fund of $100,000,000 to loan to cooperatives. It did not grapple directly with the dilemma of the surplus, which the McNary-Haugen measure attacked.

5. Served in the Division of Information, periodicals sections, of the Bureau of Agricultural Economics.

brought up for consideration. The Secretary rather indicated that he was disposed to back the Fess-Tincher bill. I very frankly told him in response to his request for my reaction that I could only repeat what I had told him last spring that the Tincher bill was absolutely unsound, that my opinion would be sustained by all good students of the problem, that furthermore it was dead as a doornail politically, and would bury him deeper than ever. Surprisingly enough he admitted that politically it was absolutely dead and that there was no hope of reviving the bill. He then asked me what I thought should be done. I told him that I could only suggest that the proposal I made to him a year ago was the one I thought merited favorable consideration at this time, and then I rehearsed my position with reference to commodity stabilization corporations and the scheme paralleling very closely the Federal Farm Loan Board.[1] He told me to examine the situation, give him a memorandum concerning same and formulate a program along the lines I had indicated.

This I have been doing the last several weeks and submitted my report yesterday. The report was received by him most favorably. Preceding this report, however, I had submitted a preliminary memorandum which he wished to take with him to the President, and which I refused to let him have. He then presented the proposition as best he could from memory in order to get the President's reactions. The President refused to make any comments and merely asked a number of questions. Among them the following:

Is this price fixing?
Is this government in business?
Is this consistent with the position the Administration has heretofore taken?

To all of this the Secretary apparently had no adequate reply, which he admitted in reporting the conversation to me. Obviously there can be no convincing of the President where salesmanship of so poor a kind is employed in selling a proposal. Before he went over, he suggested that he would like to take me along in order to present the proposal in all of its angles. At that time I was not willing to go along, but in my conversation with him yesterday I suggested that if he wished to see the President again I would be very glad to go with him on the theory that the Secretary will not be in position to present the proposal to the President in convincing manner. As a matter of fact, in this connection, reports coming from good sources indicate that the other members of the Cabinet are fed up on the Secretary and would just as soon see his resignation.

In my advice to the Secretary, I have told him this—that the thing for him to do is not to play with all kinds of proposals that come along, not to get back of even this proposal until:

1. Established in 1916 to provide credit to farmers.

1. He is absolutely convinced himself that it is 100 per cent.

2. That the farmers of this country are for the proposal.

3. That he should obtain in so far as possible the approval and support of the administration before he lines up with the majority.

However, if he obtains the farmers' support, then I advised him to break with the Administration, if necessary.

In our conferences I resorted to my usual frankness and told him some brutally frank things which he took very courteously. I frankly told him that as I met people in various parts of the country and gathered reactions from all kinds of sources, it hurt me to see how unkindly people of all grades and classes felt toward him, that it was unjustified, and that every effort should be made to change the situation. I pointed out to him that he had two courses:

1. He might follow his past policy, lead producers and their leaders to think that he was indifferent to their interests or so tied up to the Administration that he did not dare defend his own ideas, and then after this Administration is through find himself out of sympathy with the class with which he has worked during his entire life.

2. He could take a position which was positive, sound in the interests of agriculture, and perhaps break with the Administration and retire from his present position a year or so sooner then he expected, but in so doing win the respect of farmers and those for whom he has been working all his life.

He admitted that that was the situation and he went on to say that if the Western group would support him in this proposal he would go in for it and stick through thick and thin, even though it made a break with the Administration. Personally I wouldn't want to base any policy or program on a thing of that kind, because his personal attitude would probably be reflected in the rebound. In fact Mr. Russell stated, in discussing this matter with me later, that he could pick any one of 100 or 200 men who could make the Secretary do anything they wanted him to do.

Russell clearly now realizes that he is in a very uncertain position in the Secretary's office, and is disposed to be pretty critical of the Secretary. In explaining the difficulties he had in keeping him straight, he told me in this office two or three days ago of two things that recently had happened. One morning this week the Secretary was unusually happy and smiling, and Russell remarked on this. The Secretary countered by saying "Why shouldn't I be happy? I attended a party last night, had a delightful time, and among other men met John Hays Hammond,[2] who slapped me on the back and said: 'That's right, Jardine, don't let any one break you loose from your position.' When men like John Hays Hammond treat me that way, why shouldn't I feel all right?"

2. A distinguished mining engineer active in public affairs and an intimate of Presidents Harding and Coolidge.

Then Russell also mentioned the conversation he had with Mr. [Stuart Wilder] Wells of the Grain Trade in the City of Minneapolis. Wells came in one morning, greeted him rather gruffly. Russell asked him what was the matter? He said, "I have been in to see your Chief and told him what the whole Grain Trade thinks of him. We thought he was a man to begin with, but now we have lost all confidence in him. Any man who is as unstable as he is; now we are through, we are done, and I told him so. . . ."

[*no date*]

The evening of November 12, 1927, I called at the Secretary's home at the Mayflower Hotel to confer with him in regard to the price situation report and other matters that had accumulated and which could not very well be carried over during the week of my absence.

We got along famously with the report and he approved it, indicating however that we must not publish anything on the cattle situation that would weaken prices. He went on to add that it was sufficient to shock cotton prices and we simply could not take on the additional load which would follow from a report indicating declining beef prices.

We discussed [Andrew] Mellon's[3] reply with reference to [E. J.] Kyle's[4] request on the legality of National Farm Loan Associations. I pointed out to him that as far as I could see there is nothing further for him to do except to tell Mr. Kyle and his group that he had done all he could; that it was impracticable for him to go direct[ly] to the Department of Justice for [an] opinion. He indicated however that this was a part with Mellon's hidebound ultra-conservative policies in all matters. . . .

Then I brought up the question of licensing dealers generally in the United States as proposed by [William E.] Borah's bill. I reminded him of the fact that he had asked me about that measure a week or ten days before and that I gave him my opinion in regard to the soundness of it. (At that time I indicated to the Secretary my doubts as to the soundness and practicability of the measure proposed, but that I would give careful consideration to it and report later on.)

I began my discussion of the proposal by indicating the difficulties politically of putting across the Borah proposal. Without a doubt it would be looked upon in my opinion as a very far-reaching piece of paternalistic legislation. Putting every dealer in this country under Federal license would inevitably arouse the ire of all business people, and the changes of getting the bill passed would in my opinion be rather small. But more fundamental in my opinion is the fact that the wisdom

3. Secretary of the Treasury.
4. Dean of the School of Agriculture at Texas A & M.

of such a measure is extremely doubtful. There are undoubtedly a great many abuses in the retail trade that should be corrected, but we have generally taken the position that an effort should first be made to correct them through education rather than legislation. The proposal, as I see it, is contrary to the spirit of the policy we have hitherto followed, and after all I was not sure that licensing by the Federal department would increase the farmers' returns. Furthermore, it would present a huge task for the Department of Agriculture and would keep us in hot water with dealers all the time and probably interfere with the prosecution of other lines of service and research work which we have under way. The Secretary finally broke in and said, "You needn't argue this any more. I see this thing rather clearly. In fact, I got a little spanking in connection with this matter," and he pointed to the Hill. He said, "There is nothing to do, I am through as far as I am concerned. They are not going to catch me on a limb as far as this thing is concerned. Let Borah go out on the limb. I am going to play safe." I said I thought his decision was a wise one and it would be well for us to watch our step rather carefully in our negotiations with Borah.

[*no date*]

Yesterday (December 1) Russell called at my office and spent an hour and a half or so going over various matters close to his heart. Among other things he referred to the licensing matter. The thing happened about as follows: Borah went to the President with his proposal. The President listened to Borah, and said, "Take it up with the Secretary of Agriculture and get his opinion." Borah then came to the Secretary with his proposal and the Secretary spoke rather enthusiastically about the proposition. The bill from Borah was turned over to this Bureau and a memorandum went back setting forth some of the facts in connection with abuses in the trade, and the like. This memorandum was taken by [Eric] Englund[5] and used in drafting a letter to Borah formally approving of the proposal. Borah again went to see the President and it was decided the President issue a release to the press indicating his interest in the matter. About that time things broke—business men and dealers all over the country wired the President condemning the entire proposition. At the Cabinet meeting immediately following, Mr. Hoover asked about the licensing matter that had been referred to in the press. The President said that the Secretary of Agriculture had recommended the proposal as a sound one. Jardine immediately spoke up and said—yes, he thought it was a mighty wise and effective thing to do. Immediately, Hoover spoke

5. A former professor of agricultural economics who was brought into the Bureau of Agricultural Economics by Jardine to head the Division of Agricultural Finance.

up and criticized him most severely right in the Cabinet. Hoover was seconded in this matter by [James J.] Davis,[6] Mellon, [Hubert] Work[7] and other members of the Cabinet, and by the time the session was over Jardine was thoroughly spanked. Russell said he did his best to stop the letter which Englund prepared for the Secretary's signature to Borah, pointing out that it represented approval of the matter. Englund waived him aside and said he knew what he was about. . . .

6. Secretary of Labor.
7. Secretary of the Interior.

1928

Thursday, February 2, 1928.

Last Friday, January 27, at the Cabinet meeting, Secretary Hoover accused the Department of State of conspiring with the Department of Agriculture to undermine its foreign service. Mr. Hoover is reported to have been very angry and to have stated that this policy apparently was in keeping with the State Department policy which had been under way for some time to injure the Commerce Department. Secretary [Frank] Kellogg had very little to say at this particular meeting but did indicate that he knew nothing about the charges and did not think they were true. In Mr. Hoover's statement he made direct reference to Mr. [Wilbur J.] Carr, Assistant Secretary of State, as the individual who was responsible for the undesirable activities. At this particular meeting Secretary Jardine is reported not to have said anything.

After the Cabinet meeting Mr. Carr called up Mr. [Lloyd S.] Tenny[1] and gave the whole story. Mr. Jardine also had Tenny come over and told him presumably about the same story. He then went on to add that since Hoover took this position it was necessary and desirable not to antagonize him. He stated that so far as he was concerned he was favorable to the bill which placed the service in the Department of Agriculture and was not disposed to support the other bill which he thought would place the foreign service of the Department at a handicap. He said that a special effort should be made now to get the foreign bill, that since he and Hoover had jointly approved the foreign bill they would continue to do so now and not give active support to the so-called State Department bill.

The Secretary also called me over—asked me to get him first a statement presenting the differences in the two bills and also another statement presenting the reasons why the Department of Agriculture needed a foreign service and particularly why that foreign service had to be ad-

1. Chief of the Bureau of Agricultural Economics.

31

ministered by the Department of Agriculture and not by Commerce. These statements were prepared and it developed in my conversation with the Secretary that Mr. Hoover was particularly incensed over the State Department bill as he looked upon it as an attempt to undermine his Department—he had always taken the position that each Department must have its independent service and not be subject to the dominance of the State Department. According to his views the State Deparmtent would be ruled by considerations of friendly relations as between nations and this consideration would not necessarily dominate the policy of the Department. In this view the Secretary concurred. I told him we had considered this factor but had come to the conclusion after conferences with the State Department that it was not a danger in any sense. Furthermore, the bill was so drawn that we could feel quite at ease as far as our foreign work was concerned.

My first meeting with the Secretary was, as I recall, Saturday the 28th [of January], when I gave him a statement showing the differences between the two bills. The statement presenting the reasons why the Department of Agriculture should have a foreign service was given to him by me on Tuesday, January 31, just before the Cabinet meeting. I had with me a 7-page statement which I told him I would not read but would instead give him an oral statement on the matter. I asked him to place himself in the position of the President and for the next ten minutes I would be the Secretary of Agriculture. Apparently an effective statement was given him, as will be apparent from what follows.

In the course of our conversation he emphasized that he did not want to antagonize Hoover and that he was friendly to the bill which would put the foreign service in our Department, and that furthermore it behooved us to do everything in our power in this session of Congress. In this I said I was in perfect agreement. I made it clear however that this bill had grown out of, as we saw, necessity. Senator [William H.] King of Utah had objected to the other measure, and from everything we had learned had proposed to fight us indefinitely. Furthermore I made it clear that various farm leaders were of the opinion that the Department of Commerce had been instrumental in killing our bill—they certainly could not see why Senator King should object to our bill and not the Commerce bill on the same grounds. Jardine tried to assure me that he didn't think Hoover had done anything of the kind, but he said it was important that we whip King into line. He then gave Russell instructions to write certain individuals, including [Elmer G.] Peterson of Utah College,[2] to get Senator King into line in approving our bill. This Russell agreed to do. While I was still talking to the Secretary he had to leave for the Cabinet meeting.

The next developments occurred around 11:45 that same day, when

2. President of Utah State Agricultural College in Logan.

Carr called up Tenny and told him there had been another blowup in the Cabinet. Kellogg had been the first to get up and speak. He had gone over the facts with Carr and had categorically denied that the Department of State had in any way conspired to undermine the Department of Commerce. He declared that the so-called measure providing a foreign service for Agriculture had been suggested by the Deparment of Agriculture and had been worked out in cooperation with them. They had merely assisted Agriculture. . . . President Coolidge raised the question as to whether the Department of Commerce should be able to render that service. He said however that the farm population insisted upon having a foreign service in the Department of Agriculture, and since this was the case perhaps it had better be that way. Secretary Hoover then spoke up and said the Department of Commerce could render that service, but as the farm people wanted it in the Department of Agriculture, there is where it should go. He said however he resented any attempts on the part of the Department of State and Senator King to undermine Commerce. He made slurring remarks in regard to Carr's activities in trying to break down their foreign service.

Secretary Davis of Labor is also supposed to have arisen and said they had negotiated with the Department of State in regard to a foreign service. This apparently merely went to show, as far as Hoover was concerned, that the Department of State was conspiring with other departments to undermine his department.

Carr called up Mr. Tenny immediately after the Tuesday Cabinet meeting and told him the story and also told him that Secretary Kellogg was exceedingly angry. He had called up the Secretary of Agriculture and cussed him out roundly for his disloyalty and failure to support. He had then proceeded to dictate a letter which he proposed to send to the Secretary, but which he was holding. . . .

After the Friday cabinet meeting, Tenny, [C. W.] Kitchen[3] and I began working on plans as to how to meet this. We finally agreed that the best thing to do was to have the Secretary write Tenny a memorandum explaining that he was under criticism from his superiors and that a statement of the facts would help clear up the present difficulties. Nothing was done however until Tenny had his conference with Carr, Wednesdy, when Tenny and Carr went into conference on the entire matter. Carr at that time told Tenny that Kellogg had been exceedingly angry when he talked to Jardine over the 'phone, and Jardine had been exceedingly profuse in his apologies and excuses. It was therefore agreed that Kellogg should probably write a letter to Jardine explaining the facts and winding up by saying that he would undoubtedly want to place the President right with reference to the facts, and that therefore a copy of this very letter was going to the President for his information.

3. Assistant chief of the Bureau of Agricultural Economics.

I was called to the Secretary's office yesterday afternoon at about 1 o'clock to sit in on a conference with Mr. [Sam H.] Thompson, President of the American Farm Bureau Federation. The purpose of this conference was to secure Thompson's support for the foreign bill, for effective opposition to the reclamation bill, for assistance in getting the taking of the agricultural census placed where it should be, and also to set him right on agricultural price analysis and forecasts. The conference on these points was very successful, and need not be commented upon in this connection.

After the conference however the Secretary in a rather apologetic way commented upon the blowups that had developed in the Cabinet. Russell was in at the time. He went on to tell me that Kellogg was exceedingly angry because he had not supported him in the Cabinet. He told me that Kellogg had called him up and given him H____. He emphasized that he thought Kellogg expected him to support him in the Cabinet meeting, but he said he had gone on record as supporting the foreign bill with Hoover and that he could not very well go back on that position. Furthermore, he intimated that he did not know very much about the other bill. Then he went on to say that while Hoover was sore, he wasn't sore on us but he was sore on the State Department because of their continued activities over a series of years in trying to undermine him. He cited Hoover's reference to the bill that we were trying to develop with the State Department. I said, "This occurred in the Cabinet meeting? Tell us about it." And he went on to elaborate what I have written. . . .

During this last conversation with the Secretary, I took occasion to say that I thought it was exceedingly unfortunate that the State Department had been put in this light. Certainly it did not conform with the facts. We were responsible for initiating the State Department bill and seeing to its drafting. I added further I thought something should be done to put the State Department in right. I could say this because Jardine did not know I knew the facts and he could see how we felt. It was very apparent that Jardine cringed under my comments. He was somewhat apologetic and did not know how to answer. This was commented upon by Russell after the meeting. In order to crystallize sentiment in favor of the foreign bill and on other points of interest to the Department, a hearing is being arranged for Friday afternoon with leaders of various farm organizations. This is one of a series of conferences that I suggested be held with the Secretary, in order that he might keep these representatives thoroughly pepped up to their duties in support of the Department.

November 2, 1928.

Yesterday noon I took luncheon with Dr. Julius Klein of the Bureau of Foreign and Domestic Commerce. The conference was most cordial and direct from every point of view. . . .

I . . . said that I hoped we could have frequent conferences in order to develop a real spirit of cooperation between the two departments. I stated that there was every disposition on our part to cooperate with the Department of Commerce and I felt the same was true with them. I told him that I thought it was a case of recognizing, on the part of each of us, the bailiwick of the respective department. It was our job to serve agriculture and in serving agriculture we had to reach out in the domestic and foreign field and utilize every bit of data that had a bearing on agricultural problems. This meant that in many cases we would have to collect information direct, but that we could also utilize in a very great extent the data which the Department of Commerce collects in the usual course of its work. On the other hand it was the Department of Commerce's job to serve industry and commerce and in the development of agriculture, many of the facts of agriculture were of significance to business men. I stated very frankly that I thought that in doing this Commerce would find summary material developed by the Department of Agriculture and state colleges of agriculture which in most cases would be sufficient for the purpose and that it would not be necessary or even proper for Commerce to go out and do original work in agriculture. I went to some pains to make that point clear—that departments should respect one another's fields so far as the collecting of original data was concerned. In this Dr. Klein fully agreed and he assured me that there would be every disposition on his part to help work out those questions along these lines. I went to some trouble in explaining to him how we in our Department could be exceedingly helpful to them in some of their publications. For example, the "Survey of Current Business" brings together data from all sources that are useful to business men and our Bureau was supplying Commerce with quite a little of the data going into that publication and, in addition, had called attention to weaknesses in the data that were not going in, as for instance, their quotations on No. 2 wheat.

I told Dr. Klein that I thought probably our chances for a conflict would be most likely to arise in the foreign field and had been giving some thought as to how we could obviate the type of difficulty that had arisen. I told him that it was absolutely vital that the Department of Agriculture reckon with the foreign aspects of the agricultural situation and that it have a foreign service. I further told him that the thought had been crystallizing in our minds for some time that it would be a good idea to segregate our foreign service and make it stand out more boldly in the work of the Bureau. By doing that and placing some man in charge who would devote all his time to this work, it would probably further its growth and also put us in better position to maintain better relations with other departments. In that connection I suggested that a man of [Asher] Hobson's[4] qualifications might be just exactly what we would want and I did not know but that he might possibly be available some time in the near future. All of this met with a hearty reception. Dr. Klein stated that he thought it would be a splendid idea to do that and, furthermore, he thought Hobson would make a very good man for that type of assignment. . . .

December 11, 1928.

Friday noon [December 7, 1923] Dr. Klein and I had another luncheon conference. In the opening discussions a rather interesting slant was developed by Dr. Klein with reference to the tariff agitation now under way. He said he very much feared that the disposition to make things right for agriculture would lead to unreasonable tariffs on certain farm commodities, and these would rebound to the disadvantage of other agricultural products and also industrial products. For example, if a tariff were to be placed on bananas it might to some extent stop the imports of bananas, but some of the South American countries might recriminate by interfering with the export of apples or other farm products to those countries and, even worse, such a tariff might affect the export of automobiles to South America. He was wondering what, if anything, could be done to make sure that every phase of the situation was taken into account before tariffs were decided upon. I told him that, of course there were various interests to be reckoned with; that I could see that the placing of a tariff on one farm commodity might affect other farm commodities. I stated that I could also appreciate that there might be some relation between agricultural tariffs and the interests of manufacturers. I told him, however, that I thought it perfectly fair and proper that Agriculture at this time should be given every consideration and that too much emphasis should not be placed upon the interest of the industrial group. It all illustrates very prettily the difference in viewpoint between Commerce and Agriculture. . . .

Then I said that as long as were discussing matters that seemed to be pressing at this time, I wondered just how he felt about the Foreign Service Bill of the Department of Agriculture and what he thought we ought

4. American delegate to the International Institute of Agriculture in Rome. In 1929 he became the economist in charge of the foreign agricultural information service in the Department of Agriculture.

to be in the premise. I pointed out to him the status of the bill and indicated the importance of getting this bill passed without further delay. I went on to add that I thought the enactment of this bill would be an important step in ironing out the difficulties between the two departments and I hoped we could count on the support of Commerce at this time for its passage. He hemmed and hawed a little bit, but said that he too could not understand why the bill was not passed. He knew that Senator King had objected to it, but King had also objected to their measure and it was only when they induced the labor interests of Utah to build fires under King that he finally came into line. He suggested that might be a good move for us to consider. The upshot of our discussion of this matter did not leave me with the impression that Klein was unduly worried about the passage of our Foreign Service Bill. . . .

In breaking up the conference, Dr. Klein stated that he was exceedingly pleased with the conference we held. He also said that it was one of the most fruitful hours he ever spent in conference. He was quite sure that we could get together on a basis of thoroughly effective cooperation. I assured him that there would be every disposition on my part to work out the best of relations between the two bureaus and that he could count on m[e] to deal directly and frankly with all matters as they arose. We agreed to have regular meetings, possibly twice a month in order to consider matters that might come up from time to time.

1 9 2 9

February 12, 1929.

Yesterday afternoon (February 11th) at about 3:30 Mr. [Eric] Englund[1] and I were called in conference by the Secretary to discuss the farm relief program. Before we got well under way, the Secretary was handed a note . . . and asked to step out. When he came back he was thoroughly aroused because somebody had leaked information that should not be abroad at this time. He felt that probably somebody had played him false. In the circumstances, he complained that he had found it necessary to prevaricate and the plain inference from the whole affair was that it had something to do with his reappointment as Secretary.

The Secretary then asked what I had done in the way of whipping a program into shape. . . . I then told him that, in the first place, it was my opinion that whatever was done in the way of farm relief would have to take seriously into account the interest of the cooperatives. Mr. Hoover undoubtedly expects to lean heavily on them and that anything that seemed to go counter to their interest would have rough sledding. In the second place, I assured him that the relief of agriculture did not lie in short time emergency measures, but rather in the long time program which was directed at the fundamentals underlying the industry. In such a broad program I included such things as [1] thoroughly effective and energetic attempts to adjust production to market requirements; (2) a radical revision of our whole land policy, with a view to contracting the farm land area. This would embody the elimination of the present reclamation program, perhaps the transfer of the reclamation service to the Department of Agriculture, some effective control of the public domain, the strengthening of our reforestation program and other means that would result in contracting the land area; (3) energetic efforts to broaden the use of agricultural products. This program would like more

1. Chief of the Division of Agricultural Finance in the Bureau of Agricultural Economics.

[*sic*] in the field of research, but nevertheless it was fundamental in the whole picture; (4) the development of foreign markets for agricultural products and an appraisal of the foreign competition that American producers have to face. This would call for the passage of the foreign agricultural service bill and the coordination and direction of the efforts of all departments under the guidance of the Department of Agriculture in this matter; (5) promotion of sound overhead cooperative through the broadening of the research in that field and the intensification of our extension methods with the view to creating the proper attitude of mind on the part of farmers toward cooperatives; (6) a thorough checkup in our rural credit system with certain amendments to the Federal Intermediate Credit Act, in particular, that would result in making that system function; (7) overhauling of transportation rates and further development of water transportation seemed entirely feasible; (8) serious effort at taxation reduction on farm lands; (9) some specific emergency legislation of a strictly experimental nature, the purpose of which would be to try to handle surpluses that otherwise could not be handled. This measure, however, should be presented as a purely experimental attempt at solving the problem and should not loom as the big part of the whole program. Then I urged that the whole program of research for agriculture should be carefully scrutinized with the idea of strengthening it wherever it seemed necessary. In addition I pointed out the need for reinvigorating the extension service to the point where they actually succeeded in getting the farmers educated to the point where they would act on vital economic information now being made available. I insisted that if I were President of the United States and had this problem to wrestle with, that would be my program and that it would not only be the soundest program that could be advanced, but would leave the President in the most strategic position when any part failed. Furthermore, it would have the advantage of strengthening the fundamental work which we are doing in the Department of Agriculture and which is directed at the proper objectives. I went further and said that I thought a serious mistake had been made by the Adminstration in permitting all the attention being placed on one emergency measure. Naturally that would draw fire and when that failed there was nothing else to fall back on. In connection with the emergency measure, I reminded the Secretary of the memorandum I sent him before I went to the hospital two years ago, and in which I disagreed with the program laid down in the Hoover-Jardine bill.[2] I insisted then and I insist now that it is utterly inconceivable, for example, that the corn producers of the corn belt can organize the fund for the handling of surpluses. As a matter of fact the bill as it now

2. In a 1927 memorandum drafted by Hoover, Jardine expressed to the President his opposition to the McNary-Haugen bill and, in accord with Hoover's views, stated his belief in cooperative marketing as the sensible way to handle the farm problem. See Gilbert N. Fite, *George N. Peek and the Fight for Farm Parity* (Norman, Okla., 1954), p. 179.

stands provides for the participation of the Government in private business and it would be a no more radical step to have the Government actually set up the stabilization units than it was to set up the farm loan banks. The Secretary stated that there was no difference between him and me on that, but he had submitted my proposal to the "powers that be" but they turned it down and paddled him for it.

The Secretary stated, however, that he wanted his swan song to be right. He did not care whether or not they accepted it as long as the program was directed at the vital point of the situation and he asked if we would not prepare a statement which he could lay before Mr. Hoover with his best wishes. It was quite apparent from the conversation that the Secretary was kissing the secretaryship good-bye.

February 14, 1929.

In conference with John Stevens[3] last night, John told me that the Secretary was feeling pretty sore about the whole situation. The actual break, according to John, took place early in January, when Hoover was in town, at a breakfast. According to him Secretary Hoover had made certain stipulations to which the Secretary could not agree. The first one was that he must agree to certain transfers from the Department in connection with the whole reorganization program. This the Secretary said, of course, he could not agree to. The second proposal was that he should carry over until after the extra session on farm relief and then accept a position on the federal farm board. This, the Secretary felt, was heaping insult on abuse, since he had spent four years in taking the abuse of the farm interests on behalf of the Administration. Apparently at that time it was clear to the Secretary that he would not remain. It is also equally clear to me, in view of all that was told me, that the Secretary desired very much to continue and he felt he had been double-crossed. In fact, according to Stevens, he had, in an interview with former Secretary Work, expressed himself in no uncertain terms about the unfair treatment he had received at the hands of the administration. . . .

In discussing with Stevens the foreign agricultural bill and the difficulties we were having with King, Stevens suggested that we work through R. B. Carden, the Director of the Utah Experiment Station, who is a liberal Mormon and is remotely related to [Reed] Smoot.[4] He expressed a willingness to write Carden a personal letter relative to the bill, urging him to contact with both Smoot and King, if I would prepare the letter for his signature. He also suggested Frank Nebecker, Jardine's brother-in-law here in town might be able to do something with King.

3. Member of Jardine's staff and a speechwriter for the Secretary of Agriculture.
4. Senator from Utah.

Then he told me that he had a very close working contact with Senator [Francis E.] Warren, Chairman of the Senate Appropriations Committee, and that he would be glad to use his good offices with Warren on this or any other measure and, particularly, budget matters if occasion should arise. [Senator Gerald P.] Nye of North Dakota he described as treacherous, disposed to seek his own selfish ends whenever possible and ready to sell out whenever those ends could be obtained. [Lynn J.] Frazier,[5] on the other hand, he expressed as being somewhat dumb but that once sold on a proposition you could depend on him one hundred per cent. He promised to see Frazier and Warren regarding the foreign bill.

February 27, 1929.

Mr. [George B.] Christian, secretary to the late President Harding, call[ed] to see me at the suggestion of Secretary Jardine to ascertain the possibility of a position in this Bureau for a nephew of his, Chester A. Roberts, of Marion, Ohio. Mr. Roberts is a graduate of the Illinois University Grade School, was a star football player and took over his family properties in Ohio at war prices. He is now broke and is seeking steady employment. He has a family of three and, according to Mr. Christian is a very dependable man. Mr. Christian was very reasonable in the whole matter when I explained that he would have to meet the conditions laid down by the Civil Service Commission and I suggested that he have Mr. Roberts write us direct in regard to his training and experience.

The thing that interested me in my meeting with Mr. Christian were his comments on politics. He asked me who the next Secretary was going to be and I, in turn, put the question to him. He then commented on Tom Campbell,[6] indicating that he thought it would be an unfortunate selection. He then volunteered the comment in regard to Wallace that was very interesting. He said Wallace had given Harding more to worry about than any other member of his Cabinet. Wallace was always persistent in standing up for the rights of Agriculture and the rights of farmers in Cabinet and other meetings. In fact, Christian said he was very much of a personality, which made it difficult for the President to handle him. I asked him, in that connection, if he did not think a certain amount of partisanship was warranted under the circumstances, particularly when Agriculture was so seriously in the dumps, that as far as my acquaintance with Wallace was concerned, it indicated that he had a broad national viewpoint and in taking the side of Agriculture did so with the idea that he would in that way be furthering the Nation's interest. Christian agreed that that was true and he said that he was convinced that

5. Senator from North Dakota.
6. Hoover's choice to head the Civil Service Commission.

Wallace was one of the best selections that Harding had made. He also told me that Harding had asked [William S.] Kenyon, now Federal Judge, and former Senator, to find him a Secretary of Agriculture. Wallace was his choice and he said that Harding and he both agreed that Wallace was the man he wanted.

By contrast Mr. Christian referred to the attitude toward Hoover. There was practically no support for Hoover's entrance into the Harding Cabinet. Christian, himself, was the only one who supported him. Harding, however, took the position that with troublesome times ahead a man of Hoover's broad experience would prove very useful and, hence, he insisted upon his selection. He then went on to comment upon Hoover's qualifications for the Presidency. He said he was undoubtedly the best qualified man who had ever entered upon the duties of the presidency, that his success, however, would depend upon his ability to sell himself. In fact, the success of any President depended on his ability to sell himself. [William Howard] Taft was an exceedingly able man, but proved to be a dud because he could not sell himself to the public. [Theodore] Roosevelt, on the other hand, while not as able, in Mr. Christian's opinion, as Taft, was a past master in selling himself and, hence, made a real success on the job. He went on to add that he thought Mr. Hoover's greatest difficulty would be Congress. He did not know whether Hoover would be able to cope with the political alignments and interests in such a way as to keep everybody feeling sweet.

March 13, 1929.

Last Thursday (March 7, 1929) Senator [Charles L.] McNary called me to his office, the purpose of which I had no advance information. When I arrived he was very affable and gracious and said he wanted to chat with me a bit about the farm relief situation. He said he had not had an opportunity to meet the President or the Secretary[7] but hoped to do so quite soon. He had rather assumed that I had been able to confer with the Secretary and perhaps knew something of his views on farm relief. I hastened to assure him that I had not. He then went on to develop the fact that the house leaders were pressing for joint hearings on farm relief. This he opposed because he did not like the manner in which the House Committee handled their deliberations. They would be at hearings indefinitely and innumerable squabbles would develop and there would be no terminal facilities whatever. He said the Senators were disposed to put it up to the Administration to make good on their campaign promises and there would undoubtedly be a good deal of the equalization fee sentiment to reckon with.

7. Arthur M. Hyde, former Governor of Missouri, succeeded Jardine as Secretary of Agriculture.

He then said that the people on the Hill invariably ask where does the Department of Agriculture stand on the relief program. They feel that the Department, itself, is in the very best position to express sound opinions on a subject of this kind. McNary said that he would be interested in knowing if the Department did or did not wish to take the leadership in crystallizing thinking on this subject. He said if we were willing to do this, he would be glad to have us appear before his Committee and present our views. I assured him that the Department, as such, was disposed to be of the maximum help to Congress in their deliberations on this subject. I felt, however, that the Department could be of the greatest help in supplying information and answering specific questions which they might wish to lay before us, rather than for us to appear before the Committee in advocacy of one approach or another. In this connection I emphasized that farm relief, after all, was in considerable part political and the Department being a scientific institution could not well afford to be drawn into a political controversy. He countered by saying, "This is exactly what I thought would be your reaction and I think you are right. I wished to make sure however that you did not care to assume a more positive leadership in the open in crystallizing the thinking on the subject."

He then made reference to the foreign service bill and said he realized I was enthusiastically for this measure and that undoubtedly it was a move in the right direction. He, personally, had come to feel that it was a measure of much merit and he would support it in the next session. . . . I used this for my cue in indicating that it would be wise for Congress to broaden its conception of farm relief to the various situations. I elaborated upon this in some detail, pointing out specifically what might be done in preventing surpluses from appearing, in tuning up the merchandising machine to the point where it would function better, and when I had finished, he jumped up and said, "You have presented a viewpoint here that is absolutely sound and correct." He said, "You can do me a great service, Olsen. I am going to give a radio talk a week from Saturday night on the farm relief program and I would like to embody the thoughts that you expressed. Will you help me?" I assured him that I would be glad to place a statement in his hands which he might use in connection with that talk.

After my meeting with Senator McNary I tried to secure an appointment with the Secretary, but was unsuccessful until last night (March 12), when I rode up with him to his apartment with Mr. Russell. I placed before him the full story and told him that the Senator had called me at noon requesting the material which I had promised, that I found it necessary to see the Senator that evening and was going to place in his hands the statement in question. After stating the developments in my conversations with Mr. McNary, he stated that I had done just exactly the proper thing. I then asked him if he cared to read the statement which I had prepared. He said, "Most assuredly," since he was initiating his education without delay. As he read the statement, he made various comments of approval and finally wound up by saying that "after making this statement the Senator could not have much more to say," as far as he could see. The statement was thoroughly sound and constructive and he hoped the Senator would make a talk in line with the thoughts expressed. He stated, however, that these views should be expressed as personal views of mine, and not the views of the Secretary of Agriculture and of the Administration. I assured him that it would be handled in that way. He felt quite sure that the Senator would be disposed to play fair with me in the matter.

Last night (March 12) at 8:15 I called at Senator McNary's apartment at the Mayflower Hotel. He was very affable and gracious and expressed some apology for troubling me at night in connection with the matter. We first discussed the attitude of the Administration and I sought to draw the Senator out on his conversations with the President and the Secretary. He had seen both but had not been successful in getting anything very concrete from either. He said the President had told him that he looked to Hyde for his facts on farm relief matters and had further indicated that the problem of farm relief belonged to Congress and that Congress would have to find the way out. The Senator in commenting on this said that he had quite a different story before the election when it was important to get the farm support, that then he was quite ready with his promises on farm relief. In commenting on his visit with the Secretary he made it plain that he did not get anything from him and that he did not feel he knew very much about the subject. He stated that both Hoover and Hyde were, apparently, in more or less of a haze on the whole subject and did not have anything concrete to offer.

We then discussed, for a little while, some features of the farm relief bill that was before the last session and I made plain my feeling that it was not feasible to unload the problem of handling surpluses upon disorganized farmers, that certainly some of the commodity groups were not in a position to effectively organize and operate so-called "stabilization corporations." I made the further point that it was merely a subterfuge to say that the Government was not in business when it gives funds for buying surpluses and disposing of them as outlined in the bill. In that case, why not go the full length and state the Government was undertaking an experiment itself, and thereby leave it in a position to actually control that experiment. This would not be doing, in my opinion, more than had been done in connection with the Federal Land Banks. Of this he expressed approval but indicated that the agitation had been toward getting away from all semblance of Government injection in business and of placing the whole thing upon farmer controlled cooperatives.

I then picked up my statement and explained that this reflected my own thinking, and in reflecting my thinking it no doubt in considerable part reflected the thinking of the Bureau. It did not, and on this I made myself very plain, reflect the views of the Department of Agriculture nor of the Administration. The Senator said he understood that fully and I repeated that statement at least twice again during my conversation. I then read the statement to him and found the Senator in hearty accord. . . .

March 15, 1929. 3:30 p.m.

I just returned from a conference with the Secretary of Agriculture, which I have sought at least for the last week. He is so occupied with outside matters and contacts with people on the Hill, that access to him at the present time is exceedingly difficult. I presented to him the following matters, which were of an urgent nature and with which he should have some acquaintance.

In the first place I told him about the International Cotton Conference, the Agreement, the purposes of the meeting and expressed the wish that he be present tomorrow morning at ten a.m., to extend a welcoming word to the delegates. I told of my conference with Mr. Russell and his suggestion that it would be difficult, if not impossible, for the Secretary to appear at this meeting. I told him this was agreeable with me, providing I knew definitely that he could not attend. I urged him, however, to attend the banquet next Tuesday night and, if possible, take charge of that affair. I told him a decision was important since, if he were to be present, the invitations should go out in his name. He immediately countered by saying the banquet would cost him his entire evening and he did not feel justified in devoting a night to a matter of this kind as long as other pressing matters were on hand. I told him that we would not urge this upon him and that we could handle it even though he did not attend. He asked me to lay some facts before him this evening, which he might consider in connection with the talk before the delegates tomorrow morning in case he should decide to welcome them.

I then told him the story of the census, including the run-in we had with the Committee and the difficulties we were now experiencing with the Director of the Census in regard to the schedule. I told him it would be a serious matter to reduce the census schedule at this time, since we now needed more than at any other time, perhaps, information for the handling of farm relief measures for coping with agricultural problems generally. Throughout my comments along this line he nodded his head in agreement. I then suggested that it might be desirable for us to work through him in getting to the Secretary of Commerce and perhaps others in the Administration agreeable to our viewpoint. He countered, at once, by saying he would like to know just what questions the census proposed to eliminate, before he arrived at any decision. I told him I would be very glad to supply him this information.

I then moved on to the question of our office at Marseilles, sketching briefly the foreign organization we now have, the purposes of that organization, etc. I told him about the item of $10,000 obtained for the Marseilles office and told him we were now ready to appoint a man to fill this position, that this man would have to be promoted from $3200 to $4600 and since this was a large promotion we, naturally, desired his approval. He than asked if the Department of Commerce was not engaged in foreign agricultural work. I told him that the Department was engaged in foreign work primarily in behalf of industry and commerce, that they were doing some work in promoting the expansion of foreign markets for agricultural products, collecting some current information but were not analyzing the problems in a way to serve, adequately, American producers. Agriculture, as I expressed it, needed the Department of Agriculture in the foreign field, in order to give the foreign service the proper direction that it needed. The Departments of State and Commerce had organizations which could be used very effectively in this connection, but the Department of Agriculture should have an office in all of the important competing countries and in all of the important countries. He stated that the foreign service was of special interest to him, especially since the farm organizations had expressed their interest in it. I countered at once by saying that the farm organizations had been very anxious to see the Department of Agriculture expand its foreign service. He then asked what Bureau handled the foreign work in the Department of Commerce and I told him that the work fell in Dr. Klein's Bureau, but that he was in Europe. He then asked who was next in charge and I told him Mr. [Thomas R.] Taylor. He followed this with a request that I arrange a conference between Mr. Taylor, myself and him in order to consider this whole matter. It seemed rather apparent from his general attitude that he was not disposed to make any move that would prove objectional to the Department of Commerce. . . .

March 25, 1929.

Friday morning (March 22, 1929) I was surprised to receive from Secretary Hyde a brief note stating that he had left for Missouri and that he would not return for ten days. He said he had written Senator McNary that he could not appear before the Committee at this time, but that he had indicated that both Mr. Englund and I would be prepared to supply the Committee facts that we might have available.

I learned Friday that the Secretary had tried to get me over the telephone Thursday night, but naturally did not reach me as I was attending a dinner. His reply to Senator McNary was very much of a surprise to me since in my conversation with him a couple of days prior, I had emphasized the fact that it was very undesirable for Department men to testify on farm relief, certainly in advance of any testimony by the Secretary himself. In that conversation the Secretary had stated that the Department of Agriculture certainly knew more about farm relief than any other institution and that agriculture had a right to look to the Department for guidance and help. He went on to say that he thought it was the Department's job to deliver on farm relief, rather than Mr. Hoover's or the Adminstration's. With this I took very definite issue. I told him that I thought the Department should be as helpful as possible in providing available facts on various phases of the situation but in view of the political character of farm relief, it would be exceedingly serious for the Department men to be placed before the committees as witnesses.

The Secretary's leaving at this time was all the more surprising since he had arranged to accompany representatives of the cooperatives to an interview with the President. [C. L.] Christensen[8] received a note stating that it would be up to him and to me to arrange for this interview with the President. Then, in addition, a dinner had been especially arranged for Friday evening which the Secretary was to attend. The cooperatives, naturally, were exceedingly disappointed that the Secretary had failed them in this matter. They were also reported to be somewhat peeved because he had cancelled appointments with several groups of cooperatives in his office during the afternoon of that Friday.

The only thing to do was to arrange for the interview with the President and Christensen, knowing all of the cooperatives, called off their names and we all lined up in a semi-circle before the President. The President did not seem particularly at ease and stated in a very few words that he was glad to meet the group and wanted them to know that he was deeply interested in cooperatives and cooperative marketing and that he counted on the cooperatives to help solve the problems that were now confronting farmers. After his few brief remarks, Mr. [Christopher O.] Moser[9] spoke for the group, referring to the purposes of their meeting here in Washington for the establishment of a National Chamber of Agricultural Cooperatives and further remarked that he hoped there would be every opportunity to work with the Government and the various Government departments in solving the problems before Agriculture. The President came back with one or two brief sentences, in which he said there should be no question since the present administration was very much sold to the whole theory of cooperation. With that, we all filed out. The whole scene did not last over five or six minutes.

In view of the developments it became doubly desirable that I have a definite understanding with Senator McNary. I therefore arranged to see him at 3:30 that afternoon (Friday, March 22, 1929). The Senator was in very good humor and well might be because I had waited for my appointment at least a half hour while he was completing his interview with

8. Chief of the Cooperative Marketing Division of the Department of Agriculture.
9. Vice-president and secretary of the American Cotton Cooperative Association.

Farm Bureau representatives, and the press which was hot on his trail. I launched right in and told him that it would be very necessary, from my point of view, to know just what was the nature of the program ahead. I had rather gathered that the Secretary had indicated that Mr. Englund and I might appear before the Committee and this had been somewhat disturbing to me. I pointed out, of course, that we were very anxious to be of every help possible to the Committee but, naturally, it would be embarrassing for us to express ourselves on farm relief when the President and the Secretary of Agriculture had not seen fit to do so. The Senator said that he saw very well the difficulty in the situation and assured me that we had nothing to fear on that score. He said he did not propose to put us on the witness stand, but would like to have us present to answer questions of fact that might arise. He took occasion to slap the President very vigorously, indicating that he was thoroughly peeved that the Administration had withheld an expression of its position with reference to farm relief. He picked up the Republican campaign book and turned to Hoover's West Branch, Ia., speech and read the section with reference to farm relief. As he completed the reading he threw the book down and said: "This is the kind of thing on which we are asked to formulate a concrete program of relief for Agriculture."

He then swung over into the question of credit to cooperatives for physical facilities. He said that a good many wires and letters had been coming to him and it was evident to me that he was out of sympathy with the suggestion. He asked me for my personal and unofficial opinion regarding the matter, adding that Eugene Meyer was nothing but a New York Jew banker who had no conception of the farmer's needs and there would be no object in calling on him. I told him I would express an opinion or two as an individual, not as an official, since it was not fitting that I a member of one Department should criticize officials of another Department. I indicated that criticisms had been coming to us from various sources that the Intermediate Credit system was not being administered as sympathetically as possible. This was attributed in considerable part to the fact that Eugene Meyer was in charge of the entire system and to the further fact that the President of the Federal Land Banks was also President of the Federal Intermediate Credit Banks and conservative as they are, they had been a wet blanket on the effective administration of the Federal Intermediate Credit Bank. . . . He then swung over and criticized the use of the phrase "cooperative marketing." He said that after all cooperatives did not accomplish their greatest good in the marketing of a commodity, but rather when they were successful in preventing the creation of surpluses and in providing that quality of product which the market most desires. He elaborated on this in some detail and gave a splendid illustration of the fact that his education had been going forward apace during the last week or two. I assured him I felt he was right in his views of cooperation and that as a matter of fact we here in the Bureau had stressed proper production as an important function of cooperatives. He wondered whether or not some term other than cooperative marketing could not be found that would adequately cover both production and marketing phases. I told him I would think a little about it.

April 13, 1929.

Last Tuesday, April 2, 1929, the Secretary returned from Missouri for the purpose of meeting the Agricultural Committees' request that he appear before them. He did not call me over until five o'clock, at which time he told me he was scheduled to appear before the Senate Committee Wednesday morning. He was quite excited and up in the air as to just what his testimony would be. I told him I felt we could be quite helpful to him in mapping out a line of testimony if we only had a little more time, that I already had prepared a good deal of material but it would take time to lay it out in such fashion that he could readily use it. I asked him if he could not get his appearance postponed for a day or two. He seemed to take to this suggestion, but finally said the thing for him to do was to go ahead. In any event, he was scheduled to be the "vicarious sacrifice" and probably it did not make any difference whether he appeared now or later. He then told me that he was scheduled to see the President about 8:30 that evening and he would like to have certain information in advance of that meeting. He asked me if I would not prepare a list of difficulties which the Board[10] would have to face and which all argued for a board with very extensive powers. This list he insisted on my preparing, even though written in longhand. Then he also raised the question as to whether or not a statement could be prepared that he could use before the Committee. I told him that it would be difficult to prepare such a statement in view of the fact that I did not know where he or the President stood on some matters. I laid before him statements covering adjustments in production, land policy, foreign work and a number of other phases of the long-time program. He threw up his hands in despair and said it would be utterly impossible for him to get a firsthand acquaintance with such a mass of material. However, he was glad to have it. After spending an hour with him I left and later met him at the Mayflower about eight o'clock. At that time he gave me the impression that he had not formulated his ideas but that he expected help from Mr. Hoover. I am convinced that the general outline of his testimony, and particularly the statement which he read, was in no small measure shaped at the White House.

The following day, Wednesday April 3, at the very last minute I

10. The creation of a Federal Farm Board was central to the Administration's effort to resolve the farm problem and to provide equality for agriculture.

placed in the Secretary's hands a revised statement covering the long-time approach but of course he did not use it in the hearing. He fared rather badly, in my opinion, before the Senate Agricultural Committee and was placed in a number of difficult positions. On the other hand, he received a much more cordial reception by the House Committee and parried the questions with deftness and skill. When asked if he thought the Secretary should be a member of the Board, he said that if he had his way about it, the Secretary would be as far removed as possible from the Board. Later on in the course of the hearing, he was asked by Mr. [Franklin] Fort[11] two significant questions. First, he was plainly asked if he did not think that in view of the fact that many of the functions which the Board would undertake were now being performed by the Department of Agriculture, that in order to avoid duplication and overlapping they should be transferred to the Board and to this he replied "Yes." In the second place, he was asked if, in view of the fact that the Board would undoubtedly be called upon to do many things now being done by various parts of the Department, if it would not be desirable to authorize the Secretary of Agriculture to transfer to the Board such offices and activities in the Department which more properly belonged to the Board. To this he replied that he thought perhaps this would be a wise procedure. I rode back with the Secretary and Mr. [R. W.] Dunlap[12] following the afternoon meeting, and took occasion to express a little surprise at the Secretary's replies to Fort's two questions. To this he countered by saying that it did not really represent his views on the matter, but that while he could not speak for the "Big Chief," he felt that his replies represented his ideas.

Since the Secretary's appearance before the House Committee I have had a number of conferences with him that are of no small significance in connection with the farm relief program. Last Wednesday, April 10, a delegation representing the National Grain Dealers Association called on the Secretary in connection with the grain standards situation. They criticized the interpretation our Grain Division was making of the standards and made a plea for some far-reaching changes in our handling of the matter. The Secretary handled this quite cautiously and satisfactorily, although he indicated that other complaints had come to him and that he hoped to give the matter careful consideration when Farm Relief matters were out of the way. . . .

Last night, April 12, at 7:30 I called at the Secretary's apartment at the Mayflower Hotel and spent until 10:45 with him, going over phases of the long-time farm program. He took a very keen interest in the land policy phase of the matter and indicated a willingness to go along on the long-time legislation. At this point, however, when we were deciding what should be done he pulled out a copy of the farm relief bill which

11. Congressman representing the Ninth District in New Jersey.
12. Assistant Secretary of Agriculture.

the House Committee of Five had just completed and pointed out that this Bill authorized the Board to handle the land utilization question. He gave me a copy for my perusal, with the injunction that it was quite confidential. We read the entire bill and then proceeded to criticize it. The bill in this form provides two or three features that are very serious from the Department's point of view. In the first place it vests the Board with authority to undertake investigations and publish results on land utilization and other related economic questions. It confuses, badly, the investigational with the extension aspects of the Board's functions and leads one to believe that the Board is to take over a large domain of work now in the hands of the Bureau of Agricultural Economics. The most illuminating feature of the bill is the last section which authorizes the President of the United States to transfer to the jurisdiction of the Board in toto, or in part, any Bureau or division or any activity of the Department of Agriculture or other departments as he may see fit, together with the records and other facilities of such units. I protested vigorously with the Secretary against these features of the bill and the Secretary was very much inclined to agree. As a matter of fact he took pains to work out wording that would be satisfactory and said that he would go over the matter with the President this morning at breakfast. At that time the Secretary was quite in harmony with my views on the subject and was disposed to use his good influence in getting the adjustments made in the bill. It remains to be seen if the President is not altogether responsible for these phases of the bill.

I discussed with the Secretary the possible accomplishments which might be effected through stabilization corporations and he agreed that the Board would have real difficulty in delivering in the case of commodities that were not cooperatively organized and that, furthermore, the government would be in the business of fixing prices within limits and that the present setup was really a fiction. He admitted that my suggestions of the Government actually stepping in and taking over the function of stabilizing prices was probably a sound approach, but could not receive administration approval. There was some discussion of the debenture plan[13] and I told him that the boys had reported back that the Senate Agricultural Committee seemed very friendly to this proposal that, in fact, the Committee had the impression that Mr. Hoover might be friendly to the debenture proposal. To this Mr. Hyde shook his head and said this was very unlikely and then he pulled out [Walter] Newton's[14] letter, together with the questions which the President had noted on an attached slip, as indicating that the President could not be

13. The debenture plan, championed by the National Grange, called for the issuance of treasury certificates to exporters of surplus agricultural products representing the difference in production costs at home and abroad. These certificates could then be used in the payment of tariff duties. In Congress an effort was made to include the debenture plan in the measure creating the Federal Farm Board.

14. A former Minnesota congressman who was a secretary to President Hoover.

favorable to the debenture proposal. He then raised the questions as to whether or not our men had supported the debenture proposal. I told him they were sent over there to present facts in response to questions and not express opinions in regard to the bill and certainly not to take a stand either for or against it.

This morning, April 13, we are confronted with press releases, for which the Senate Agricultural Committee is in no small part responsible, indicating that the Department experts . . . had given testimony supporting the debenture plan. . . . In order that the whole matter might be placed fully before the Secretary, I arranged to take Englund over with me this morning and discuss yesterday's session. The immediate reason for calling was that Senator McNary requests that the testimony of our boys before the Committee yesterday be printed, even though given in executive session. To this I violently objected and the Secretary agreed with me. The Secretary then stated that the White House had gotten the impression that the Department men had testified in favor of the debenture plan and he, himself, was quite a little disturbed about it. I told him that the Department's men had not been authorized to testify in favor of or against the plan and that I had Mr. Englund here to state just what had happened. Mr. Englund then recounted some of the things that had happened and the Secretary seemed quite satisfied that we had not been indiscreet. He said he realized that it was an exceedingly difficult thing to handle and that, however neutral we might be in our statements they probably would be misconstrued, as he was in his testimony before the Committee. He then called Newton of the White House on the phone and made about the following statement. "With reference to the news report that Department men had favored the debenture, he had the Department men now in his office and from their statement he concluded that about the following had happened. The Committee had asked the question, 'If prices of agricultural products are to be raised through relief legislation what, in your opinion, would be the most effective method of raising prices, the equalization fee plan or the debenture plan?' To this our men replied that if it was the purpose of Congress to raise prices it seemed to them that the debenture plan was simpler in operation and also would probably cost less." Mr. Hyde went on to comment that a statement of this kind could not very well be avoided in the circumstances and, of course, lent itself to misinterpretation. He raised the question with Mr. Newton as to whether or not the Department should not withhold sending up any of its men to the Committee for further testimony. To this Newton replied that it would not very well do for an Administrative Department to refuse to give Congress such information as it might request. The Secretary then agreed that we should go forward with the preparation of the report on the debenture plan and use this as an excuse for keeping away from the Committee if it could be diplomatically done. . . .

April 16, 1929.

April 15, 1929, 5:30 p.m. I just returned from a conference with the Secretary and he asked what progress we were making with the report on the debenture plan. I told him that the material was practically ready for submittal to me and that I would get it to him in the morning. I also told him that Mr. Taylor of the Department of Commerce had called me by phone and said that they too had a request to report on the debenture plan. The Secretary seemed a little surprised at this and called for Newton's letter. He went on to add that he thought the situation was an extremely unfortunate one, since the testimony of our boys had undoubtedly resulted in convincing four or five members of the Committee that the debenture plan had real merit. Senator [James E.] Watson [from Indiana] reported to the President that the sentiment for the bill had been considerably strengthened by their testimony. I told him that I had gone over the testimony and that the boys had been cautious and had only answered such questions as they were forced to answer and that their statements were all properly hedged. He said he recognized this but it all went to strengthen the difficulties of the situation. He seemed somewhat worried that they would now jockey the debenture plan into the bill and in case the present McNary Bill were turned down, then the Administration would be put into the position of having to accept the debenture plan. This, evidently is causing the Administration considerable worry. I asked him about our conferring with the Department of Commerce and presenting reports that were quite alike. He, to my surprise, indicated that he thought there might be some advantage in having somewhat dissimilar reports, but he noted the fact that Commerce was making the report and said he would get in touch with them before he sent forth his statement.

I then told him that I had before me a copy of the House bill and that it contained two sections that were particularly obnoxious to me and to all friends of the Department. One section was that authorizing the Board to conduct extensive investigations in the economic field and the other was the clause authorizing the President to transfer, in whole or part, any office or Bureau from the Department to the Board. He tried to minimize the danger in that connection and said he felt quite sure that nothing adverse could happen for the next four or eight years. I countered by saying that if there was no danger in that and if it were assured that the Department was going to render the services requested by the Board, why introduce these disturbing sections in the bill, which would clearly give the impression of trying to undermine the Department's work. He made some reference to inter-bureau jealousies and I indicated this was not inter-bureau jealousy but that it was striking at fundamentals and the permanent work of the bureau and of the Department. He then said, "Well, I would hardly have the guts to tell the Presi-

dent that this was all wrong, but perhaps you would." I countered by
saying that if the opportunity were afforded I would have no hesitancy in
telling the President just what I thought of these phases of the bill. . . .

April 25, 1929.

About Wednesday of last week (April 17) matters waxed more than
hot in connection with the debenture plan. The attitude of the Administration swung from one extreme to the other. One day they were
hot and the next day they were cold. Undoubtedly the disposition, at the
outset, was to leave the door open to take a neutral position which
would prevent the alienation of the support of certain groups and, at the
same time, take a rather definite position later on.

The Secretary admitted that the President had given the Committee
encouragement in believing that he might be friendly to the debenture
plan. I took pains to tell him that Senator McNary had recounted to me
their conversation with the President in the course of which he, Senator
McNary, had called attention to the fact that the debenture plan was of
course a subsidy and, therefore, impossible. The President, however, did
not react as he expected but countered by saying that he was not against
all subsidies, that there might be conditions under which a subsidy might
be acceptable. This remark by the President was what led them to believe
that he might be friendly to the debenture plan. Later on in the week,
however, it became more and more apparent that the President was
determined to take a definite stand. We had drafted the original letter so
as to leave the Secretary in a more or less neutral position. I told the
Secretary that it would be right important for us to know where the Administration stood in the matter, in order to properly draft the letter. If
they wished to take a neutral position, the letter would be drafted one
way. If they were going to take a decided position against the debenture
plan, then of course it would be drafted another way.

Thursday, April 18, in my conferences with the Secretary he suggested that it might not be a bad idea for me as Chief of the Bureau to
give him a vigorous report against the debenture plan, which he could
transmit to the Committee. I at once countered by saying that would
place the Bureau in an impossible position. It would throw us into the
midst of a political scrap and that was what we had persistently tried to
keep the Bureau out of. I stated my opposition so vigorously that he did
not press the matter any further.

Friday morning, April 19, the Secretary called me on the telephone
and made the brief remark, "Give her the poison," and from then on it
was quite apparent that the Administration wished every argument
against the debenture plan developed to the fullest extent. In my last visit
with the Secretary, Saturday night, April 20, before the letter finally

went up to the Hill, I called his attention specifically to the weaknesses in certain statements which were made for which he was fully responsible, among these were his statements on diversification and also the concluding two sentences of the letter, in which he referred to the bad results that might follow from another period of inflation. In connection with the concluding paragraph, he told me, confidentially, that Walter Newton had urged him to retain the sentences to which I objected. To this I countered by saying that I did not think Mr. Newton was correct in his appraisal of the reaction that would follow from that kind of statement. Nevertheless, the two sentences to which I objcted were left out of the final draft. . . .

[no date]

Last night (June 6) I called at the Secretary's Office about 5:15 and after a visit with the Secretary on various matters he invited me to take dinner with him. We spent a couple of hours at the Army and Navy Club in a very delightful chat on various matters. In the course of this conversation certain points were made in regard to farm relief legislation now about to be passed. In his opinion there was no doubt but what the Senate would accept the bill pretty much as passed by the conferees. The very fact that the Florida legislature had instructed its Senators to line up for the bill there is no question, according to the Secretary, of its final outcome. We touched upon the question of Section 9[15] and I again reiterated my position that this was a very bad thing from the viewpoint of the Department and that I was still hopeful that something might be done to eliminate it. He did not express himself very fully but indicated that he felt there would be no real menace to the Bureau. . . .

The Secretary became quite personal and reminiscent in regard to his political history. He told of a news item that had been sent to him by Mr. [Claudius] Huston,[16] stating that Mr. Hyde was very high in the President's favor and undoubtedly could have anything he wished. He sent the clipping to the President with the comment that he wanted him to know that he appreciated the compliment but that he was not in the market for anything whatsoever. At the conclusion of his Kentucky and Tennessee campaign trip, which he found interesting enough but rather lonesome because he was out among people with whom he was not personally acquainted, he returned to Washington and found the Republican National Headquarters teeming with men who were in the field for

15. Section 9 granted the Federal Farm Board authority Olsen claimed would duplicate or transfer work already being done by the Bureau of Agricultural Economics. See entry for April 16, 1929.

16. An Assistant Secretary of Commerce during the Harding Administration and a prominent Chattanooga businessman and Washington lobbyist active in Republican politics, particularly in the South.

political preferment of one kind or another. The whole thing disgusted him and he left as quickly as possible, vowing that he would have nothing further to do with politics and, yet, he said, once the virus is in your system it is impossible to resist. He said he had no idea of coming to Washington on his present appointment, but the urgency with which the matter was pressed upon him and the smoke of battle had a real appeal. He went on to remark in this connection that a number of people, whom he knew, had actually approached Hoover with reference to some place, which of course was apparently the worst possible move with the President. From his observation, he remarked, he was sure that the President would not be influenced in the least by the pressure that was brought to bear for the appointment of individuals on the Board, but it would represent his own personal opinion of the men. The Secretary was again very complimentary of the Bureau and its work and gave every indication of wanting to strengthen, maintain and support it. The very fact that he is coming to us for rules, regulations and suggestions on the setup of the Board is, in itself, right significant. However, the danger is here and only the future will tell the story. . . .

June 17, 1929.

. . . I brought up the question of the Marseilles office and told the Secretary that we were embarrassed because we could not go ahead with our plans, even though funds were available. "Well," he said, "it was quite apparent that the Big Chief was of the opinion that the foreign service should be handled by the Department of Commerce and that made it quite difficult to go forward with our plans." I countered by saying it was unthinkable that this Department could give up its foreign service or that Agriculture would permit it to happen, that as far as I was concerned I was willing to defend the thesis that the Department of Agriculture was the only Department to represent its service in the foreign field. He remarked that he had not known the President for any length of time prior to his appointment, that as a matter of fact he had met him only twice prior to his coming to Washington as Secretary of Agriculture, and that as soon as he could establish a somewhat more intimate acquaintance with him, he felt it would be far easier to handle a delicate matter of this kind.

At the time, a Mr. [Charles S.] Wilson[17] of Hall, New York, was in the Secretary's office. It has been rather noticeable, lately [*sic*], that some of his personal friends, either from Missouri or elsewhere, have been camping in his office when I have arrived. Wilson stepped out after

17. A professor of agriculture at Cornell University who became a member of the Federal Farm Board representing the fruit interests of the northeastern states.

a few introductory remarks and after [F. H.] Spencer[18] had submitted to him what appeared to be a list of candidates for the Board. As I passed out of the office, I hobnobbed and chatted with him, making a very slight reference to the passage of the farm relief bill. He perked up at once and asked me what I thought of it and what I thought would be the policy for the Board to pursue. I made a comment or two and he proceeded to make a note of it. Is Wilson a candidate for the Board, or just what is his interest in this whole matter? . . .

July 3, 1929.

Last night I took dinner with the Secretary at the Army and Navy Club and had a very worthwhile visit. He was in a very good frame of mind and was disposed to be quite confidential.

We discussed, in some detail, the Federal Farm Board and I did not try to worm out of him the names of the additional members, simply because I realized it was the wiser course not to seem too inquisitive. I congratulated him on the setup of the Board, so far as it was appointed, and he countered by saying that the President deserved the major credit for the selection. He said he thought, in this case, it was good politics to select a Board of outstanding men, as had been done. He said, confidentially, however, that he thought the President had some real difficulties ahead and that probably the rock on which his ship would sink would be his failure to recognize his political obligations, that he was living in a realm of idealism and was not recognizing the fellows in the front trenches who had, somehow, to be rewarded. The President did not think the pivotal positions should be awarded to men of that type but he did feel that he could not hold the support of the party workers if they were not given at least minor appointments. I told the Secretary that I felt there was a great deal of truth in what he said, that personally I felt it was very desirable to select men on the basis of their merit and I had to respect Mr. Hoover for taking that attitude. On the other hand it behooved a person in his position to be sufficiently practical and pragmatic so that he did not undermine his support. I told him that I sensed that he, the Secretary, was winning the President's confidence and assumed that he would have an excellent opportunity to direct the President's thinking along the right lines in this connection. He frankly admitted that the President lacked a sense of humor, took things seriously in the highest degree, in fact could not discuss anything but business matters, when he should relax and talk about frivolities. He cited, for example, that on the trip which they took to the fishing camp two weeks ago,

18. Secretary to the Secretary of Agriculture.

the President talked four hours about the Farm Board on the way out and, after they began fishing, the same old story was trotted out.

We discussed the situation in the Department and, particularly, the help he now has. He said that he would need a man to serve as his contact man with the new Federal Farm Board and asked me for my suggestions. I told him I would be glad to give it some thought. . . . He said he thought it was advisable not to put in too many Missouri people near him, although it was mainly Missouri people he could draw on as his close friends. He asked me to give serious thought to a man for that office, as well as for the contact work with the Federal Farm Board. He said that he could not afford to give too much of his time to the Board, that there were innumerable things in the Department that should have his attention. I urged him to gather about him a staff of men upon whose judgment he could depend, that it was impossible for him to examine all the matters that came before him and that he must have someone upon whom he could rely. He said he realized that this was the case and that was the reason why he was anxious to have me help to find two good assistants. He also asked me if I would not give thought to matters within the Department as a whole, that might need his attention. . . .

In speaking of Federal Farm Board matters, he referred to Carl Williams[19] in a rather joking way. He said he liked him very much, but was amused with the way Carl tried to indicate he was not interested in the job. He said he was sure Carl wanted the job very badly and cited the following as an illustration of that fact. After they had been over to see the President, Carl had said to him, "You must see to it that the Chief does not press me too hard in this matter because I really cannot afford to accept." The Secretary said, when a man talks that way you may be sure that he is fishing pretty hard, that later on Carl indicated in no unmistakable way that he wanted the job. Then the Secretary explained how [Charles C.] Teague[20] had come to accept. He said it was true that Teague declined, but the President immediately wired some of Teague's friends in California and they, in turn, put pressure on Teague to compel his acceptance.

In commenting on the President's lack of humor, he said he had been able to get a real chuckle out of him on just one story. In talking about the research work of the Department, the President had asked what type of things the Department was doing. The Secretary countered by saying it did the widest range of things, but among others they tried to determine if the hog would gain more weight if the feed was brought to him than if he had to go to the feed. This struck the president's funny bone and he had a good laugh about it.

19. A member of the Federal Farm Board who had been active in the cooperative marketing field and was a former president of the American Cotton Growers Exchange.
20. President of the California Fruit Growers Exchange.

July 25, 1929.

Wednesday evening, at 7:30, July 24, I met the Secretary at his office in response to a request that I confer with him on his Baton Rouge speech. He was in his usual good spirits and free in expressing himself on anything that came along. I had occasion to ask him about some action of the Federal Farm Board, to which he replied that he did not know and that he would not be apt to know about the details of the Board's action. That prompted me to ask what arrangements he was making for an understudy to represent him on the Board, to which he replied that he expected to eliminate himself as much as possible from the Board. . . .

This discussion gave me a good opportunity for bringing up the matter of the relationship of the Department to the Board and the possibility of inroads being made upon the Department. I told him I was somewhat uneasy about the intimations that had come to me through members of the Board in particular, and others, that the Cooperative Marketing Division would be transferred. I asked him if there was any truth in that. He said there was considerable thought along that line and it might well be. I then told him I thought it would be a very serious mistake, that there was no excuse for it, that the Board did not need the serious research work under its jurisdiction, but it needed a staff of economic advisers who were something more than merely cooperative marketing advisers, but in which there would be a group of cooperative marketing men who could do the trouble chasing, could interpret the studies of this Bureau, plus any other material, plus the situation surrounding a cooperative and lay before the Board its concrete suggestions for a program of action. That it did not call for a program of work which I had in mind, that is the serious intensive studies that call for a year's application to a problem and perhaps the resources of the whole Bureau, instead of one division, which certainly could better be done in this Bureau. Furthermore, I asked him if he knew what had happened to the standing of the Federal Trade Commission and the Tariff Commission. I told him I believed it was generally felt that the findings of the Tariff Commission were partisan and were not taken anywhere near as seriously as the investigations of the Bureau of Agricultural Economics on tariff. As a matter of fact I had just been told by one of our men who was in Canada that the people up there pooh-poohed the findings of the Tariff Commission but viewed with the greatest respect any statement made by the Department on this subject. As far as the Federal Trade Commission was concerned, most students of the problem felt that its findings were colored and did not stand for independent fact finding. The chances were that the identical thing would happen in the case of Cooperative Marketing work if it were put under the Board, because certainly the Board would be subjected to more pressure than either of these other two commissions. The Secretary asked me if I had discussed this matter with any members of the Board. I told him I had gone over it to some extent with [James C.] Stone[21] and Teague. He then said that he wanted me to see other members of the Board on the subject and he was sure that they would wish to give me an opportunity to present the case before the Board in full session. Furthermore he was in agreement with what I had said. I mentioned, however, at that point that his own attitude as Secretary of Agriculture would go further than anything else in determining whether or not his Department was to be invaded or remain intact as a virile going institution and that I hoped he would interest himself, personally, in this matter. I said the same thing applied to many other matters, for example, the foreign work. I said much of the opinion that this Department should take a very positive part in foreign agricultural work. I told him I thought there was something of a menace confronting us on this score and it behooved us to watch our fences. I told him that as far as I was concerned, I was willing to defend the thesis that this Department had a very important place in the foreign field and that Agriculture would not be served until it took that place. I again urged him to make a special study of this matter and come to his own conclusions as a result of such a survey, that I had no fear of the outcome with a man who faced the facts fairly. He then said I need have no fear about his position, that he had already been convinced of the fact that we should be in the foreign field. He said however, "You know what my difficulties are. The President thinks he knows something about this subject, coming from the Department of Commerce and naturally he had something of a bias. My influence with him on this is not very great because I have disclaimed any special knowledge on the matter." The Secretary said the real approach in this matter is through the Federal Farm Board, who are now running ace high with the President. He said, "Convince them of your position and it will go far to effect the right kind of a solution." In that connection he said he wanted me to get acquainted with the members of the Board. He said, "Above all, I want you to know [Alexander] Legge[22] and want Legge to know you. It is important you go with them to Chicago and take my place on the Board at the Grain Hearing, and then go down to Baton Rouge and hobnob with them on the train and, in that way, get a firsthand contact with all of them."

In connection with the organization of the Board, I made reference to the kind of economic advisory staff which they would need and suggested that they might want to reach in and get men like [Mordecai]

21. Vice-chairman of the Federal Farm Board and former president and general manager of the Burley Tobacco Growers Association headquartered in Lexington, Kentucky.

22. Chairman of the Federal Farm Board who was president of the International Harvester Corporation.

Ezekiel[23] and some other good men. I told him I had no objection to their taking individual men who would be of outstanding value to the Board, because I recognized the tremendous job they had on hand, but I did object to any invasion of our organization which would tend to break it down. To this he countered that he did not think that we should be too generous in releasing men like Ezekiel and others who were pivotal men in our organization. He said he wanted the Department kept intact and its staff maintained in the highest degree of efficiency, and that he was not so sure that he would like to see Ezekiel go over to the Board. . . .

August 13, 1929.

On my return trip from Baton Rouge, I fell in with [L. J.] Taber of the Grange. Our discussions became quite confidential and free. He told me very frankly that he had his fingers crossed on the Federal Farm Board and what it could do. He said that during the past two or three months he was in touch with farm leaders all over the United States and he did not believe there were more than eight or ten who expressed the hope that anything much could be accomplished. He felt sure the Board would have a peck of troubles to wrestle with, perhaps even upon the readjournment of Congress. . . .

Taber gave a very intimate and confidential picture of the happenings in connection with the debenture. He was somewhat unhappy that there had developed a complete break between him and the President, but he went on to add that it perhaps helped the Grange more than any other single thing during the past several years. His narrative brought out the tremendous pressure brought to bear by the President to change his position. He said he had been in consultation with Hoover several times and at the outset was led to believe that Hoover was not so diametrically opposed to the debenture plan. The day before the release of the now famous "Hoover-Mellon-Hyde" statements [denouncing the export debenture proposal] he was in consultation with the President and told him that he would be glad to transfer the debenture question to the tariff, if the President so desired. He left with the understanding that this was the way it would be handled. When the next morning the President's vitriolic statement came out, as he put it, he was absolutely dumbfounded. The news men rushed to him and tried to get an extended statement from him, which he refused to give. He indicated to them, however, that his position had not changed. That same morning Newton called up and asked him what he was going to do about contacting with Congress and men on the Hill and shifting the debenture fight to the

23. Engaged in statistical analysis for the Bureau of Agricultural Economics and soon transferred to the Federal Farm Board.

tariff. He countered rather savagely that that was an unfair question to put, in light of what the President had done over Sunday, and as far as he was concerned he had no further moves to make in that direction.

I should have added that Senator [James E.] Watson was the man who induced the President to adopt the course he had. Watson urged that it was good policy for him to attack his friends, rather than his enemies. Taber admitted this was good strategy provided you got away with it, which of course he did not succeed in doing in this case. Taber also knew that Secretary Hyde had submitted two statements on the debenture, one taking a neutral position, and another bitterly opposing the debenture. He knew too that Hyde had asked Newton what type of statement he wished submitted and Newton asked him to submit the two statements.

Taber stated that in approaching the President a man was put at a tremendous disadvantage. The President, naturally, would sit back and maintain his silence and the visitor was put on the defensive. He also pointed out how easy it was for various individuals to shift their positions. In that connection he called attention to how Watson had urged that issuance of a rabid statement by the President would jar loose about eight senators, but he did not however reckon with the friends the debenture would win as a result of that statement. [William E.] Borah,[24] by the way, had worked very closely with Taber and he had stated to him that he would go down the line and not waver in the fight.

August 14, 1929.

Yesterday afternoon about 3:30 I was notified by the Secretary's Office that the Secretary and I had been requested to appear before the Federal Farm Board at 11:30 this morning. I later on ascertained from Mr. Spencer that the Board wished to discuss the transfer of the Division of Cooperative Marketing. I protested that there was very little time available for preparation and this morning I told the Secretary that we should work for a postponement until next week, if at all possible. With this he fully agreed.

Late yesterday afternoon I visited with the Secretary about the projected conference with the Federal Farm Board. He made it very plain that he feared we were scheduled for a transfer. He agreed that we should put up our best argument in a friendly way. I pointed out that there would probably be a reaction from the country if the division was transferred, but to this he rather expressed gratification. He said, however, that it was important that the protest come from the country rather than from us, showing, in this way, that he has splendid political

24. Senior Senator from Idaho.

acumen, which has been so evident in every discussion we have had. I told the Secretary yesterday afternoon that the more I thought about the matter, the more I was convinced that it was an unsound move from the point of view of the Board, the Bureau and also the Department to transfer the division. The transfer would involve a disruption of an important piece of work which correlated closely with other lines of work and, in presenting it to the Board, I would emphasize the need to lay before them a complete picture of what we were doing and the way these various lines of work intertwined. With this he agreed fully and expressed his desire to have me make a thoroughly effective argument. I also pointed out to him that the transfer of the division would serve as an entering wedge into the Department and it was difficult to say just where the drive might ultimately lead. For one thing I was convinced that there was going to be a concerted effort on the part of the Department of Commerce to obtain the foreign work. . . . I told him that the Commerce boys, naturally, had the President's ear because they were close to him during his eight years of Commerce administration. Furthermore, I told the Secretary that I thought it behooved him to watch the moves that were not always what we would approve in order to strengthen their Department at the expense of some one else. The Secretary asked me to state frankly what I had on my chest. I told him then that, as far as Dr. Klein was concerned, I felt he should not assume that he always played fair. He had not been known to do so in the past and there was no reason to believe he was disposed to play fair with us in the future.

I then reminded the Secretary of the statement made by Secretary [Ray Lyman] Wilbur[25] at Boise on the transfer of unallotted public domain to the states and ultimately the transfer of the National Forests to the states, which had now been coupled with a savage attack on the Bureau for its opposition to reclamation. . . . He stated that the important thing was to know just where the President stood. He was going over to see him that same afternoon. In this connection he made the statement that he had had a chat with Secretary Wilbur about the matter and that Wilbur had expressed his willingness to go along with him in a demand for the purchase of about $500,000,000 [worth] of lands for reforestation, annually. I asked him, bluntly, how he could harmonize this proposal with Wilbur's very clean-cut intimation that he wanted the National Forests turned over to the states. He admitted that these statements could not be reconciled, but they were part of some other things he accepted from Wilbur. I urged upon the Secretary the need of watching this situation with the greatest care and that it was an opportunity for him to come out in a thoroughly telling and effective way as the champion of the people's interest in this question of natural resources. . . .

25. Secretary of the Interior who was president of Stanford University.

August 23, 1929.

Last night the critical meeting was held in the Secretary's Office on the proposed transfer of the Cooperative Marketing Division. A delightful dinner was prepared by Dr. [Louise] Stanley[26] and helped create an atmosphere that was friendly and helpful. As a matter of fact the Board's attitude, in general, is one of real friendliness to the Department and to the Bureau, also to me personally. There was some preliminary kidding about the operation that would be performed, etc., but we settled down and had a pleasant social visit during the dinner hour. . . .

At about 7:45 o'clock dinner was entirely completed and the Secretary moved to begin our discussion of the matter in hand. I brought in various sets of material and was kidded somewhat about keeping them until midnight or later reading all of that stuff, but I had them all comfortably assured that they would not be bored with a lot of reading, that I, myself, was something of a talker and was disposed to talk. The Secretary very briefly and, in my opinion, all too briefly opened the matter, stating that we were there to discuss the pros and cons of the proposed transfer of the division and that I would set forth the facts. He said he hoped that I would be given opportunity (in keeping with the request that I had made of him in the course of our little jaunt around the Speedway) and that they would permit me to complete my direct statement without interruption. I then launched in and talked from perhaps 7:45 until 9:30, practically without interruption. I was assured in advance, by the Secretary, that it would be perfectly proper for me to speak with the utmost candor and directness on all points involved. This I proceeded to do and I held the attention of every man (some taking notes) throughout the entire period. The points which I made are presented in the outline attached[27] and were very materially elaborated upon by me with considerable fervor, and at times possibly with a little emotion, but never I am sure, and the Secretary assured me, in such a manner as to indicate that I was in any way peeved or unreasonable. The burden of my statement was that it was the job of the Board and the Department and all Federal agencies to serve American agriculture, that in any effort to serve Agriculture it was essential to lay aside any personal consideration, that if it was logically sound to transfer a unit from this Department to the Board, there should be no question as to the action that should be taken. Right at the very outset, however, I made it very clear that, in my opinion, it was absolutely unsound to transfer the fundamental research in cooperative marketing to the Board, that on the other hand it was thoroughly sound to transfer to the Board the service

26. Chief of the Bureau of Home Economics.
27. Since the essence of Olsen's remarks is presented in this entry, his outline is not included.

and extension work of that division and that undoubtedly the Board should build up what I choose to call an economic advisory staff which should, to be sure, include a substantial group of cooperative marketing specialists, well trained, experienced in research and competent to advise, but also men who could be helpful to the Board in an economic advisory capacity on the wide range of subjects they would have to meet. In stressing the objectives of the Board, I made plain that they would make a mistake if they permitted their attention to be concentrated too much upon cooperative marketing and not, at the same time, such things as better adjustment of production to demand, the withholding from agricultural use lands that were now unnecessary, eliminating waste in the general field of distribution and the like. I stressed the fact that the Board, from a reading of the law, from a consideration of the debates in Congress, from the sentiment of the public in general, was evidently intended to be an action and strategy board to translate into action the services and research findings of this Department and other Departments and that it evidently was not intended that it should supplant or supersede other departments and their work. It was something new, super-imposed upon what other various Government departments already were doing. I spent a little time in pointing out how this function could and probably was being accomplished by the Board through the organization of cooperative clearing houses, stabilization corporations, through educational and service agencies, through its various units, through pronouncements on questions like overplanting of this or that crop and in the light of probable price trends, etc. On the other hand the Bureau was distinctly a fact finding service institution and, in that field, could function with efficiency which could not be done by the Board. I spent some time in elaborating upon the crop estimating work and the additional technique that we were striving to develop in that work, the market news work and the new problems arising in that, the standardization and inspection work, warehousing and other things of that nature. I then swung over to the research activities of the Bureau and dwelt at some length on the pivotal lines of economic research in the field of land policy, in the fields of price analysis, transportation, finance, the independent marketing machinery, and finally came to the discussion of cooperative marketing research, upon which I dwelt with considerable emphasis. In that connection I stressed the distinction between intensive research and general service research, the former, in my opinion, being something that we were preeminently qualified to do, the latter being the kind of thing the Board should expect to do. . . .

At the conclusion of my statement Teague and some other men made the remark that this was a very able presentation of the matter and wanted me to know that they were anxious to have the facts. . . . Mr. Legge, I think, was the first man to make some comment. He got off on a rather peculiar tangent right at the outset. He remarked that I had made a very interesting statement and had given him a valuable picture of the wide scope of our activities, but, he said, "Why don't you fellows learn to talk to the farmers? Now, today, I went over a statement which you prepared on the wheat situation and after reading page after page, I finally concluded that it all meant this, a few simple facts which could have been simply stated and which would have meant a great deal to the farmer, if he only sensed those facts." He said something was wrong when we did not succeed in getting our stuff across to the farmer. After he had a full opportunity to express his views and one or two others had injected something in that connection, I made about the following statement. "Mr. Legge, I am not going to quarrel with you for a moment on the point you make. I recognize as well as you the importance of presenting our results in a manner that producers, themselves, can understand. It is not an easy matter, but it is something that should be done. We are working along these lines and we are going to do our best to simplify the statements to the point where they can and will be understood. But here is one thing I want you to have in mind and that is the economic science is different from the physical and biological sciences. The laws and principles of economics do not operate with the same regularity and definiteness that we find in the physical and biological field. The human equation enters into it and we have to use "ifs" and "ands" whether we want to or not, because no other course would be safe and, in my opinion, the big job before us is to educate farmers to think in economic terms so that they would reckon with these "ifs" and "ands" and take them into account in their operations, and in that connection let me suggest that it is going to be advisable for your Board to hedge some of its statements with "ifs" and "ands" because any other course will inevitably bring grief." A number of men chimed in and said, "Olsen is right." Teague, Carl Williams and Stone said I was right, agreeing that much could be done to interpret our material for the presentation to farmers. . . .

September 3, 1929.

Sunday night, September 1, I was called on the telephone about ten o'clock by Mr. Newton (of White House) from Rapidan[28] and told that the Secretary wanted to speak to me. The Secretary evidently had been thinking about the Packer Consent Decree hearing and thought it would be desirable for Mr. [John R.] Mohler,[29] him and me to meet the next day and go over the whole situation, to which I agreed. The following day we arranged to get together at noon and took lunch with the

28. President Hoover had his retreat on the Rapidan River in the Blue Ridge Mountains of Virginia.
29. Chief of the Bureau of Animal Industry.

Secretary at the Army and Navy Club. In the course of that conversation the Secretary made it clear that he had been asked by the President to handle this hearing and while it might be looked upon as in the nature of buck passing, to a certain degree, nevertheless he felt it our duty to step to the front, provided in that way a useful service could be done for the Administration. He did not feel, however, that we need put ourselves in an indelicate position in the handling of the proposition. We agreed on the handling of the details and the procedure and then chatted lightly about Rapidan and other matters.

During our visit the Secretary made the interesting comment that Rapidan was helping to loosen up the President socially to quite a degree. He was now finding it possible to unbend and tell stories with the rest of them. The night before they sat around and told Negro stories for a couple of hours. The President himself told two or three which seemed to be real evidence of mellowing on his part.

Following our dinner, the Secretary and I drove around some in his car and in the course of that visit he confided that the President had asked him to handle a number of important speeches throughout the country, since he was the real speech maker of the Cabinet. Naturally he expected him to discuss agricultural themes and this would afford a splendid opportunity to get before the President in a concrete and full way the position of the Department on some of the important issues. He pointed out how the President had already agreed to the program of controlling production through outlook reports. He felt that by the right kind of maneuvering and educational processes it would be possible to get him to support our land policy, and a number of other things. . . .

September 30, 1929.

On September 20 Dean [Edwin F.] Gay[30] came to Washington to meet Alonzo Taylor[31] on the foreign service work. He immediately got in touch with me and we arranged for an evening session. . . .

In the course of my visit with Dean Gay that evening I developed in detail the part which we felt the Department of Agriculture should play in the foreign service. In this picture I specified definitely (1) responsibility for the development of estimates of acreage and production in foreign countries, (2) studies of production trends and potential competition in competing countries, (3) current market news service comparable to that which we have in this country, (4) issuance of production outlook and

30. Dean of the Harvard Business School who was advising Legge on the functioning of the Federal Farm Board. For a discussion of Gay's role, see Herbert Heaton, *A Scholar in Action* (Cambridge, 1952), pp. 215-16.

31. Director of the Food Research Institute at Stanford, having been selected by Hoover in 1921 for the position.

market outlook reports, (5) studies of consumption and demand tendencies in important consuming countries . . ., (6) extension of Federal standards for agricultural products and checking on quality of products arriving in foreign countries, studies of pack and packaging along lines now performed in this Bureau. Dean Gay indicated his approval of all of these activities as part of the work which the Department should do.

The next forenoon (September 21) at ten o'clock we went into conference with Dean Gay, [Asher] Hobson,[32] Taylor, and [E. G.] Montgomery,[32] [C. W.] Kitchen and I representing the Bureau. Dean Gay made a rather effective statement at the outset, in which stress was placed on the fact that the Board would insist on having certain information in regard to conditions abroad, that the Department of Agriculture would be counted on in a large measure to supply those facts, that the Board however did expect all departments to make their proper contributions. He referred to the controversies that had maintained between the Department of Agriculture and the Department of Commerce and expressed his conviction that that controversy would have to be settled. He then asked Hobson to state the progress that had been made by the two departments during the past week. Hobson gave a brief review of where we stood, using as his text the proposed amendments to the foreign service bill. . . . The discussion later centered on what was meant by "market outlook service" and both Taylor and Montgomery developed in some detail their position that market outlook reports were reports issued perhaps once or twice a year and in the preparation of which data collected by the Department of Commerce would be used. They stressed the idea that the Department of Commerce should collect the current market news data on tone of market, as they put it, stocks and the like. Hobson stressed that the market information service, in his opinion, included three things: (1) crop estimates, (2) market news, (3) price analysis.

I permitted the discussion to be carried on between Gay, Hobson and the Commerce men for perhaps three quarters of an hour, in order to let Hobson develop our position as far as possible. I then injected that evidently there was not a complete meeting of minds as to the meaning of outlook service. Montgomery had insisted that it was not our business to provide the public and the trade short-time interpretations of the outlook, as that was something they could do themselves. Taylor disagreed with Montgomery and I stated that I thought Taylor was correct. It was the business of the several departments to render any service that would enable people to perform their business better. . . . Toward the very end, when it was apparent that we would have to adjourn for luncheon, and we had not come to some agreement, Dean Gay empha-

32. Chief of the Foreign Agricultural Foundation Service in the Department of Agriculture.
33. Chief of the Foodstuffs Division, Department of Commerce.

sized that it was going to be of the utmost importance for the Departments to get together, that the Board would not tolerate the condition that obtained, they had insisted on having the facts. He said that he had seen Legge this morning and Legge had said that if we could not come to an agreement between ourselves, that he, [Robert P.] Lamont,[34] and Hyde would have to settle it with the President. I understood Gay to say that Legge, Lamont and Klein[35] [would see the President] and that naturally gave me a somewhat different impression than I should have had of this move. However, even with Legge, Lamont and Hyde as the party seeing the President, it was apparent that the little club was being swung again, because naturally the three being appointed by the President and Legge and Lamont being particularly close to the President, who already was prejudiced in favor of Commerce, would make the odds pretty much against us. We agreed to the modification of the bill, with the understanding that we had of the meaning of the bill as revised and it was agreed that Hobson and I should write a definition of the market outlook service. . . .

October 3, 1929.

Last night at 4:30 [*sic*] the Secretary asked me to come over and, as he leaned back in his chair, he said he had been gazing some more into the crystal ball. There were developments ahead. He said there were two schools of thought on this farm problem. One school said, "Prevent the surplus and in that way increase farm prosperity." The Administration was supporting that school. The other school said, "Control the surplus and do not worry much about the prevention of surpluses." The objectives of both schools were to increase farm incomes and rural prosperity. If you adopted the thesis of the second school it was thoroughly logical to stand for debenture, McNary-Haugen and other governmental contraptions, to artificially elevate prices. He said the scrap was anything but over and the debenture was coming up sure as pop in connection with the tariff measure. In fact, he was none too happy and optimistic about the whole outlook. He asked me what I thought of his making a cracking speech on that subject out at Ames [Iowa], October 24, at the time of the Country Life conference. I told him that I thought the whole subject was loaded with dynamite, but he knew best what he wanted to do. I asked him if he was prepared to face the West on the proposition of preventing further expansion of farm acreage. He said the die had already been cast, as far as he was concerned, and he had nothing to worry about on that score. He realized, however, that a speech of that kind would bring down a heap of criticism on him from [Henry A.]

34. Secretary of Commerce.
35. Now Assistant Secretary of Commerce.

Wallace[36] and others, but he was not afraid of that. He asked me to prepare a speech for his consideration, which he in turn could lay before the President. . . .

We discussed somewhat the work of the Board and he in a very playful mood laughed about the mental evolution through which members of the Board had passed. He asked me if I had ever been a candidate for public office. I told him "No." He then said, "Then you can not quite understand." He said that when a person is suddenly thrust into the limelight, and his photos are placed in the paper from coast to coast, a lot of nice things are said about him and his chest just naturally swells, as well as his head. He thinks he is somebody. That is human. He went on to say that very shortly, however, when the bricks begin flying pretty freely, you become disillusioned and you find you are a very human sort of fellow and not very much different from the ordinary run of men. He said the Board members are just beginning to pass into that second stage and the past two weeks of hearings on the Hill have had a very chastening influence upon them, but he said the questions that have been raised and the attitude shown while they feed one's sense of humor, nevertheless tend to give one [a] focus as to what may be ahead. The Board, the Secretary said, just does not know what it is up against and it has got to be reaching out and doing some very vigorous things, if it is going to stand the gaff of public opinion. I asked him what he had specific reference to and he said, take for example, the wheat situation. The Board permitted themselves to be manuevered into a position where the radicals took charge of the organization of the wheat corporation, with men like Bill Settle,[37] wild [Myron W.] Thatcher[38] of Minnesota. These organization heads are now sitting on the lid and propose making themselves members of the Executive Board, which he said is utterly impossible. Really, what the Board should do, he rather jokingly suggested, is to throw overboard their plans and start anew under section 15, under which they would declare there are not enough cooperatives through which to work and were going ahead on their own basis, setting up an organization, selecting their own men and shaping policies according to their own ideas. I countered by saying that he, the Secretary, had been making some progress in his thinking, as I had the temerity to suggest that was about the only way they would get some things done. . . . He rather chided me for being so radical in my thinking, but I countered by saying that it was satisfying to know I had a very apt pupil. Then he very confidentially said that, as a matter of fact, they had had a secret night session, at which the suggestion had been seriously discussed, that the

36. At the time editor of *Wallaces' Farmer*, a leading farm journal published in Des Moines, Iowa.

37. President of the Indiana Farm Bureau.

38. A farm leader in the northwest who was manager of the Farmers' Union Terminal Association in St. Paul, Minnesota.

Board announce quite soon that they would assure to the farmer who sold his grain between now and January 1st, $1.50 a bushel, that they would take the necessary steps to see this was actually brought about. I asked him if this was all in joking, or if they were really serious. "No," he said, "there was really serious consideration of this but the idea was not accepted." He asked me what I thought of it. I told him that I would have serious difficulty in harmonizing this proposal with the position that the Administration had taken, that there should not be price fixing or Government in business, because if that was not a clean-cut case of fixing the price, I did not know what price fixing meant. The Secretary said, of course, that it was utterly impossible to adopt a program of that kind. The whole episode, however, illustrates the fears under which the Board is laboring.

November 11, 1929.

Yesterday I had a most delightful visit with the Secretary at his office and, as usual, matters of peculiar interest came up for consideration. The Secretary launched into quite a tirade on the Federal Farm Board. He said it undoubtedly was a most unusual Board from the point of view of the knowledge which individual members had of specific cooperative organization. Each member of the Board seemed to be satisfied to be something of an authority on his particular commodity in the cooperative marketing field, but when it came to the broader phases of the agricultural situation and when it came to political aspects of the problem, he had come to the conclusion that they were sadly wanting. He had fairly paced the floor and importuned them to broaden out their policy and get away from the piddling loan making work which they were now doing. He said that in Missouri he had very effectively attacked the Wilson administration for the bad loans they had made during the war, playing up the inefficiency of the administration in handling matters, and he felt quite sure the same thing would happen in this case. If, on the other hand, they would step out and move to organize agriculture in a thoroughly big way, they could at any rate create a psychology that would be helpful in disarming criticism and have tremendous value from the political aspects of the matter. In his opinion the farm problem was political quite as much as economic and they could not afford to ignore that fact.

1 9 3 0

On Saturday, January 25, about three o'clock, I had a brief conference with the Secretary and after reporting to him the developments in connection with the Georgia survey item of $5,000, he swung on me and said, "Now I have something for you. I took up the matter of the foreign service bill with the President and I am through." The Secretary said the President rather resented the matter being brought up again, saying there were altogether too many units functioning in the foreign field and this proposal merely complicated that situation. The Secretary played upon the political consequence and showed the President the letters which he had signed. This seemed to irritate the President a bit and he explained that he was virtually jockeyed into the signing of those letters, the situation being such that he had no other alternative. The Secretary said he knew when he had had the hot end of a poker in his hand and he was not, himself, going to make any further fool moves. I asked him then how we stood, were we to drop the work, mark time or continue with our present appropriations. "Well," he said, "that is one thing on which I did fail to get a reply. For the time being I think you had better mark time but," he said, "I am going to take this up to the Farm Board and it is up to them to make the next move." He went on to say that he felt sure the President's reactions probably reflected the activities of one Julius Klein. I stated that I was perfectly astounded at the President's attitude and that he would rue the day when he took this position. The Secretary said he agreed but he said, "The important thing now is for you and the rest of us to keep ourselves in position where anything that happens cannot be pinned upon us." He urged very strongly that that be done. . . .

Last Monday, January 20, I had the Secretary over to lunch at the Lafayette Hotel and at that time I gave him the history of our relations with Commerce, of the reactions following that fight, both in Congress and out of Congress. I stressed the fact that there had been a coming together in viewpoint and that Mr. Hoover had seemingly approved that and I stated, as forcefully as I could, the danger of reopening a sore which had been surprisingly well healed. The Secretary, at the conclusion of my rather comprehensive statement said, "You are absolutely right and the President is making a mistake. I will do what I can." At that particular session we had quite a round on the question of "equality for agriculture." I accused him of muddy thinking and he, playfully, did the same with me. Nevertheless, I succeeded in shaking his disposition to step out and tell the world that the day of economic equality for agriculture had arrived. This conference was preceded by one held with the Secretary in the lunchroom of the Senate. The Secretary was very friendly from the very outset, but when I got into a discussion of the foreign service situation he was somewhat phlegmatic and indifferent. I attributed this to the fact that he was holding a reception at his home and was thinking more of Mrs. Hyde's problems than his own problems at that time. At any rate I did not make much headway in getting him roused. That was accomplished at the lunchroom the following Monday, January 20.

March 3, 1930.

Last week at the luncheon which the Secretary and I had at the Lafayette Hotel, we went over the foreign service situation. I left with him the memorandum criticizing the compromise proposal and suggesting that the original proposal with certain amendments should be vigorously sponsored by the Federal Farm Board. He expressed his usual favorable attitude and said he would take the memorandum with him for study on the Chicago trip. The Secretary criticized very severely the last compromise proposal which he said was merely truckling to Department jealousies; that the service belonged in either one department or the other and there was no use to try to straddle and build up part of it in one department and part of it in the other. I urged very strongly that he take this matter in hand, since the whole situation was becoming very embarrassing. The very fact that the Kiplinger Agency[1] commented as to it, showed it was gradually becoming a "mess." He was very much interested in the Kiplinger item and said, however, that we would have to be a little patient while the cotton and wheat situations were being straightened out. In the course of the discussion on the wheat situation, he pulled out of his pocket a little pencilled note of the President, which was a suggested telegram to Arthur Cutten.[2] The telegram went on to say, that it was reported that he had been very active on the bear side of the market during the recent period and that it was somewhat difficult to understand his attitude in this matter, and raised the question as to whether

1. A Washington press service which published an agricultural newsletter.
2. Prominent Chicago businessman and director of several large corporations.

or not he thought he was really operating in the public interest, when he took a position of that kind. The telegram was in pencil and considerably scratched and the Secretary said that, when the question arose as to whether he or Legge should send the telegram, the Secretary grabbed it and said he would be delighted to send that telegram—which he did. The Secretary went on to add that he thought that original note of the President might some day be worth framing.

The Secretary is, clearly, worried over the developments in the agricultural situation, and the probable effects of those conditions. During the course of the visit, which we had at the Army and Navy Club a few days before, at which time there was a downward revision of about 25¢ in [O.C.] Stine's estimate of the May price of wheat, it was considered by him as meaning the loss of perhaps forty or fifty Congressmen. Of course this was in a jocular vein. The Secretary has expressed, on several occasions, the thought that the Board has gotten itself into a very uncomfortable position and evidently he drove forward along that line vigorously at the Chicago meeting Saturday, which resulted in reversing part of the Board's policy. . . .

March 11, 1930

. . . On Sunday (March 9) about four o'clock the Secretary called me by phone, incidentally, in addressing me said "Hello Ole" and explained that he had been called over to the White House and for that reason had not been able to see me in the afternoon. He asked me if I would not come down in the evening, which I consented to do. When I arrived at his office in the evening we entered upon a cordial chat on friendly matters. First of all the Secretary told me about the invitation of the President to him and Mrs. Hyde to take dinner with him. Mrs. Hyde was ill. He explained that fact and the President said, "Come over any way. I want to see you." So, the President, Mrs. Hoover and Secretary Hyde occupied the dining room alone and the chat was very friendly, cordial and intimate. The conversation according to Hyde developed the fact that the President was very much worried about the reactions of the East to the farm program. One of the most important New York papers, such as "The World," and I think "The Sun" were going out with vigorous editorials criticizing the President for his price fixing program and, generally, the President was not happy over the outlook. The Secretary emphasized that the President was clearly worried and he said that he had reason to be. . . .

March 31, 1930

The week beginning March 17 I had a number of conferences with the Secretary regarding the foreign service work. The Secretary, in these conferences, make it clear that he was in thorough sympathy with our viewpoint, that he fully recognized that Commerce was trying to pull a fast one. He felt, however, that it behooved us to play the game in such a way that the charge of "obstruction" could not be hurled at us. He intimated very definitely that he had no objection to pressure being brought to bear to pass the foreign service bill. That, of course, had to be handled adroitly.

When the Lamont memorandum of March 21 came in, he evidently felt a real victory had been scored. At that first meeting I did not sense the full import of the memorandum, as I did not read it. On further examination it became apparent that the proposition was to have the appropriations go direct to the Department of Commerce. When I called the Secretary's attention to this fact a few days later, he rather pooh-poohed the idea and said we simply could not take an arbitrary position in this matter, that Lamont had assured him that the Department of Commerce was playing square and would go ahead and carry out the program. I, of course, insisted that this was intended as a first step in effecting the transfer. However, I said, "You are the doctor and if it is your wish to go ahead on this basis, that is how it will be done." I suggested that a memorandum to Mr. Lamont be the supplemental letters of both Mr. Legge to Mr. Lamont and Mr. Lamont to Mr. Legge. This he agreed to. That resulted in the letter which The Secretary addressed to Mr. Legge under date of March 25. It was also at the Secretary's suggestion that I included in that letter the thought that wording should be provided authorizing the Department to transfer its funds to the Department of Commerce for the purposes stated. The Secretary made one slight change in the draft which I submitted, which did not change its tenor. He made it very clear that it was his view, Mr. Legge's view and understanding that the appropriations were to run to this Department and not to the Department of Commerce and that is the point on which I insisted. He said, furthermore, that if they violate the understanding and agreement, you have a perfect right to object and I expect you to object.

After the hearings on the Hope bill (H.R.3921)[3] last Wednesday (March 28, a.m.) Mr. [John C.] Ketcham[4] called me out of the Committee room and said he had a very satisfactory visit with Mr. Legge. Mr. Legge told him about the arrangements and assured him there was every desire on their part to have the service developed by the Department of Agriculture and he felt sure the program would be satisfactory. He said, very confiden-

3. Introduced by Clifford Hope of Kansas, calling for creation of an inspection service for canned food.
4. Michigan congressman.

tially, that the President had taken to task some one over in the Department of Commerce, whose name he did not have. He did not think, however, that it was Dr. Klein, for trying to hog things and bulldoze the Department of Agriculture. . . .

April 8, 1930

Last week, just before the Secretary left for New York, I had a very brief visit with him on the foreign service matters. He approved of the plan outlined and then followed me as I was about to leave. He asked, very confidentially, what I thought of [Samuel R.] McKelvie.[5] I told him that I thought McKelvie had been rather given to too much talk. I did not know but that that might be said of others as well. At any rate, he had gone off on a tangent on a number of matters. The Secretary countered by saying that he did not know but that McKelvie would go out and try for a senatorship, and it was a problem of finding a man to take his place on the Board. The Secretary asked how I thought [William M.] Jardine would do. I said that there was some question, at this late date, whether Jardine would accept a place on the Board and I thought that probably his appointment would bring some reactions because of Jardine's past "Hoover background." I expressed the opinion that Jardine was not a searching thinker on these matters, that I did not know that he would bring either political support or searching analysis to the work of the Board. Then he referred to the question of Earl Smith[6] as a member of the Board. I told him I did not know Earl Smith personally, very well. I had met him but that I thought politically he would be an asset and my general impression of his judgment was good.

The Secretary then asked me what I thought of Jardine as Secretary of Agriculture. I looked at him with amazement and said I did not understand the question. He said, "Answer it." I said, "I can not conceive of there being any need of answering it. You certainly are not thinking of a successor." The Secretary said, "What do you think of him in that capacity?" I said, "Frankly, I would consider it unfortunate to reappoint Jardine as Secretary." He had naturally gathered up a good many enemies during his four years as Secretary. He came in under certain distinct disadvantages and he went out disappointed that Hoover had not seen fit to reappoint him as Secretary and I figured that it would be embarrassing to the President to appoint him at this time and Jardine would not prove an asset to the Administration. In this he rather agreed. He did say that it was quite true that these were objections in Jardine's case and he asked me to give it some further thought. I pressed him again as to his intentions and he said, "Well, I am not cut out for this kind of work and this is not my particular field. I do

5. Former Governor of Nebraska and a member of the Federal Farm Board.
6. President of the Illinois Farm Bureau Federation.

not see why I should burden myself with something that is more or less foreign to me." I went on to assure him that he had demonstrated an unusual aptitude in grasping the problems now before Agriculture and he had gotten away in good shape and it would be a sore disappointment to us in the Department, if he were to leave.

May 10, 1930.

Wednesday (May 7) I had two conferences with the Secretary that were right significant. In the forenoon we discussed, among other things, the most recent developments in the foreign service matter. On direct question the Secretary told me that he had called Secretary Lamont the Monday before and told him that neither he nor I had anything to do with the fuss on the Hill. Secretary Hyde went on to say that he felt quite sure that Lamont did not believe him.

Secretary Hyde was, frankly, in a somewhat depressed frame of mind which grew out of his feeling that the Administration was not putting up a vigorous fight. I at no time found him so frank in his statement of the fact. He said he stood virtually alone and that he had just come out of a conference with Administration leaders and found them lukewarm in support of his approach. He felt sure that the appointed time had come to fight and that choice ground had been found on which to pitch their tent. . . .

The Secretary said, "Now I want you to understand that there is nothing disloyal in my attitude. I am thoroughly sold on the President and I am anxious to help him, but I do feel that if he would fire some of his close advisers, such as [Walter H.] Newton and [George] Akerson,[7] he would be much better off." "As a matter of fact," he said, "it all goes back to the nature of the President. He has high ideals, scientific attitude and he fails to appreciate the need for a stiff front. That fact illustrates one of the dangers, of course, of forcing him out into the open. If you got him out into the open on one issue and then if he failed to maintain that position, it would do more harm than if he had remained in the background from the outset." The Secretary expressed deep resentment over the fact that McNary and [Frederick] Steiwer voted against the confirmation of [John J.] Parker[8] and he said he was not altogether sure but that he was ready to reverse the position which he had taken in regard to a national forests matter and in which both those Senators [from Oregon] were interested. He said there was nothing that he wanted worse than a good Assistant Secretary, that he realized that he would be called upon to enter the campaign this fall and he needed some one to carry on here. He has asked on various occasions previously that I help him find a good Assistant Secretary.

7. Both were secretaries to the President.
8. Nominated by Hoover for a seat in the Supreme Court and turned down by the Senate.

May 10, 1930 [a second entry].

I confronted the Secretary with the attached item[9] and asked him if he was losing his mind. He smiled and said, "Young man, do not have any worries on that score. I am not crazy enough to take on that assignment." In that connection he said, "You may be interested in knowing that I was slated for the Vice Presidency at the Kansas City convention. I did not want the assignment and would not have it. Why would I want to be a mere wallflower with nothing in particular to do? Furthermore, the fact that the Vice President is always in danger of becoming the President would, in itself, be enough to frighten me off." I countered by saying that the country could fare worse in such a contingency with some one else succeeding. He appreciated the compliment and went on to say, "You have no idea what a gruelling and grind the President is subject to, because he is of a sensitive nature, takes things to heart and is all the time subjected to terrific strain and criticism."

May 13, 1930.

About Friday, May 2, the Secretary called me on the inside phone and asked me if I would not come right over. He was in a good frame of mind and after discussing Department matters he said he had just had a call from Lamont and that Lamont was very excited in regard to the foreign service situation. Lamont stated that the foreign agricultural service bill in both houses had been revived and, to their consternation, had a very favorable position in both Houses. Lamont evidently intimated that some one over here had been active in this connection and that was the purpose for calling me over.

The Secretary got up and said, "Now, Olsen, I do not care if the bill does pass, but it is very important that neither you nor I be in any way implicated." I spoke up and said that it did not surprise me that a ruction was developing on the Hill, that, as a matter of fact, I had forecast that months ago. I had forewarned him in a memorandum and in oral conversation that they were playing with dynamite when they reopened this issue and I assumed that thought had also been conveyed to the President. Naturally I could not help it if the farm organization leaders of this country and Congress took exception to the moves that were now being made in this field. I assured him that my influence was of little moment in connection with a matter of this kind, that if I had the power to arouse Congress to kick over the traces on this issue, I should not be here in the Bureau but ought to be where I could capitalize on such capacity. The Secretary smiled and said, "Well I wanted to be sure that I could tell the Secretary of Commerce that

9. A clipping from the *Washington Daily News,* April 30, 1930, stating that Hyde was a candidate for chairman of the Republican National Committee.

the controversy was one over which we had no control and the farm interests had just naturally revolted against the move. . . .''

This same day the Secretary spoke about the Chamber of Commerce fight. He seemed quite enthused about the whole matter. He said the fight should be the making of the Administration. Months ago he had urged Hoover to step out and had called his attention to the fact that a fight was impending. He went on to say that Hoover had now to choose his position, either he would be aligning himself as a conservative and be rated as such, or he would have to stand out as the leader of the liberal part of the Nation. As far as he was concerned there was no question, but that the President should align himself with the masses and with the liberal point of view. He thought the Chamber of Commerce fight was very significant in that it had brought such men as [John] Brandt of the Land O'Lakes out into the open aggressively supporting the Federal Farm Board program. He felt that the thing to do was to forge ahead and secure the complete support of the agricultural interests.

The morning of the river trip, Saturday, May 3, the Secretary was especially confidential in his remarks to me. I think it was as we went out to lunch that he put his arm around me as we walked down the corridor and said the Big Chief called him over in regard to the fight that was under way. At that time the Secretary had told the President that he had made up his mind that "fight" was the only thing that would save the Administration. He, himself, was ready to step out and vigorously espouse the Administration on all counts. He assured the President that he had absolutely no ambition to ingratiate himself with the public and that if his activities should prove harmful to the President he would be ready to step out without delay. The President countered and said that he was glad there were some fighters in the Cabinet and that he realized that the Administration had to put up a fighting front. The Secretary was elated because, he said, up to now he never had assurance from the President that he would really fight. (This reaction does not, however, find support in the Secretary's comments to me Wednesday, the day he left for Texas. Even at the train, when I saw him off, he said that he was still standing pretty much alone for an aggressive program and he seemed just a little bit dejected, I thought.) . . .

Wednesday, May 7, the Secretary asked me to take a boat trip down the river. He got hold of [Elton L.] Marshall (solicitor of the Department of Agriculture) and we three went together. He took with him on this occasion the minutes the Chamber of Commerce meeting. We read them and had lots of fun commenting on various moves that had been made. On this occasion he remarked about our previous trip with Mr. [Elbert H.] Gary.[10] He said, "Gary is just one hundred per cent for you and your men. He was very enthusiastic about the conference he had had with you and the assistance he had received in that way." Some remarks were made upon the President's

10. Retired president of the U.S. Steel Corporation.

disposition now to fight. In referring to the Parker matter, the Secretary stated that the President was of course worried that the vote would go against him and had asked the Secretary to prepare a pungent paragraph which he might use. (I asked the Secretary the following week if the pungent paragraph had been produced. He said "Yes,' I placed it in his hands, but I guess he won't use it.")

We steamed up and down the river for about three and a half hours and spent quite a little time playing pitch, to which the Secretary is an addict. He is one of the most human individuals I have ever met and makes most delightful company on an outing of that sort, being informal, hearty and chummy in every way.

May 29, 1930.

Last night I saw [Louis J.] Taber[11] at his hotel room and he went over the whole foreign situation with me. He, of course, feels that he is in no small measure responsible for the happy outcome of the whole matter and is, therefore, fired with enthusiasm to carry through. We discussed the possibility of a veto and he expressed some doubt as to that. He had seen Senator McNary a day or so ago and the Senator had replied that he had not given it any thought and did not think there was any possibility of that. He saw him, however, a little later and at that time the Senator suggested that he arrange to see the President. He asked me what I thought of it and I said I thought it would be very helpful. He said he had been trying to get [Sam H.] Thompson[12] to come in but so far had not been successful. He rather thought Thompson was laying low, but for what reasons he did not know. He said he would arrange to see Legge today. He did not know but that he might write Hyde and would give the matter of seeing the President further thought. He went on to comment very frankly as to the President's characteristics, his feeling against [H. C.] Wallace and the Department and he went on to add that he thought he would make a very serious mistake to allow his venom to rule him now. I asked Mr. Taber if he thought it would be passed over the President's veto and he thought that might be rather difficult. For that reason he was very anxious that both Legge and Hyde might be in a frame of mind to urge the President to sign.

We got into quite a frank discussion of Taber's relations with the President. He in some detail narrated how the President tried to take him into camp on the debenture, how he held out and finally it came to a break. The President on one occasion when he was trying to browbeat him into submission said that he, Taber, was the first man he called in at the time he became Food Administrator, that he had known him as a friend for fifteen years, but that developments now seemed to be indicating a parting of the ways, or

11. Master (president) of the National Grange.
12. President of the American Farm Bureau Federation.

something to that effect. Taber countered by saying that he realized that there had been a close association and he regretted what was happening now since he realized that Grangers had in no small measure been responsible for his election. He went on to comment on the scrap between Hoover and Wallace over the foreign service and how he was brought into it. On one occasion Wallace had him out, with Ketcham, to the Wardman Park apartment to discuss ways and means of promoting the bill and late in the evening, when returning, he stumbled on to another man who was, in 1922, President of the California Farm Bureau Federation and later became a member of the Department of Commerce Staff. Taber remarked to him that a man out as late as that was open to suspicion, and the other fellow countered with a like comment. Taber said, "All right you tell me what you have been up to and I will tell you what I have been up to." This man said he had been conferring with Hoover, trying to devise ways and means of defeating Wallace's plans to set up the foreign agricultural service. Taber went on to describe the last meeting with the Secretary, just before he went to the hospital and how on that occasion the Secretary (Wallace) had said that the Department of Agriculture had given the Farm Bureau Federation at least two million dollars worth of advertising through its publications and in other ways and not a cent to the Grange, but that from henceforth that was going to be set aright. Taber expressed some feeling about the tie-up between the Extension Service of the Department and the Farm Bureau Federation and said that they had not been dealt with fairly by [C. W.] Warburton.[13]

June 3, 1930.

This morning at ten o'clock I had my first conference with the Secretary since his return from the Southwest. The visit opened with some light chatter regarding his fishing exploits and he was in a very fine frame of mind. He showed me photographs of a shark which he had landed and assured me that a story that had been circulated in regard to a shark having five or six little ones after it was captured was true and he even consulted the dictionary on that point. He went on to add that they went down in a private car of the Missouri-Pacific Railroad. Of course, as he said, paying their railroad expenses and that the Coast and Geodetic Survey had a large boat placed at their disposal. The group he went with was of course the Missouri group.

The Secretary then swung off and said, "I want to go to Cabinet, but I do want to speak to you about the foreign situation. Frankly, Olsen, we are in a terrible mess in this matter. We are all under suspicion. They suspect me. They suspect you and they suspect all kinds of people in the Department. They have gone so far as to prepare an analysis of the whole episode

13. Director of extension work in the Department of Agriculture.

to illustrate that the various moves made by the Department of Agriculture in the last several months have all been with a purpose of forcing the passage of the foreign service bill. They insist that what had happened could not have taken place unless there had been a master mind behind the drive to put it across. Furthermore, they knew that some one had been up to the Hill and undone what they were firmly convinced they had been able to do in calling Ketcham off. They were sure that it was a Department of Agriculture employee and, of course, were trying to locate the culprit.'' We did not have very much time, but I at once launched into the various points that the Secretary made. I said, in the first place, it was a laugh that Commerce people now tried to find a goat for their folly. I reminded the Secretary that I told him months ago that this was dynamite and that it would surely cause a world of trouble. He agreed that was the case. They knew that was the case and yet they went ahead with their foolhardy plans. It was perfectly preposterous to try to work out a case that the concessions we had made were with a view to bringing about the passage of the Act. I had, to be sure, with him objected to various silly proposals that had been advanced but all with a view to finding a basis that was tenable from our point of view, as well as from their point of view. It was my purpose to develop that basis and go forward and try to work it out as best we could. As a matter of fact it was I who suggested the bringing together of the offices and placing our men under the general policy supervision of the commercial attaches. That certainly did not indicate any unwillingness to provide a working basis. As a matter of fact I had geared up the machinery to get to work on that program. The Secretary chimed in and said, ''You are absolutely right. I know that to be the case and it is ridiculous that that view is urged.''

With reference to the second point I told him it was not strange that Agriculture moved almost as a man in this matter. It was deep seated, going back for a whole decade or more, and there were plenty of agricultural leaders ready to seize upon a situation of this kind. The Secretary chimed in and said, ''I knew even a man like Henry A. Wallace, alone, could have set the prairie afire. As matter of fact Earl Smith of Chicago told me that Wallace had bombarded him with wires urging action in the matter. In addition to that [Cully A.] Cobb of Atlanta, Ga., had been tremendously aggressive and active. Those two men alone could mobilize the agricultural forces. . . .''

Then I asked the Secretary whether the President was going to sign the bill. He said, ''I do not know, but I am afraid he will veto it.'' Then I launched in and said: ''If you are a friend of the President you will see to it that he will not veto this measure. There has been enough turmoil created already by the sheer foolishness of his adviser. The veto of this measure will tear the lid off and open up old sores that good progress has been made in healing as a result of the Board's work. The thing for the President to do is to sign the bill and take it sweetly.'' The Secretary said, ''You are right and that is going to be my advice to him. This thing is loaded with dynamite.

However, if he asks me for a letter asking for a veto, and he is determined, I will give him such a letter." I said, "Mr. Secretary, don't you do it. You can not afford to do it. The agricultural interests will look upon you as not supporting their cause and their department and it will hurt not only you but the President. It is your job, as the agricultural adviser of the President, to see to it that he does the right thing. . . ."

June 5, 1930

. . . Yesterday (June 4) shortly before noon I took over some letters on the foreign service and handed them to the Secretary as he came out with [R. W.] Dunlap. He said, "Come on get in my car, I am going over to the apartment." So, I rode over and he commented most of the way on the Indiana trip, the gruelling grind he was being subjected to in making these various trips and the danger of stubbing his toe but, he went on, laughingly, to add, "I do not permit any worry to settle on me because any time they are ready to let me out I am ready to go and there are lots of interesting things to do." In fact, he was rather craving the opportunity to go into hiding for a half year or so and visit with the denizens of the sea.

Then as we reached the hotel he said, "I have another item that will interest you." He said, "I believe the President will sign the bill." I expressed some joy at this. He said, "Now wait, don't be in a hurry. Besides that there is another thing that is to be reckoned with and that is we want to get at two or three traitors over there in the B.A.E. and I want you to help me." I laughed and said that certainly was a good joke and he was in very good humor. He said, "You know it reminds me of the story of a Methodist revival meeting. In reporting on the meeting one of the leaders remarked that it had been very successful. They had not, it was true, succeeded in getting any new converts but they had succeeded in separating three undesirables from camp." With that he walked into the hotel. . . .

It was reported to me today that the farm representatives saw Mr. Legge yesterday in regard to the measure and that Mr. Legge, while he sputtered somewhat, indicated that he believed the measure would be signed.

June 14, 1930.

Senator [Henry J.] Allen's[14] secretary, Mr. [Clarence H.] Judd, called Miss [Grace] Leonard[15] on the phone early last week and said the Senator wished to speak to me about the foreign service. Later on Mr. Judd was placed on the phone and he told me that Mr. [George L.] Kreeck of Kansas

14. Junior Senator from Kansas.
15. Olsen's secretary.

was interested in obtaining an appointment in the foreign service. The Senator was anxious to know what the possibilities might be. Mr. Judd asked me to give him some idea of what our program would be and this I did. He indicated that Mr. Kreeck had been a Minister to Paraguay and had been promised a position in the foreign service by the Department of Commerce. Since the foreign service however was not to be in the Department of Commerce they were not in position to take care of him.

A day or two later I was with Secretary Hyde and he said that the Senator had been in touch with him in regard to a Mr. Kreeck but the discussion did not proceed any distance.

Thursday, June 12, Mr. Judd called at my office and bluntly and flatly and simplemindedly stated that the Senator was very anxious to find a place for Mr. Kreeck, that the Department of Commerce had promised him a place in the foreign service but that when the foreign service bill of the Department of Agriculture passed, that made it impossible for the Department of Commerce to carry out their terms. For that reason they were coming to us to see if we could not find a place for Mr. Kreeck in the service. I, of course, told Mr. Judd that we were in the field for good material for the foreign agricultural service, that it was not to be a very extensive service but we were going to push ahead very vigorously and we would be glad to consider Mr. Kreeck's qualifications. I urged him to have Mr. Kreeck write us, giving a statement of his background and I also told him it would be desirable to obtain a Civil Service status.

This episode ties in with confidential information which Mr. Englund obtained from Mr. [Milton S.] Eisenhower.[16] Eisenhower had told him that one of the Senators had been promised by the Department of Commerce most anything he wanted in the new agricultural foreign service, providing he would do their bidding. It is a beautiful illustration of how Commerce has tried to bribe senators to do their dirty work in defeating the foreign agricultural service bill, clearly indicating a willingness to sell out the service itself in order to obtain support.

June 14, 1930 [a second entry].

. . . Yesterday noon the Secretary asked me to go to lunch with him. We went over to the "Ugly Duckling" on the Hill. He was in a ruminating frame of mind and pondered deeply on the difficulties of doing anything for Agriculture. He very frankly stated that he thought it was virtually impossible to get cooperation from farmers as a whole because they had not been brought up to the level of thinking. He made certain reference to driving them into line, all of which gave me a good opportunity to comment that, after all, action had to come out of farmers themselves, but should be on

16. Director of Information in the Department of Agriculture from Kansas.

the basis of right information and right guidance and that meant research and extension of the kind that had never before obtained. . . .

On the way back from lunch, the Secretary became exceedingly confidential. He said, "Now, Olsen, I want you to answer the question I am going to ask you now as frankly and as daringly as you always answer my questions. You have undoubtedly observed that I have reached out a little bit into the political aspects of things. You also know that I am deeply interested in helping Agriculture and championing its course. Am I, or am I not making a mistake by reaching out this way into the political arena? In the second place, even though I did not agree with the President in all matters would I not be making a mistake if I broke with him? Is it not far better for me to do as I am now doing, going along trying to educate him and bring him to see the proper course to follow with reference to the industry?"

I said to the Secretary, "It is quite apparent that you are being looked upon more and more as the political adviser of the President. That comment is coming from a wide range of sources and it is generally felt that you are by all odds the astute political observer and adviser in the Cabinet. A good many of us have realized to an increasing degree that you have a capacity for winning friends in the political field and we recognize that is a real asset. We have also been elated with the interest you have taken in the problems of Agriculture and the keenness with which you have analyzed those problems and attacked them in cooperation with us. Your political astuteness associated with your analytical powers make you an exceedingly effective man to handle the problems of the industry. I am frank to say that I, personally, have been just a little concerned with the degree to which you have been devoting yourself to strictly political matters. I have not felt altogether easy and happy about such remarks as this, 'Well, it is very apparent that Secretary Hyde is the political fence mender of the Hoover Administration and, goodness knows, there are plenty of fences to mend.' The difficulty is this, as I see it: if you become known as the political fixer for the President and the President is not in the good graces of the agricultural people as a whole, then are you not damaging your opportunity for helping Agriculture? Now, as to your attitude toward the President, so far I have felt you have done the right thing. The President is in power and you should work through and with him. It becomes very necessary, therefore, that he think correctly along agricultural lines. Certainly your chances of influencing his thinking are better if you go along with him than if you break with him. I think you have made very substantial progress in reshaping his thinking. I think you have unlimited opportunities still ahead of you. If I were in your position I would daringly strike out with him along all the vital pivotal lines and drive him to an acceptance of the correct daring and effective position. If he failed, after such attack, to adopt a constructive position with reference to Agriculture, then I think you have a time at which to consider a break with him."

In the course of this conversation, the Secretary said, "Some people seem to forget that after all I was not a Hoover man originally. I have been associated with the Middle West. There was no reason for picking me for this position. I knew nothing about Agriculture. I very frankly told you and I told the President that I did not know anything about Agriculture, but I had this one advantage, that I did not have a number of bad brands on my back. For example, I did not have a McNary-Haugen label, but, after all, it was not logical, from some points of view, to select me for this assignment."

June 30, 1930.

Saturday afternoon (June 28) I was called over to the Secretary's Office for a conference. This followed a conference in the forenoon here in the Conference Room of the Bieber Building on outlook, at which both Legge and Hyde were present. We did not have very much time, but the following developments took place.

Secretary Hyde reached for a document on his desk and he said, "You are asking for the appointment of Mr. [Louis G.] Michael in the foreign field. I have reasons to doubt the loyalty of Mr. Michael. I am afraid he is a socialist and if there is one thing that I stand for it is loyalty to American institutions and the American form of Government." I said, "That is a very unusual statement. What is the basis for it?" He said, "Well, here is a letter which Mr. Michael wrote to a representative of the Amtorg Corporation at New York." The Secretary proceeded to read the letter. It dealt with a conference which we had with a group of Russians in my office some time last winter, at which Mr. Michael was present. The letter made reference to me, contained one or two opinions, and finally wound up with a rather indiscreet sentence, in which Mr. Michael stated that he was interested in the communal farm development of Russia, that he wished them to have all the information available in the Department in order that this experiment might be given an adequate trial. The Secretary stopped at that sentence and said, "That does not look good to me." I stepped in at once and said, "I can tell you all about that conference. The Amtorg people got in touch with me and asked if they might come down to see me. I told them they might. I brought them to my office and asked Mr. Michael to come in because of his knowledge of Russia and the Russian language. I told them about the Bureau's activities and said I would be glad to put them in touch with people in the Department, as well as State College people in general and expressed a willingness to be helpful in every way. I did this after carefully weighing the whole matter and concluded that the only proper thing for this Department to do was to be helpful to this group. I had been in touch with the State Department in regard to the matter and had never been warned not to [have] contact with Russians who came to this country. If we feared contamination from contact with Russians, then the thing to do was to keep them out at the border and not permit them to establish offices in New York, Washington and elsewhere." I said that as far as Mr. Michael was concerned, I had asked and instructed him to help me in handling this group. I had told him to be as helpful as possible, but considered that the sentence to which reference was made was indiscreet but was mere applesauce and the kind of thing that I or any one else might be guilty of writing. I knew positively that Mr. Michael did not have any socialist or anarchistic ideas in his head. He had not been a student of the problem and it was ridiculous to base any conclusions or charges against him on the ground of this one single sentence. I said, "Furthermore, Mr. Michael was of such a character and disposition that once you told him what to do, he performed as a most faithful dog." I then proceeded to rehearse the history of the Wallace-Hoover Administration, how Mr. Michael had been brought in to serve Mr. Wallace, that he had carried out his instructions faithfully and had been effective, helpful and it certainly was unreasonable to permit any of that past to be used against him. As soon as Wallace died, Mr. Michael was told that his functions had completely changed, that he would devote himself to foreign research matters and that he had as a matter of fact assiduously [sic] applied himself to those matters. The Secretary went on to say that of course he recognized that it was a serious charge to make against any man, stating, "I am speaking to you in the utmost confidence and only you but I do feel that it will be a very serious matter for the Government to employ a man who is fundamentally opposed to American Institutions and who may, literally speaking, be a viper at one's breast." He said, "I suspect if he is inoculated with these ideas you will find his desk covered with books on socialism and I wish you would go over it and make an examination this afternoon. If I had time I would go with you." I said I would be glad to do it.

That same afternoon I went over to Mr. Michael's office and did what I usually do not do, went through his desk, through the matter on top of his desk and bookcase and made a list of the material I found there. . . . As a matter of fact his desk was littered with pencil notes and material on Poland and other countries which he has studied.

The Secretary asked me if I would not return that same evening. I promised to do that but he did not call. The next morning, Sunday, the Secretary called and I met with him around eight o'clock and remained with him until around ten p.m. We had a very delightful visit on a great many matters. In the first place I went over the tariff statement and made a number of suggestions which pleased him. He frankly admitted that the material we had supplied had been exceedingly helpful. In fact he had based his statement almost altogether on our material and to a very slight extent on the material supplied by the Tariff Commission. . . .

Then I said, "Now a word about Mr. Michael. I went through his desk, bookshelves and all his material, as you requested, and here is a list of the material I found." I read over the attached list and said, "There was no evidence whatever of his being socialistic or anarchistic in his views. Further, I am more than ready to vouch for him. He was the most faithful man I had had anything to do with." What I said seemed to satisfy the Secretary and he did not counter very much. He asked, however, whether or not Stine had been critical of Hoover and the Administration. He said there had been some suggestion that he was disposed to speak vigorously in criticism of the President. I told the Secretary then of the experience we had with Jardine and that Stine did not mean anything by it, that the men were in the habit of reacting on anything that came along and, personally, I did not see why they should not to a certain degree. We could not expect to muzzle men of the calibre of Stine whether they were in the Government service or not. On the other hand, I recognized it would be quite improper and impolitic for Stine or any of the men to speak in a disparaging way of the President. In commenting on the criticism of Jardine the Secretary immediately said that so far as he was concerned he would not expect any one to hold off criticizing him if they were so disposed. He swung over then and said he thought it would be very desirable for Mr. Michael to go into Russia and make a study there if he went abroad. I pointed out to him the difficulties. He said of course he realized he could not go over in an official capacity, but there might be some other way to handle it.

Monday night when we were sitting in the conference room on the final revision of the outlook the Secretary came in and chatted about the outlook and other things. As he left he asked me to come into his office before I went home. When I reached his office he handed me the Michael document and said he had decided to accept my recommendation and approve the appointment of Michael for the European assignment. He suggested, however, that we make sure there was no foundation for the charges that had been made. I assured him we would be glad to do that.

I called up [W. W.] Stockberger[17] a day or two ago regarding the difficulties on the Michael case and he said, "This is once that I can not be frank with you and give the full story. Certain things have been given me in confidence." I said, "All right, I will not press for the facts." After my visit with the Secretary and his disclosure I made up my mind it was all right to call on Stockberger. So, with [C. W.] Kitchen, I called on Dr. Stockberger last Sunday afternoon and told him what transpired. He then told me the Secretary had had him in and had indicated that charges had been made against Michael, evidently at the behest of Commerce. He was quite sure that a memorandum had been submitted by Commerce to the President and that Hyde, in turn, received that memorandum from the President. He was also equally convinced that it was nothing but small spite work, growing out

17. Director of Personnel and Business Administration in the Department of Agriculture.

of the passage of the foreign service bill and the Secretary indicated that he felt that such was the case. Stockberger felt that the course that I had mapped out, of urging an investigation of the charges and freely facing the facts, was one that would turn the trick completely with the Secretary. This was the attitude I had adopted from the very outset and Stockberger's view merely confirmed me in the plans that had been laid. . . .

September 5, 1930.

Last week, about Wednesday (August 20), the Secretary decided to go to Chicago, and I went to the Depot with him and en route he picked up Mr. Legge and the three of us rode down together. As soon as Legge got in the car Hyde said they had learned through grapevine sources that [Arthur] Cutten and some of the big boys at Chicago were disposed to go into the market and help boost prices but that the regulations of the Grain Futures people served as a "wet blanket" upon Exchange activities. If the Secretary would remove the limitations upon trade there could probably be quite a little activity launched on the bull side. He asked Legge what he thought of it and whom he could trust in Chicago. The Secretary said he was rushing out to see Cutten and a few of the fellows and wanted to be sure that he was getting the right men. Legge rather definitely reacted against the suggestion from the very outset, stating that it was a pretty risky thing to trust one's self to that "band of thieves" as he described it. He just figured that they were setting a trap and he urged the Secretary to be right cautious. . . . The general impression I got was that the trip was being made by Secretary Hyde, and was approved and engineered by the White House, all of which goes to show that the Administration is in desperate straits to bolster agricultural prices at this time.

Friday, August 22, the Secretary returned and I visited with him at some length regarding his Chicago trip and other matters. He told me he had visited with Cutten and some of the other boys. Cutten had maintained that as the market was now being operated it was a strictly seller's market. The Secretary made the statement that he was absolutely convinced that the farmers had been cheated out of ten to fifteen cents per bushel on their wheat for the last year by reason of the manipulation resorted to by those fellows. For one thing, the ability to deliver, as he stated, seven different grades of wheat on a contract gave the seller a bloody advantage. The miller was not disposed to use the futures exchange to buy his wheat when he had no assurance of the quality of wheat delivered him. Hence that in itself, according to the Secretary destroyed a great deal of buying power. I countered at once and said I did not think the future exchanges were to function as merchandising markets, but primarily as hedging markets. If you were going to use them as merchandising markets, you would take all speculation out of them and speculation was necessary to strike a balance between supply and demand conditions. I do not believe the Secretary clearly sees this point. He said, furthermore, that he was convinced that the near futures were purposely and unusually depressed in order to buy the wheat from the farmers on an abnormally low basis. Quotations to farmers are made on the basis of the near futures and in order to hold them down they kept large stocks of wheat on hand at Chicago as a depressing influence. Furthermore, the Secretary said he was convinced there was a lot of sculduggery going on in the mixing of wheats. Cutten and others maintained that there were all kinds of limitations and he wanted the grades toned up to cover that situation. The Secretary had a chart which Dr. [Joseph] Duvel[18] had given him showing how several grades of grain go into the elevator, ranging from No. 1 to sample grade, and go out as mostly No. 2 and 3. The Secretary went on to say he was now convinced that the grain traders were a bunch of scoundrels and that he was going to throw a bomb into their camp. He stated that he recognized the dangers in that kind of procedure. "One thing," he said, "with Newton at the White House the situation was materially complicated." Newton was what he is because of the grain trade, that from a business and professional point of view and he did not blame Newton for being their good friend and supporting them, he would not respect him if he were not. He said, however, that it was a further complication. "Furthermore," he said, "you must remember that the President himself was Secretary of Commerce at one time and has always worked closely with groups of the grain trade sort and, naturally, his leanings would be somewhat friendly to them." The Secretary was convinced, however, that if the President once saw the iniquity of the situation, we could count on him to do the right thing. The Secretary called in Solicitor [Elton] Marshall while I was there and told him to look up all the laws and find out what authority he would have to raise some "Ned" with the Grain people. He also asked me to obtain similar information from the warehouse and grain divisions. . . .

September 22, 1930.

Under date of Wednesday, September 17, I was called over by the Secretary to sit in on a conference which he was holding with Mr. Legge and representatives of the Chicago Board of Trade. The representatives were [James C.] Murray, Vice President of the Quaker Oats Company, [Peter B.] Carey, Vice President of the Chicago Grain Exchange, Mr. Cutten, Secretary of the Exchange, and a fourth man whose name I have forgotten. The burden of the Secretary's request was that they modify their rules so as to make the contract more favorable to the buyer. He made a point that, at the present time, as many as seventeen grades were deliverable on futures

18. Chief, Grain Futures Administration, Department of Agriculture.

contracts, and that the delivery of grain on contract was also a factor more favorable to the buyer than to the seller.

September 27, 1930.

It was apparent that the Board of Trade representatives were disposed to use this opportunity for loosening up on the Grain Futures Administration. They stressed the unfavorable influences which reporting transactions to the Grain Futures had on the speculative temper of the trade, that this was a bear influence and they hoped this restriction would be taken off. Furthermore, they suggested that the tax now levied on grain transactions should be removed, as that was also a deterrent to trading. The Secretary did not give any encouragement along those lines while I was there, although he asked me to make inquiries regarding the tax item. This I have done. . . .

A few days later on, the whole situation took quite a new angle. It developed that the White House, with the Secretary, had been working on a clue to Russian activity in the market. Several times while I was in the Secretary's Office, the Secretary engaged in conversation with Newton and the Russian situation was the matter under consideration.

Following the Secretary's public statement on this subject, we chatted about the whole matter and, among other things, the Secretary said that he was more and more convinced that short selling was immoral and should be absolutely prohibited; that if it were not immoral for the Russian Government to sell short on our markets, then the question of propriety of short selling by any one was a matter of moment. More and more I have been impressed by the fact that he is drifting to a pretty strict position on the futures exchanges and it would not surprise me if he finally clamped down the lid to prevent all short selling.

Yesterday afternoon (September 26) he chatted a bit about his experience on the Russian problem and referred to his visit with Vice President [Charles] Curtis and a number of other contacts. Vice President Curtis had a man at his office who claimed to be able to deliver, in Stalin's handwriting, the very document in which he had said was stated the purpose of the Soviet with reference to the United States. That purpose was to capitalize on the present business and agricultural unrest in this country to foment disturbances and wreck our institutions in so far as possible. It had been stated that the International Harvester Company was riddled with Russian spies. The evidence behind statements of this kind could be had for a consideration of eight or ten thousand dollars. I commented that the proposition looked a little fishy, that I would look at that bird twice before I would cough up ten thousand dollars to have his spurious evidence, if it proved to be such. The Secretary recognized that he had to be very careful. Just as I was leaving he said that a minister or a priest, I do not recall which, was calling to discuss the Russian situation. So, it is apparent that at this time the Administration is using its utmost efforts to collect every bit of evidence that will tend to disclose an organized effort on the part of the Soviet Government to demoralize conditions here.

November 10, 1930.

Yesterday afternoon and evening I spent with the Secretary at his office. He was busy unpacking several boxes of books that he had shipped in from the Missouri home and arranging them in book cases. I commented that that was rather incriminating evidence that he expected to stay here for some time, to which he countered that he at least wanted to be comfortable and contented for a month or two that it would take to find his successor. The Secretary took a great deal of pride in poring over and showing me books he had collected on religion, the family Bible, and the family record in the Bible, which showed two members of his family, his father and grandfather, collectively, having lived over 187 years.

After a while we sat down to our coffee and I then asked the Secretary, point blank, what he thought of the business situation. He countered by saying that I flattered him by even asking him, when such men as Andy Mellon had frankly stated that the whole situation now had become so worldwide and so confused that no one knew what was really the cause and where we were really headed. The Secretary expressed, however, the need of greatest caution in every way, because he felt sure that rocky times were ahead. I asked him, now that the election was over, what they really expected to do to assist in a constructive way in correcting the situation. I told the Secretary that I, personally, had become exceedingly weary of all the optimism air that had been spread by the Administration and now the "Buy More" talk. . . .

In the course of that conversation, and right at the outset of our afternoon's discussion, following my statement of impatience with the "statement making" of the Administration, the Secretary said, "Now what I am going to say, I will deny if you ever repeat it," but, he said, "If the President has one weakness it is his childlike faith in the efficacy of mere statements." The Secretary elaborated by saying there had been altogether too much talk and that the country was tired of statement making. . . .

Over the dinner table at Harvey's we had some further confidential chatting. He frankly admitted that the political situation was in a very bad way. The Federal Farm Board was undoubtedly headed for a savage attack. The Secretary frankly stated that in the circumstances probably the wise thing to do would be for the "Chief" to have a few of the Republicans join with the Democrats in assuring that the next Congress would be organized by the Democrats. That would place them in a position of carrying the burden, if they resorted to a program of obstruction. In discussing the matter, I expressed the thought that the country would probably expect the Administration to make the most of it under these trying conditions, that if it went through this session with a constructive program in a daring sort of way and met only rebuff, there might be some excuse for saying, "Very well, take over the load yourselves." The Secretary countered by saying that the President probably would not be disposed to adopt such a course. During the course of the conversation I reminded him of the statement he made to me shortly after he came in, when we were discussing the price forecasts, "that after all the important thing was to be right in the matter of our objectives. In some cases we could arrive at things by the direct course and in other cases an indirect, longer course might prove necessary." This comment grew out of the discussion of the ethics of the principle that was involved in this particular matter. About at this point, in the course of the dinner, he said, "Olsen, you know Clarence Poe?"[19] I said, "Yes." The Secretary said, "He has recently written me and criticized me pretty severely for my political activities, stressing the fact that in taking this active part in politics I have injured my chance of helping Agriculture. Now, I know that I am not in the closest touch with the scientific work in the Department, I am not altogether sure that I am in heartiest sympathy with all the scientific work of the Department. I am thoroughly sold on the economic work and that is the part of the work which is vital at the present time. What is your reaction to Poe's criticism? Tell me frankly how you feel about it." In defending his position he went on to say that as a member of the Cabinet, and as a member of the party it was his duty, as he saw it, to defend the program of the party and to help translate the party's program into action. I recalled in the back of my mind that somewhat similar questions had been put up to me by the Secretary some considerable time ago and I answered him about this way. . . . "Now, if it is necessary for the Secretary of Agriculture to break with his Chief, or take violent issue with his Chief within the family, I think he should do it and should not feel called upon to support him irrespective of the soundness of his position. Now, as far as your relations with the Department are concerned, I am going to frankly state that I think you are in a very difficult position. You are a two-headed monster of the kind that no one really understands, Dr. Jekyll and Mr. Hyde. You can not be the whole-hearted head of the Federal Farm Board and at the same time a whole-hearted Secretary of Agriculture. There is here, whether you have recognized it or not, a fundamental difference of viewpoint in some respects, and in some respects there is a conflict between the Department of Agriculture and the Federal Farm Board. Let us be frank, I have wanted to talk to you about this for some time. The Federal Farm Board is a partisan body set up to further the aims and objectives of

19. Editor of *Progressive Farmer* and a leading figure in southern farming circles.

cooperatives in competition with and to undermine other agencies. This is a fact which you can not deny. In starting out on your program as a Board you launched out vigorously on the position of building up huge nationwide cooperative associations to replace existing agencies. You loaned huge sums, oft times on a loose and reckless basis, according to general impression. At any rate the outside public, the various trade groups, look upon the Board as an arch enemy and look upon the Federal Government as somewhat of an arch enemy intent upon undermining them. They speak of themselves now as outcasts, as far as the Federal Government is concerned. Now, contrast that with the attitude they take toward the Department of Agriculture. They look to the Department of Agriculture for standards, inspection services, market quotations, stocks, movement, data on crop estimates and research. We, in turn, look to them for cooperation in order to get these data. Without their cooperation we can not perform these services, but they do not carefully discriminate between the Federal Farm Board and the Department of Agriculture. We are all Federal Government and intent upon their destruction and they go so far as to say that 'while we recognize you mean well within the Department of Agriculture and we like you and will work with you, still we feel we can not trust you any more because you must be under the domination of the Federal Farm Board and must be subject to the far-reaching legislation that the Agricultural Marketing Act represents.' In short, there is a conflict between the two institutions which we must not overlook. The Department of Agriculture is a public service institution serving all groups. It must be on friendly terms with them. It must have their cooperation. The Federal Farm Board is making that relationship for the Department of Agriculture well-nigh impossible.''

I continued a little further stating that, ''The antagonism is not confined to trade groups against both the Federal Farm Board and the Department of Agriculture, but there is the basis for the feeling of competitive conflict between the Department of Agriculture and the Federal Farm Board. The Department of Agriculture, mind you, is an institution that has rooted itself deeply in our Agriculture and its national life. It is a marvelous institution with all its faults. It has the scientific point of view and has made marvelous contributions in all our sciences. It is looked upon by leaders in Agriculture for leadership in agricultural matters. Is this great Department of Agriculture going to abdicate in favor of an institution that is, admittedly, dominated by political situations, the outgrowth of political strife and turmoil?''

We did not cover all of this at the dinner, but some of it was continued in his office and he pulled out a book and took rather copious notes while the discussion was on. So, the lid is off, so far as that phase of the problem is concerned, but his reactions were good. He said, ''I am now more than ever convinced that I have no business trying to serve two institutions along these two different lines. If I am to be Secretary of Agriculture, that is what I ought to be." I said, "I agree."

Then we had some discussion as to what amendments to the Agricultural Marketing Act might be made. He said, "I would like to throw out the whole stabilization feature of the Act. It is unworkable." I countered by saying, "It may be, but if you throw that out what have you left as a farm relief measure? The enemy would say that was a frank admission that the Act was a failure. Furthermore, if you are going to get down to brass tacks and face the situation, then let us step out and substitute the things necessary in the picture." He said, "What are they?" Then I again stressed the various elements in a program, farm reorganization drive, land utilization drive, a taxation drive and the various things that would figure in a thoroughly constructive program.

As I view the conversation we had, today, from this vantage point I am ready to query whether or not I may have been just a bit too frank on the entire matter, but, on second thought, no, if the head of your Department is not entitled to the honest convictions and reactions of his pivotal men, he is in a bad way.

November 19, 1930.

In conversation with Kitchen about my visit with the Secretary on the unemployment situation and the weakness of the Administration's policy, he told me *very, very confidentially* that Ethelbert Stewart's[20] private secretary had told a very good friend of his that the President had forbidden the Department of Labor to release its findings on unemployment and had ordered Stewart to doctor, for the public, his statement on unemployment. This order came direct from the President.

November 22, 1930

. . . When I saw the Secretary yesterday afternoon, he expressed some little surprise at the reaction of the Russian representatives to his remarks. It was the first he had heard that they regarded it as a basis for international episode, but he said he realized there had been some criticism about that part, at least, of his speech. . . . In speaking about the episode, the Secretary tried to repeat what he had said. It seems that he had referred to the economic policy with reference to the unloading of wheat which had ruined prices, that the whole Soviet movement went much deeper, it was a menace to civilization in that it struck at our fundamental institutions. It nailed to the cross, as he eloquently put it, our concept of religion, home and the

20. Commissioner of Labor Statistics.

sanctity of private property, etc. He said, as far as he was concerned, he had no wish to conceal anything whatever he had said in that connection. He stood by it, but, of course, if it should become embarrassing from a national point of view, that might be a little different. He said, however, that he could not see where this particular episode could injure the Administration. In that connection, I countered by saying that it was a very inconsistent policy, so far as I could see, to admit Russian representatives, give them free access to Departments and everything else in this country and then look upon them as horrible monsters unfit to associate with in any way. I told him that it certainly put us in a very difficult position when these people came to us for information, and as long as we were doing that, why should we not counter by sending a man or several men to Russia to study that situation intensively and come back with seasoned conclusions based on adequate information. The Secretary countered by saying that one or several men could not do very much in appraising that situation but, in any event, I put in my plea for a scout or two to get at the Russian situation. . . .

1931

January 8, 1931.

On Tuesday afternoon (January 6), following a conference on the alfalfa seed verification project, I had a very intimate visit with the Secretary on the current situation. . . . He looked tired and I told him he looked tired. He countered by saying "Olsen, I have never been so low as I am now." I said, "What do you mean?" "I mean that I am depressed in spirit." While I can not quote the Secretary verbatim now, he went on to develop the fact and general idea that the outlook was not a bright one. I chimed in and said that I had to confirm what he said. The Administration was not in good favor in the sections where I had been. Even in California there was a disposition to say critical things about the Administration and Mr. Hoover personally. In order to point things up in a definite, concrete way I asked the Secretary what position he proposed to take with reference to the Public Domain Commission report.[1] He said, "I have the material on my desk and I do not know what to do. I am saying to you what I am not saying to anyone else. I like [Ray Lyman] Wilbur personally, but he is making my position almost untenable. He is obsessed with the reclamation idea, the expansion idea, and he is dominating the views of the Commission. Naturally, as a close personal friend of the President, he carries weight with him." The Secretary went on to add that he had spoken rather frankly to the President and had urged upon him that he take a vacation for a while. The President did not take at all kindly to the suggestion. I then chimed in and said that I realized that all was not well, but that probably the appointed hour had arrived when his opportunity had come. I could not imagine that he had in any way shifted his position with reference to our land policy and if he had not shifted his position, the sound thing was to go forward and maintain it. He countered at once by saying, "Olsen it is one thing to have convictions and another thing to aggressively stand for them

1. The commission proposed to return some public lands to the states, provided conservation guidelines were accepted.

and support them. As long as I am a member of the Cabinet I have got to and will be loyal to the President. The President in the present situation, with the local interests of the East, must count on the West, and that is what he thinks he is playing to in this move." "The West," the Secretary added, "in my opinion is domineering and unreasonable but is getting away with murder. At one time the Public Domain is purely Federal in their view when they want to urge Federal appropriations for its development, but these same interests have no difficulty viewing it from a State point of view when it is to their interest to do so and demand their share of the boodle, whether in the form of grazing fees or what not." In short, the Secretary expressed rather deep resentment against the attitude shown by western representatives generally. I told the Secretary that I appreciated the position he must take with reference to the President, but that I had to take exception to the idea he had expressed of loyalty. I told him very frankly that I thought the President and the Administration was in a bad way politically and that the only moves that would put them right, if anything could be done, were certain daring strokes that they might take. Certainly the President at the present time could not count on the West. The Farm Board program had proven a dud, was severely criticised, and very little was expected from it, that more and more the sound, thinking leadership in Agriculture was thinking of just the very things which we in the Department at present stand for—far-reaching adjustment in the field of farm reorganization, land utilization, taxation and the kind of things that take quite a while to work out but which are basic in any fundamental farm program. I told the Secretary, very frankly, that I had seen men like [Henry A.] Wallace and that Wallace stated that he admired the Secretary, thought he had a lot of capacity. . . . Wallace expressed the idea that the Secretary had the qualities of leadership, and I told the Secretary, "I am sure Wallace feels as I and others do, that you are in a very strategic position to step out on some major matters and help put them across." I told the Secretary that I had sent a copy of the "Land Utilization and the Farm Problem" bulletin to Wallace and he expressed the idea that the time was ripe for a real major move in this direction. I said to the Secretary, "I am telling you all this very frankly because I want you to know how some people are reacting to the situation here. Frankly I am more than ever of the opinion that you have now an unusual opportunity. I think you should take a very definite stand against the Public Domain Commission report, you should take it with the Commission and with the President, and I hope that as a result of the position you take, that you as Secretary of Agriculture will step out and provide leadership for a real program along this line. There is no reason why you should not call a national conference on land utilization, which would stress the withdrawal of sub-marginal lands, the reforestation of lands of that kind, as major matters for consideration, and deal with the public domain and reclamation as subsidiary issues. In doing this I think you would attract to you strong interests throughout the country that would overshadow the influence of the group that stands for the other policy."

Just before we had to break up this conference, in response to a call from Secretary Wilbur, the Secretary made this rather significant statement, "I think perhaps what I may do is to tell the Public Domain Commission, when it meets here next week, just how I feel about the matter in no unmistakable terms, report to the President the position that I have taken and tell him that it is impossible for me to yield my convictions in this matter, that if I am a handicap to him now that I shall be very glad to eliminate myself from the picture." In short, my appraisal of the situation right now is that at no time to date has the Secretary been so near stepping out as he is at present. I feel sure that he thinks the cards are stacked against Hoover and the Administration and that little perhaps can be done to stave off the disaster. . . .

January 10, 1931.

. . . Last night (Friday, January 9) we met with the Secretary at eight o'clock in his office. It did not take long to get under way. The Secretary was in good humor and with him we went into the very heart of the Public Domain Commission's report. The Secretary asked Major [R. Y.] Stuart[2] what his primary criticisms were. The Major stressed, primarily, the failure of the report to reckon with watershed protection and the failure to recognize that the states could not handle the matter and that the Federal Government alone could handle a real program on land conservation. . . . The Secretary called on me. I went down the line and spent a half hour in dissecting the report and I think convinced the Secretary that the Commission was on unsound ground from an economic point of view, unsound ground from the point of view of the Administration and unsound ground from the point of view of public sentiment and, finally, it was the worst piece of dynamite they had ever had in their hands. . . . The Secretary very clearly is in a dilemma. He does not conceive it in the least. He said, "You fellows laugh and say it is an opportunity of a lifetime and it is the tightest squeeze in which man was ever placed. I want to be loyal to my Chief and I want to be loyal to my convictions." To this I countered, "You are loyal to your convictions when you go down the line and do not mince matters. It is an opportunity in a lifetime." The conference was very satisfactory and the Secretary, I feel quite sure, will be willing to go forward. The Secretary asked me to ride home with him. The Major had a car of his own. On the way the Secretary said, "Olsen, I am just about driven to this conclusion. I think I will gather up my evidence and I will go over first to Wilbur, throw it on his desk and say, here is my position and the position

2. Chief Forester.

of my Department. You are not only wrong in an economic way, but you are also wrong within political ideas. If you want to bring [Gifford] Pinchot[3] right out to the front, you can not do anything more effective than what is proposed in this report." He said, "I could not say this to Stuart because I know Stuart and Pinchot are very good personal friends, but I am saying it to you, Olsen." I countered by saying that when I stressed the rousing of the conservative sentiment in this country by this report I had Mr. Pinchot particularly in mind. The Secretary said, "Then I think I will lay my cards before the Commission. Then I will go to the President and say, 'These are my views and my convictions. I can not take any other. I do not want to embarrass you, Mr. President, and if my views in any way are making it impossible for you, just count me out of the picture.' "[4] I countered by saying that that was of course a very dramatic way of presenting his views, but I thought it would be a very effective way of bringing the thing to a head and driving the President to take the position which he should take. I urged the Secretary, by all means not to pass up an opportunity of a lifetime and I felt, when we parted last night, that an important decision was about to be made.

January 12, 1931.

Saturday evening Major Stuart, Dr. [L. C.] Gray[5] and I spent the evening with the Secretary on the public domain report. . . . We adjourned at ten o'clock with the understanding that we would meet Tuesday in the afternoon to prepare the memorandum. In the forenoon Dr. Stuart called me and told me that the Secretary was seeing the President at one o'clock or thereabouts and he would be seeing Wilbur a little later, but I should hold myself in readiness for a conference with the Secretary around four o'clock. About a quarter to six the Secretary called and asked me to take dinner with him. We went to Harvey's and over the dinner table he told me that he had a very busy afternoon and that not all of his time, by any means, was taken up in the discussion of the Public Lands Commission report. As a matter of fact, he had not been able to touch upon it with the President, because the conference with the President had been on the Wickersham report[6] which is scheduled, he told me confidentially, for release this week. It is very apparent that the Secretary is quite disturbed about the Wickersham report and its political significance and he made the statement that with all the other troubles that we now have, including the troubles that will grow out of

3. Chief Forester during Theodore Roosevelt's presidency. A leading figure in the fight for conservation under national auspices, he was in his second term as Governor of Pennsylvania at this time.
4. The Department of Agriculture believed that turning large portions of the public domain over to the states, besides being a poor conservation practice, would put more land into production and add to the plight of agriculture.
5. Chief of the Division of Land Economics in the Bureau of Agricultural Economics.
6. The report examined prohibition and the enforcement of the 18th Amendment.

the Wickersham report, why call down on our heads difficulties with the Public Lands Commission. He said he had visited with Wilbur and put up to him very strongly the political aspects of the matter. Wilbur did not seem to be overly impressed but still the Secretary was not sure but that he had registered somewhat with him. I raised the question as to why Wilbur saw fit to take a position such as he was taking, when he must know relatively little about the problem. I told the Secretary that the reactions I got in California indicated there was little confidence in Wilbur's knowledge of this question. The Secretary looked at me a little severely and said, "Why raise that question when the question may well be raised why the Secretary of Agriculture, with his automobile background, would be any better qualified to pass upon the question." The Secretary made a few comments regarding the President, which I thought were quite interesting: the only thing that could save the Administration would be a marked comeback in business conditions and he was skeptical that they would come back unless some unusual things happened in the next six months and, secondly, that unless the President did the dramatic thing of unloading upon the Democrats and Progressives impossible problems with which he was confronted, such as the liquor question and others [his chances for reelection were slight]. The Secretary said that if he were the President, and he has even suggested it to the President, he would let the opposition go ahead and organize Congress and then lay upon their laps this whole bunch of problems with which to wrestle during an extra session, which he admitted was quite likely. I commented somewhat upon what appeared to be somewhat of a change in the President's attitude toward his job, and which is reflected in his comeback on the Power Commission[7] and his comeback on the appointment of the Secretary of Labor.[8] Hyde said that these moves were hopeful. He made this comment, however, that the document which went up on the Power Commission matter was altogether too wordy and only one paragraph had any punch. The whole document should have been short, containing one syllable words, short sentences with punch, drive and smash that would make those fellows sit up and take notice. He went on to add that he had, months ago, advocated a vigorous fighting attitude on the part of the President. As a matter of fact he was the only one who had advocated that attitude. He thought possibly there had been some change in the President's attitude and that a little more vigor could be expected. . . .

This morning, at noon, Stuart and I met the Secretary in his office. He

7. On January 10, 1931, Hoover sent a message to the Senate declining to resubmit the already approved nominations to the Federal Power Commission of George Otis Smith, Claude L. Draper, and Marcel Garsaud. The Senate had requested Hoover to return the certified copies of the resolutions consenting to their appointment. Hoover refused to permit what he considered a "fundamental encroachment by the Senate upon the constitutional independence of the Executive." The commissioner continued to serve and the proponents of public power, who sought to embarrass the President, in turn experienced a rebuff.

8. William H. Doak was selected by Hoover to replace James J. Davis as Secretary of Labor in December 1930.

said he had an appointment with Chairman [James R.] Garfield[9] at 12:45 but he wanted to see us for a moment. He had a visit with the President this morning, in which he stressed the weakness of the report particularly from the conservation point of view and the political danger of reaction on the part of the conservation forces. The President countered by saying that he understood the membership of the committee represented the conservation interests. Garfield himself was a conservationist, [Elwood] Mead and others. This counter of the President evidently caught the Secretary somewhat unaware and he admitted that he did not make a very vigorous rebuttal on that point. He went on to add that it appeared that Wilbur had reached the President before he and had evidently discounted with the President the objections which he expected would be raised. The Secretary then went on to outline his line of procedure. He had redrafted the letter somewhat and was going to hand the letter to Garfield this noon. In the letter he had incorporated a paragraph stating that his position was based upon the work of his Department and these bureaus had not been heard and certainly the Commission would wish to avail itself of the information which these Bureaus had. In that way he would be able to reserve his position and not be drawn into an inevitable conflict with the President. It would be perfectly all right for us as Bureau chiefs to aggressively support our program. I did not lose much time in countering with this thought, . . . that in my opinion it was absolutely vital that the Secretary step forth before the Commission and represent the Department viewpoint, particularly in view of the circumstances as here obtain. Stuart backed me up. The Secretary then suggested that perhaps the thing to do was to merely reserve our decision and let the report go forward and transfer the whole matter to the Hill. The answer to that is clear—if the report is one to arouse the agricultural and conservationist groups of the Nation, the brunt would fall on the President's head. Hyde admitted that would be the case, but he had done the best he could to warn the President and he did not know what more he could do to stave that off. We finally countered with this thought—suppose the report goes to the President, is approved by him and is submitted to Congress; in what position are we as Bureau chiefs to fight on the whole matter. The Secretary said there was no reason why we could not aggressively submit our views to the committees. The Secretary admitted he had not thought of that contingent, and at that time he rushed out, saying that he would want to see us sometime this afternoon when he got back. . . .

February 27, 1931.

. . . Yesterday I went out to lunch with the Secretary and in order to get far removed so that no one could find him, we went to Child's at Union Sta-

9. Secretary of the Interior during Theodore Roosevelt's administration and chairman of the commission to study and recommend to the President the best way to manage the remaining public lands—about 250,000,000 acres.

tion. It is very apparent that the Secretary is sensing that he is to be on the firing line to help shape political sentiment in favor of the Administration. His feelings toward the independents in Congress are extremely bitter. In fact, most of the luncheon hour was monopolized by him in expressing his criticism of that attitude. He is a very strong party man and he thinks the objectives of good Government can be accomplished through party organization. Men like [George W.] Norris, [Robert M.] LaFollette [Jr.], etc., according to his views, are useful elements in the picture but should register their views through the party councils at the time of the convention and the formulation of the party's platform and once the die is cast they should be good soldiers and go forward and support the program. Nothing could be accomplished by the party without a united front. I countered that sometimes the party did not stand for public interest and should be criticized. He countered by saying, "That is the job of the opposition party." He said he admired independent, vigorous men like Borah and Norris, but he certainly did not approve the treacherous policies they adopted with reference to their party. . . .

On our return to the office yesterday, the conversation swung around to Legge leaving. I asked the Secretary if a successor had been found to which he replied "No." I asked him if a successor had been found for any of the other members who would be leaving the Board soon. He said "No." I asked him if it was not going to be embarrassing for the Administration to have a flock of resignations turn up at present. Then he looked at me and said, "Will you accept a place on the Board?" I said I was not in a jocular frame of mind and did not propose to answer silly questions. He said, "I want to know how you feel about it?" I said, "If you are in earnest—I have a desire to be of real constructive help to agriculture but I feel very sure that my opportunities for doing that constructive something are quite as great in my present position as they would be in any capacity on the Federal Farm Board." Then he countered with another question, "Which would you rather be, Secretary of Agriculture or member of the Federal Farm Board?" I said, "If you are putting that question in order to enable you to arrive at a decision for yourself, I well tell you unhesitatingly that you have the great and real job right where you are, and if you know what is good for yourself personally and good for the cause of agriculture you will stay put."

March 30, 1931.

Last Friday the Secretary and I took luncheon together at the Raleigh. I wanted to edge in on him at once with reference to Bureau matters, but he wanted to discuss the political situation. He told me, confidentially, that he suspected that the enemy was about to make an attack upon him personally. We discussed the nature of such an attack that they might make on him on purely personal grounds. I told him I did not think it strange that the enemy singled him out for special attention, since it was quite apparent that he was the political brains of the present Administration, that naturally they would want to get him. He then developed the fact that the attack would either be developed on the failure of the Federal Farm Board or his decision with reference to the Russian situation. The Secretary raised the question as to whether he should wait for the enemy to attack him or he step out aggressively and attack the enemy, particularly on the Russian issue. He feels very keenly on this program and believes that Russia and her program is an absolute menace to the future integrity of this country. He believes we should adopt a program of strong nationalism, incorporating in that program anti-communism, antagonism to the League of Nations, and to the World Court; the building of a strong Navy and other elements of a like nature. I told him I thought the spirit of nationalism in this country was very strong and that he probably on most counts would get pretty strong support. I also told the Secretary that there was a thing of getting too excessive on a matter and that the Administration, as I viewed the matter, was thoroughly inconsistent. At one time it would advocate adherence to the international court and the dismantling of the Navy and then, on the other hand, support a tariff program which was nationalistic in the extreme and which, in my judgment, was going to get us in a great deal of difficulty. I gained the impression that he is laboring with Hoover and other leaders on this subject, with a view to shaping a course strongly nationalistic in flavor.

The Secretary went on to develop the facts in the Russian case. He reminded me of the visit he had in Senator [Charles] Curtis'[10] office with a man of Russian origin, who at that time stated that importations of rum were being made by the Russian Government on a certain ship and that enemies were planted in munition and aircraft factories of this country for the purpose of sabotage. This man had offered to supply the detailed evidence in connection with munitions and aircraft factories for $5,000. He needed $2000 to help capture the opium shipment. Hyde took the matter up with the narcotics division of the Department of Justice and all they could make available under Government regulations was $400. This was not enough to employ the necessary men to check on the shipment. The boat came in and they did recover several lots of opium but not the amount of $2,000,000 worth which was reported by this informant. Hyde went on to point out, in conversation, that the recent difficulties at an Akron aircraft factory confirmed almost to the letter the information that was given to him last fall. They, of course, captured the scoundrel by placing Government mechanics along side of the suspected man. All of this goes to confirm Hyde in his conviction that the Russian Government, as a Government, is out to undermine our basis of civilization. He would like to step out with a story but he fears that his inability to reveal the name of his informant and his other sources of information would tend to discount anything that he might put out. My comment on this was that I believed there was a possible

10. A former Senator from Kansas now Vice-President of the United States.

menace in the Russian situation. . . . I added, however, my doubts about the wisdom of his aggressively stepping out on a program of this kind at this time, when millions of men and women in this country were in economic distress and were disposed to lean quite a little that way in their thinking. Furthermore a statement of this kind, I suggested, would be construed by his enemies as merely another red herring strewn across the matter to confuse the issues. Secretary Hyde seemed to see both these points and we proceeded to our other discussions. . . .

April 15, 1931.

Yesterday morning I found the Secretary in a very good frame of mind and we discussed, at the outset, the land utilization conference proposal. I told the Secretary we had to have a decision now if we were going to hold the conference this spring. He said he had taken it up with the President, that the President was not opposed to it but did express some doubt as to the values that would accrue. The President has an idea that these conferences do not get very far and he referred to the conference which Wallace called in 1922 as being without result. I explained that the situations were not parallel and that we were in position to formulate a concrete program of land utilization at this time, whereas it was quite difficult if not impossible to formulate a concrete working program back in those days. I said, "Then it is my understanding that we will go forward with the preparation for the conference," and he said "Yes." I said, "The important thing is when will the conference be held?" "Well," he said, "I do not think it can be held this spring. For one thing, I am going to do some fishing. Mrs. Hyde, according to present plans, will leave on a U.S. Transport for Japan. I will be sailing with her and then I will be fishing off the coast of Mexico." We spent some little time going over the itinerary of Mrs. Hyde and I said, "This suits me one hundred per cent. There is no need of trying to put on a big national conference without ample preparation and I, personally, feel we really could not expect to get by with it now before July 1." We then agreed that October would be a desirable month for the conference and the Secretary suggested that I go forward with the preparations. . . .

May 4, 1931.

Saturday afternoon (May 2) I was with the Secretary in the afternoon and after we chatted a little while, he suggested we go over to the Washington Hotel for our coffee. . . . We wound up on stools in the basement of the Washington Hotel and I told him then of the visit we had with Mr. [William R.] Castle of the Department of State in the morning.

Castle had suggested that Jardine, possibly, be assigned to the London conference in order that this country might be represented by brass collar men much as the other countries were. Hyde said that was interesting. I said, "I think that suggestion comes from the Chief." Hyde said, "You know the Chief really likes Jardine very much and, at the same time, I think he does not have a great deal of confidence in his ability. You know the Chief undoubtedly helped get the $25,000 a year salary from the New York people for him at the time he was lifted out of the Cabinet and since then the Chief thought Jardine might possibly be put on the Federal Reserve Board in place of [Edward H.] Cunningham and he asked me to sound out sentiment on that point. I did so and found there was no sentiment for Jardine at all." I also told the Secretary about Jim Stone's[11] suggestion that McKelvie engage a suite on the *Leviathan* with a conference room in order that the delegation might hold conferences on the way over. Furthermore he raised the question of taking a secretary along for dictation on the boat. I told Jim that I had not given the matter any serious thought but I did think our main job now was to analyze the material we had and clear up thinking so that when we went into the conference we would be able to express ourselves on the various points that were up. Just why we needed a special conference room on the boat to do that was more than I could see and particularly at this time when the Government was bearing down on the expenditures so vigorously. Furthermore it might not set so well with the farmers of this country if they knew delegates were engaging $500 suites on the *Leviathan*. The Secretary said, "I know how you feel about it and I feel the same way but those fellows over there have the idea of show." "But," I said, "I do not want it." But, the point is that the Farm Board is not going to overlook any opportunity to parade themselves as the important ones in the show. That raises in my mind the further question as to whether I should raise the issue as to who should be the chairman of the delegation, if there is such a thing as Chairman. This I have not discussed with the Secretary.

The Secretary's plans now are in a worse muddle than ever before. Mrs. Hyde takes the U.S. Transport *Grant* for the Orient and will be gone several months. She will land at San Francisco July 16 and insists that he be there to meet her. Carol[12] returns the middle of June and that puts another crimp in his plans. It begins to look now as though the Secretary will cancel his European trip. What hurts the Secretary still more is the fact that he is going to find it expedient to cancel the projected Panama trip. He said [Patrick] Hurley[13] had offered to make available a fine boat with a personnel of about 140 men which would take him from New Orleans to any points around Panama and especially good fishing grounds, but after further reflection it had become apparent that it would not be politically expedient for him to avail himself of such facilities. . . .

11. Vice-chairman of the Federal Farm Board who succeeded Legge when he resigned as chairman in March 1931.
12. Caroline C. Hyde, the Secretary's daughter.
13. Secretary of War.

In my judgment the one outstanding factor that would probably prevent the Secretary from going still higher is his family situation. He laid it bare in a most surprising way the day following the dinner he gave the President and Mrs. Hoover. The story was part of another illustration of what has impressed itself upon me—that there are very few whose paths are strewn with roses.

May 4, 1931 [*a second entry*].

Under date of Monday, April 27, at 2 p.m., at Senator McNary's request I went to his office to discuss the wheat situation. . . . Senator McNary told me that he had been up to see the President with regard to the London wheat conference and insisted that it was important for this Government to be represented, for political reasons if for no other, since of course the farmers had a right to feel that this Government was overlooking no possibility to better the situation. The Senator very frankly said that he did not think anything could come out of the conference, but he thought attendance would have a very wholesome effect. He said he told the President that I was the man who should attend and that I knew more about the wheat situation than any other man. The President, he said, took kindly to the suggestion and he hoped I was willing to take on this assignment. Then the Senator went on and said, "Now I would like to know how you feel about some of the moves that have been made. As far as this Wheat conference is concerned, I have no confidence in the Federal Farm Board. The President told me to go over there and talk to them about it and I did and they had no ideas, such as you do." He said, "Talk about a group of supermen—it is laughable." He picked out [Charles S.] Wilson particularly for comment and said, "He never did have an idea." The Senator went on to say that he thought the Federal Farm Board program had broken down, that they could not get anywhere on the stabilization approach, and he wanted to know just what I thought. I told him, rather frankly, that I thought the Federal Farm Board program so far had not brought us very fruitful results and that I did not see how they could expect the results they had in mind to follow from the program that had been laid down. I discussed with some candour the effects in the standardization field, the cooperative marketing field and I even touched upon their more recent efforts to horn in on the field of this Bureau and, particularly, their efforts in acreage reduction and the like. It was very plain to me that the Senator was disgusted with the Federal Farm Board setup and was looking for support to his views. He also told me that the President had seriously suggested the wisdom of these sign-up campaigns to reduce wheat acreage. He wanted to know what I thought about it. I told him, frankly, that there was a radical difference in thinking between us and the Federal Farm Board. We did not see how a domestic basis could be realized. The Senator said, however, that the President had urged the matter very strongly and would like to know how I felt about it and then he left with me some material . . . which he said he would like to have me analyze and report to him on it. He asked me if I had any objection to my name being used in that connection. I said I did not think it would be well for me to figure in the picture for obvious reasons, but that I would be glad to give him, for his own personal use, a critique that would be helpful to him. Senator McNary also asked me to supply him material on the various phases of the wheat situation and to suggest the kind of things that might be done in a legislative way. He said, very frankly, that he did not see very much that could be done legislatively. I told him I thought, in the main, he was correct but there were certain things that could be done, about taxes, land utilization and the reforestation of lands. He thought it was rather foolish to talk about planting lands to trees, that we had too many trees right now. I told him that was not a remedy in itself, but was just one of the many things that should be done to gradually improve the situation, that after all this whole problem was a long-time problem that had to be worked out in the field of competition adjustment and until we began to think the same way along those lines, we would be muddling around. He agreed and, more and more, I think that Senator McNary will probably line up with the program of strengthening the activities of the Department.

August 27, 1931.

Tuesday (August 25, 1931) before Cabinet meeting I placed before the Secretary the beef cattle outlook report. I should explain that this report had been revised by the boys in keeping with the suggestions I made and that I, personally, went over it and carefully eliminated all price forecast, but did retain outlook which was reasonably favorable to the feeding of beef cattle. The Secretary read it, got my point, saw the optimistic phases of the report and then commented about as follows: "About two years ago the President went right straight up in the meeting we had on price forecasting." (I gathered it was a Cabinet meeting, although I am not sure as to this.) "He (the President) stood rather vigorously against forecasting of any kind and yet was sufficiently vague so that I really did not know what position I should take. I came back, and, as you recall, I told you of this conference and the need of great care in the handling of forecasts. I did not forbid them but it was understood that we should be very careful. As a matter of fact, I am in favor of this sort of thing." I reminded the Secretary that in keeping with that policy I had made it a point to lay the price situation and other price forecasts before him and that we had, jointly, gone over them and edited them and I understood that policy had his approval and to this he did not demur. The Secretary asked, "Did you see the President's message that he sent me?" I said, "I did not see it, although you quoted from it.'' The Secretary said there was no mistaking the President's tone, that he went very far in intimating that we had violated his instructions and he went on to add that this matter now had to be handled with the greatest care. . . . That evening I tried to see the Secretary but he had a group with him and I did not want to open up the subject in the presence of others. So last night (Wednesday, August 26) when I went over to see the Secretary I got the full story. He had taken the report up to the President and the President had said ''Thumbs down.'' It is true that this report is of an optimistic character but no one could forecast what was likely to happen. Everybody had been wrong and, for that reason, he did not think there should be any forecasts but a mere statement of the facts and let the other fellow draw his own conclusions. The President went on further to comment that what would happen in case the farmers acted on the basis of this forecast and then the prices went down? Secretary Hyde interpreted that to mean that the President expected a further drop in prices and in the business situation. He said, ''There is of course some justification for the President's decision. We have all gone wrong on our forecasts.'' He spoke about the wheat forecast in the fall of 1929 and how we had worked with the Federal Farm Board and how the Farm Board had probably used our data and our forecasts in arriving at their position. . . . He said, ''You have been wrong on lots of your forecasts. You can not expect anything else under these conditions. Why not face the facts and call it all off?'' I said, ''That is true. There have been some mistakes and it could not be anything else, but you will find on examination that the forecasts in this field have been unusually good. I am going to have an investigation of them made and will present to you a report, because the facts will have to be known. We are taking a very serious backward step when we kill the Outlook service. Without it we cannot formulate plans of adjustment and you are going to throw overboard what we have been developing since 1923.'' I said, ''Furthermore, this is going to have violent reactions, the Land Grant Colleges, private and public agencies throughout the country have accepted the service and are strong for it and will protest violently. The President can not afford to bring upon himself any more criticism at this time.'' ''Well,'' he said, ''That may be, Olsen, but this is an Executive Order—loyalty above anything else.'' I said, ''Yes, Arthur, and when I come to your office and say you are all wrong on this or that, am I loyal or disloyal? There is no question about whether that is loyalty. That is all I am asking you to do in this case, is to fight it through and prevent the President from taking a position that can be only detrimental to a cause and to him personally.'' He said, ''I dislike to have this happen but do not see any way out at present. You will have to about-face and let people draw their conclusions but if you wish to write letters to your State people, quoting your understanding of the facts for their own use, with the understanding that they do not quote you, it is all right with me.'' I said, ''But, where does that leave me when it comes to an actual showdown? You can not keep a fact of that kind secret or under cover and I prefer to deal with this in a clean-cut and above-board manner." He said, "Perhaps you could issue a statement to the effect that now that the world is so badly upset it is impossible to make forecasts and for the time being they are discontinued." I said, "That will not let us out. In the first place, we will not subscribe to the statement and in the second place, some one will ask why. The only thing I can do is to carry out the Order literally, take out anything of an interpretative character, let mere facts slide along and let the reaction come." He said, "That is perhaps all you can do but remember let the reactions come of their own free will and check through me." I said, "I understand." (What I want to make clear in so many words is that the Secretary made clear he was in sympathy with our position and that, furthermore, he would not be averse to the strategy which was intimated because he went on to say that perhaps the reactions that came in might be useful in an education way—meaning to the President.) . . .

The Secretary said, "Olsen, what are we going to do about the situation this fall?" I said, "What do yo you mean?" He said, "Everything is wrong, the Farm Board vigorously and violently attacked and they are going to wipe it out; the Federal Farm Loan banks crashing and if things keep on this way the whole system will go to pieces; agitation for such things as debenture and equalization fee and so on." In other words, he gave the impression of being a man who is badly harassed by all of the problems that are pouring in on him and which he could not dodge. He has been exceedingly friendly since my return and no criticism has been directed against the Bureau in any respect.

October 1, 1931.

The Saturday before Labor Day I spent some time with the Secretary in his office and on the evening of that day he suddenly bobbed up in the lobby of the Cairo Hotel and called for me at my room. He asked me to come down in the lobby and meet him. He had been working on his "Review of Reviews" article[14] and I had given him some suggestions in the afternoon. He had been revising that article in light of those suggestions and asked if I would not listen to his pencilled statement. I made a few running comments as he read, but reserved my comments until we got into his car. It was a hot evening and he told his driver to hunt the breezes out in the country side. We drove from eight until about 11:45 and had a most intimate discussion of many matters. . . .

The Secretary made it clear that evening that if he was free to do so, he would resign over night. It is very clear that he is chafing under the strong hand which Hoover is exerting on the activities of the Department. He is not

14. "Agricultural Teeter Board," an article by Hyde, appeared in the October 1931 issue of *Review of Reviews*.

free to go ahead and do what he would like to do and what he should do as the head of the Department. He remarked that the Chief would act on matters with which he was not acquainted or which should be left with him to handle and this proved embarrassing. His remarks were not stated in this blunt fashion but that was the implication in what he said. (Mr. E. E. Hall[15] since then has remarked on two or three occasions that the Secretary is working under real difficulties because of the President's insistence on "having his fingers in the pie" on everything.)

We discussed the political situation and the Secretary was clearly pessimistic. He said he thought the best thing the President could do was to declare to the world that he would not be a candidate again and go still further and let Congress organize Democratic and carry the full onus for the present situation. Very confidentially he made the statement that Coolidge no doubt had his eyes upon the nomination and he made me a bet that before a great while Coolidge would make a public statement disavowing any intention of seeking the nomination, but all with a shrewd political purpose of getting himself in an advantageous position if a jam developed in the convention. I took him up on the bet with the understanding that he had to prove that Coolidge's statement would be made with that motive in mind. He left it at that and said, of course, no one could prove any man's motive. (Just a day or two ago the Secretary called me over the inside phone and asked me how my finances were. I told him I was managing to live. He pressed me rather hard and I said, "What have you got on your chest?" He said, "I want you to pay off the bet and give me the hat I won. Have you not seen the article in the *Saturday Evening Post* by Calvin Coolidge?[16] He has done just what I told you he would do.") Ever since then the Secretary has kidded me about the hat and about the bet. I told him he still had the job of proving that Cal made the statement with the motive he suggested. . . .

In one of my more recent conferences with the Secretary, in which I have pressed him on land utilization he had told me confidentially that he was making headway with the Chief and he now thought that he might be getting a statement from Wilbur stating the Department [of the Interior] would cease to urge further expansion of irrigation projects in the agricultural area. He went on to add a hope that he could get out of these conferences with the Administration's approval a strong program of land utilization in keeping with our general thought. . . .

October 19, 1931.

Saturday, October 17, I had a short visit with the Secretary in his office, at which time I pointed out to him the embarrassing situation with

15. An assistant to the Secretary of Agriculture.
16. "Party Loyalty and the Presidency" by Coolidge appeared in the October 3, 1931, issue of *Saturday Evening Post.*

which we were placed with reference to outlook. I told him quite a number of complaints had been registered with us and that it was making it exceedingly difficult for us to function as we did not know how to proceed to make these outlook reports of interest and value to the extension forces, and furthermore that it left the Federal Farm Board free to invade our field. I told the Secretary that at this time we might say some very constructive things about cotton, wheat, etc. I also pointed out to him some of the statements which the Federal Farm Board had been making in their outlook reports and placed before him the section of the Agricultural Marketing Act which forbids cotton forecasts. He noted this and said it was really a prohibition on price forecasting and what Congress had in mind was that individual members of the Board might resort to price forecasting with cooperatives but only in a personal service capacity. He admitted that it was unreasonable and unfair to place us in this position but he went on to say that the only thing he could do was to lay it before the President and have the President call Stone over and tell him where to head in. This he evidently did not feel disposed to do, but I told him that sentiment would undoubtedly roll up and make this a very embarrassing situation. He countered by saying, "Let the reaction come." . . .

The Secretary also told me he had a thought of a political nature which he wished to lay before me for my reaction. Very bluntly he said, "Do you think the farm organizations would be willing to lay aside equalization fee and debenture and the like in exchange for a vigorous land utilization program?" He went further and asked me if I would be willing to put this up to Chester Gray.[17] I told him that I did not know that it would be wise for me to put it up to Chester Gray. I was willing to admit that these proposals had slim chance of passing over the President's veto, but I expressed a doubt that it would be a judicious move to attempt to trade with these farm organization leaders in this way. I told the Secretary I was convinced that the farm organizations as such were very much sold to the land utilization program and if put forward vigorously and supported it would go far to nullify any efforts for equalization and the debenture fee. I then asked the Secretary why he was thinking along such bold lines. He told me he had told the President that he would like to have an hour or two with him to discuss some matters with him in a very personal and intimate way. The President told him to come over to dinner, which he did and they went into a number of matters. He laid before the President the land utilization plan and the desirability of shutting down on further homesteading of public domain, shutting down on reclamation, contracting the land area by land acquisition, reforestation and the like, and the President's reactions evidently were very good. He said the President had already run afoul of the Columbia River lobby which was said to have $100,000 available for their use and he was dead set on opposing them. The Secretary also said his hand had been strengthened in the handling of the drainage district crowd. All in all he

17. Washington representative of the American Farm Bureau Federation.

figured the President was in a frame of mind to support the land utilization program but of course as a politician it would be a king strike for him if he could negotiate a deal with the farm organization leaders such as I have just described. I asked him if he had brought [Ray Lyman] Wilbur of the Interior Department into the picture and he said it was a very delicate matter to bring a close friend of forty years standing into the picture. He had, however, made up his mind to see Wilbur personally.

A little later on in the week I told the Secretary I had had both Chester Gray and [Frederic] Brenckman[18] of the National Grange in my office and had tactfully felt around on the program they were going to support this winter. In the discussion it developed that they did not feel too strongly that they could pass their pet measures and they were both disposed to go very far in supporting the land utilization program. I suggested to the farm organization leaders that it would probably be better to swing back to one large conference as there was so little time before Congress adjourns. In this they heartily agreed. At such a conference arrangements would be made to develop in a concrete way the specific segments of a land utilization program with a view to presenting it vigorously in the next session of Congress. It is very clear that the Secretary is wrestling with the problem and I take it still hopes to go through with the land utilization conference.

November 28, 1931.

Late last night the Secretary called me over to his office and was visibly disturbed. He said, "I have something on my mind, but I do not know whether I dare tell you." I said, "Have you reason on the basis of your past experience, to doubt me?" "Well," he said, "here it is." He picked up a typewritten document, which he said was the President's forthcoming message, saying, "Now remember this has reached practically final form and was handed to me for my reaction." First the Secretary read a section which was about as follows: "I recommend that Congress take the necessary steps to reorganize the Department of the Interior and in that reorganization provide for a Division of Education, Health and Conservation. Authority should also be provided for the transfer to the Department of the Interior from time to time various units that might properly function in that Department." The Secretary went on a little further and read another section from the message, about as follows: "I recommend that Congress take the necessary steps to develop the Grand-Coulee Pumping project in the Columbia River Basin, with a view to developing the reclamation and especially the hydraulic electric resources of that great body of water. I also recommend that Congress take the necessary steps to carry out the necessary program on the Cove Creek Tennessee River project."[19] The

18. National Grange's Washington representative.
19. Norris Dam, the first dam constructed by TVA, is on the Cove Creek site.

Secretary said, "Now what do you make of that?" I said, "I am not sure that I see quite all the implications. Read it again." So he read it again. "Now," he said, "what are the conservation bodies in the Federal Government—Forestry, Biological Survey, Chemistry, Parks, Reclamation, etc. Evidently the President is running absolutely counter to the thinking of all of these conservation bodies that have been so aggressive in the past that I cannot comprehend it. Furthermore, he steps out and advocates in the face of all the surplus problem we have had, in face of all criticism of the reclamation policy, in the face of the position I have taken and the conference just held, and recommends the development of the Columbia River Basin project." I countered by saying that it was incomprehensible, that the only way that I could explain it was that the President did not know that he was running counter to the powerful streams of public opinion today and it meant merely additional political suicide, and that if he persisted in this viewpoint, I went on to add, it made his (the Secretary's) position almost untenable. The Secretary at that point added that if the President adhered in this view he had only one alternative and that was to be on his way to Missouri forthwith. We discussed the matter a little further and I said that I thought he owed it to the President to pound his table and state in no unmistakable terms that he was on the wrong path and did not know what he was doing. . . . He then asked me to get in touch with Dr. Gray and see what information I could get on the Grand-Coulee Development, as well as Cove Creek. I had both Dr. Gray and Mr. [W. A.] Hartman[20] at his office at nine o'clock, at which time we had a session and developed the full facts regarding the reclamation features of these projects, and the Secretary was more than ever convinced that he should take a vigorous position in opposition. He then suggested that we go to his apartment and there we remained until one o'clock. . . .

This afternoon, November 28, about 3:30 the Secretary called me over again and was in a very good frame of mind. He had his visit with the President and had called him on both points and evidently shocked the President into a realization of what he was about to do. It developed on the first point that what the President wished to do was to focus attention upon the creation of a new Department of Education. He realized there was opposition to this move and in order to divert some of that opposition he had grabbed for some collateral issues such as public domain and conservation, etc. He had made the mistake, however, of grabbing the hot poker when he included conservation, and the Secretary evidently succeeded in convincing him that he was on dangerous ground. He expressly stated that there was no thought of transferring Forests to the Department of the Interior and the Secretary was rather of the opinion that the word "conservation" would be completely eliminated from his message.

With reference to the Columbia Basin project, the Secretary made

20. In charge of land settlement studies in the Division of Land Economics, headed by L. C. Gray.

about this comment: "Between us girls, I am convinced that the President had been told that he would not have the Washington delegation in the convention if he did not make this recommendation in his message." Hyde said that he told the President that he thought he was on very precarious ground, that in his judgment the State of Washington was not committed to the Columbia River Basin Project, and he went on to develop the sentiment that was abroad against reclamation. He said he had succeeded in convincing the President that he had better eliminate all reference to the project but he wished to have some additional supporting evidence if I could corral some evidence of the opposition, particularly in the State of Washington. That accounts for the messages I have just sent to [Albert S.] Goss[21] and to [William A.] Schoenfeld,[22] which read as follows: "Please forward air mail available resolutions and any other evidence disclosing opposition States Washington, Oregon, Idaho to Columbia River Basin reclamation project." The Secretary went on to say, "One of these bright days I am going to commit suicide—I am going to say that where you find a western senator in the Senate, there you will find a land steal," or words to that effect. His point being, of course, that the senators from the western states were merely catering to the voracious expansion elements in their respective states. The Secretary feels that he has won his battle and that the message will not carry these objectionable features.

December 7, 1931.

Saturday afternoon (December 5) following my request that Mr. [C. W.] Kitchen and I be permitted to see him for a few minutes regarding certain matters, Mr. [Ernest] Hall called and said the Secretary would like to have me come over but come alone. So, I went. The Secretary picked up a draft of a letter and said, "I want your opinion of this." I proceeded to read the draft of a letter to the President in which the Secretary in unmistakable, direct and forceful language took issue with the President on his Message as to the Columbia River Basin project. At the conclusion of the reading I made a number of suggestions, all of which he incorporated. He asked me then what I thought of the letter and I told him I thought it was a masterpiece and a masterstroke. Then I asked him, "But, why are you writing it?" He said, "I will tell you. If the President puts out his Message in its present form, it is questionable if I can remain in the Cabinet." I then asked, "Why does the President insist on his position?" The Secretary then got up and pranced around and said: "Well, here is a document on the Columbia River Basin project and on page 3 or 4 it reads as follows," and then he quoted from a statement of Hoover as Secretary of Commerce heartily endorsing

21. Master of the Washington State Grange.
22. Pacific Northwest regional representative of the Federal Farm Board stationed at Portland, Oregon.

the Columbia River Basin project, stating that it was thoroughly justified from a reclamation point of view. "The trouble is," Hyde continued, "that Hoover is now confronted with a commitment which he made at a time when he was a seeker of office." "Then too," he said, "you must not overlook the fact that Hoover is a German. Now there are two kinds of Germans. There is a German that corresponds to the cock of the walk. He rules or ruins. Or, there is the German that is the market garden variety of hams. Now draw your conclusions." The Secretary then said, "I have one more question to ask you. If after presenting this protest to the President he retains this item in his Message but says that it will be quite all right with him if I, Hyde, continue to express my views on this subject, can I under any circumstances consistently remain in the Cabinet?" I told the Secretary that was a hard question and I wanted to think about it before I could give my answer. A card party in the adjoining room interfered with my giving a reply and that concluded the discussions of Saturday.

About seven o'clock I took Tom Cooper[23] over to the Secretary's Office and we had a very interesting visit regarding the conference. The Secretary at that time evidently was conversing with [Walter] Newton about the Columbia River Basin project and was saying some rather vigorous things, so I kept Tom out of the office in order to give the Secretary complete latitude in his telephone conversation. When I came in he was winking knowingly at me. We settled down and shortly began chatting about the land utilization conference and committee appointments. The Secretary in the course of that conversation made it clear that he thought the committee should be set up and operating very soon. He was especially interested in the Advisory Legislative Committee and expressed the idea that the Chairman should be a strong man with a lot of political backing and should, preferably, come from the Northeast where he could influence the dominating vote or from the Pacific Northwest where he could mobilize the favorable sentiment of that region. We finally hit upon the idea that it was probably desirable to have a representative of the Grange or the American Farm Bureau serve as Chairman of the Advisory Committee. The Secretary turned to me and said, "Now, Ole, I think it might be well for you to skip up to New York and see Rockefeller, Jr. You are going to need some money to finance this party. You do not want to overlook the sinews of war." I countered by asking just how it might strike some if it were known that Rockefeller money was being used to finance this party. The Secretary looked at me and said, "There are ten commandments with which you no doubt are very familiar. There is an eleventh one which you evidently have not learned so well and that reads as follows. 'Do it but do it in such a way that you are not caught at it.' "

Shortly thereafter we parted company and again stumbled on to each other in Childs down at Pennsylvania Avenue. The Secretary nodded to me as his group was going out and we stepped over to one side and then he

23. Dean of College of Agriculture, University of Kentucky.

whispered that he was too late, that the President had released the Message to the Press at four o'clock. I said, "For heavens sake then get your letter into the President's hands irrespective of that." He said he was going to see him in the morning. So the next morning, Monday, he spent a good bit of the morning with the President. In the afternoon Kitchen and I had a brief session with the Secretary but he was in a hurry so we did not have much time for discussion, but following the conference with Kitchen the Secretary said he would like to see me just a minute. . . . "Now," he said, "just a little progress report from me. I went in to see the President this morning with the letter in my hand and started out by saying, 'Mr. President, this matter I discussed with you is of such deep importance that I feel that I would be derelict in my duty if I did not use my utmost efforts in placing it adequately before you.'" The Secretary said that as he was about to hand the President the letter, the President said, "You need not worry about any immediate need for discussion of this matter now. I think I have modified my Message in such a way that you will be entirely satisfied for the present." The Secretary showed me the paragraph in the President's printed Message which stated that the President would submit to congress a special Message on the question of reorganization and reclamation. "So," the Secretary continued, "we have won the first round but this may be the beginning of the end. We have burned our bridges and there is just one course ahead." The Secretary went on to say that it was now vital that we take the letter that had been drafted, elaborate upon it to develop fully and vigorously the philosophy of the agricultural program for which we were standing and show the place of irrigation and reclamation in that program. He said that would have to be done before much of January had gone by. I added that I thought, too, that it was desirable to have our friends active and watching and checkmating any developments. He said that is all very true but remember that our first duty is to see whether we can not influence the President's thinking.

December 14, 1931.

. . . Last night (Sunday, December 13) I called at the Secretary's Office about eight o'clock. After a few breezy exchanges I made the remark that from all the signs it seems that the Administration had gotten itself as completely mired as possible. The Secretary looked at me quizzically through his squinting and made his statement: "H.H. can not be re-elected." I countered by saying I thought he never made a more truthful statement, that the Republican party was surely sunk from all the signs now available. The Secretary said, "Come on let us put on our hats and go over to the Mayflower." We went over to the coffee shop, sat down at one of the tables and chatted until eleven o'clock. Other matters came up in the course of that conversation: I remarked that I thought the President's message had been very unfortunate, had not only painted an exceedingly dark picture but it failed to put across a program that commanded confidence. Furthermore I told him I could not understand the conception of politics that prompted him to advocate the reduction of reparations and the revival of the War Debt Commission. I went on to say that if the Republican party expected to win they would have to step out in a daring way as never before and reverse the politics for which they were now standing in no uncertain terms and supply a leadership that would command confidence. The Secretary seemed to agree with all of this one hundred per cent. He said that as far as he was concerned the President's Message did not paint in unusually dark colors, the situation, but it fell down in putting up a lame program. He said if the President had merely painted the doleful picture and then said to the Democrats, "Now here is your job. Fix it up," he would be sitting pretty. Instead of that he had merely put up his several proposals for the Democrats to shoot at and riddle. He said that any advocacy of reparations reduction at this time was exceedingly unwise and he went on to say that if it were his business there would be about four or five planks in his program: (1) Attend to our own business and quit trying to save Europe when we had all we could do to save ourselves; (2) serve notice on the world that we are not going to be drawn into their fights but that we were going to keep ourselves well armed for any eventuality; (3) admit that there were badly rotted spots in our economic body; that these had to be cauterized and corrected and that inroads on the Treasury was not the way out; thousands, if not millions, had taken their losses and it was up to others to do so; (4) cease senseless injection of Government into business and restore the emphasis upon private initiative. This, in general, seemed to be the line of thought he was following. I said that in the main I would subscribe to many of his thoughts, that I would have some reservations and, furthermore, that I felt he had not stressed certain matters that had to be reckoned with. Also, I stated that it was about time that the spirit of independent thinking and statement manifested itself around Washington. It was not only the Civil Service people, like myself, who found themselves wet blanketed in their duty and right to speak freely but I certainly felt that men high in Administrative circles gave the impression that they were no longer able to speak their mind. . . .

The Secretary went on to remark that H. H. somehow had the way of saying the wrong thing and he clearly indicated that the situation now seemed hopeless. "You know," he said, "he has a childlike faith in statements and I think his actions grow out of a natural timidity to strike out, and also out of a compromising policy which has brought him where he is today." Then the Secretary told me how last Thursday (December 10) following the diplomatic dinner at the White House the Cabinet members with their wives had adjourned to the President's quarters for refreshments. As that little party broke up the President tapped Hyde on the shoulder and asked him to step into his office. Hyde said his heart sank into his boots, thinking that he would have to listen to some more of these hopeless statements to which H. H. was given. When he stepped in he found Pat Hurley there and the situation looked no better, but in the course of another half minute Walter Brown[24] stepped in and he then thought things looked interesting and, sure enough, H. H. trotted out his twelve points on cooperation which he read in his simple childlike way. Hyde went on to say that the statement came out considerably modified from the original draft. He said that in commenting upon it to the President he said, "The statement is all right. It is merely nailing to the mast the statement, but the trouble is that the foundation is defective so why nail it to the mast?"

The Secretary went on to say, "Olsen, you know I sometimes feel very uncomfortable under the present situation. I can not agree with the position taken by H. H. and yet I must seem to agree. I do not believe that I am as yet jockeyed into the position where it can be said that I am approving these several policies but how can I avoid it if I continue in my present relationship?" I spoke up at that time and said that I thought he had been very successful in preventing them from tying the tin can on him but there was grave danger of his appearing in that light, but in the public mind he would be associated with the President's policies and even though he remained silent on them he would be construed as approving unless he stepped out and took a forceful position on the various questions. What that would ultimately lead to, of course, was another matter. . . .

[*no date*]

Late yesterday afternoon I had a visit with the Secretary on two or three very interesting matters. . . . During the course of our conversation I slipped under his nose the letter to the Secretary of State regarding the French preferential tariff. I introduced this by saying that it was a letter of importance and interest and I wished he would read it with great care. After he had read the letter I made an oral statement in which I condemned the indifference to what was transpiring in this field and called his attention to the detailed memorandum which I had sent over to Mr. [Herbert] Feis of the Department of State and in which we had registered our objections, and I told the Secretary it looked to me like a case of selling out the American farmer and if the matter became known it would become a veritable bombshell and I then added, as a matter of fact the letter had been toned down by the elimination of certain statements that indicated that the failure to protest the German treaties had undoubtedly encouraged France to make a similar move and would undoubtedly encourage other nations to do the same. I went on to say that this had been taken up with us by the Economic Adviser of the Department of State and in the course of that conference a veiled statement had been made that led us to believe that the President had

24. Postmaster General.

indicated to the Department of State that he did not wish to object to the treaties and was thinking only of the European situation. At that point the Secretary pounded his desk and rather forcefully said, "It was not the President—I know that it was not the President who took that position. It could have been no other than 'Henry L. Muttonhead (Stimson).' " The Secretary went on to express his feelings regarding "Muttonhead" and his messing things generally. As a matter of fact I gained the impression that he had in one of the Cabinet meetings taken issue with him in his advocacy of measures to aid Europe, irrespective of their bearing upon the United States.

December 19, 1931.

. . . At the outset of the conference yesterday afternoon Secretary Hyde said, "Well, Olsen, I have demonstrated that I am the greatest jackass in America." He said, "Earlier this week we were over to the White House and after the dinner the President got me off to the side and said: 'Well, at last, for the first time in my experience, the financial crowd have gotten together and are going to act. The life insurance people, the big banks are going to support the market. The life insurance people have already amassed a poll of $100,000,000 and there is more to be had.' " He said, "I thought about it and realized here would be a good opportunity to make a pile but I passed it by and then last night (Thursday, December 18) Mrs. Hyde and I were at dinner at the White House and the President again called me aside and said: 'It is going through.' " The Secretary continued, "I had at least ten or one dozen stocks which I bought that would have made me a little fortune because you know what the stock market did today." As a matter of fact the stock market went up as much as ten or twelve points on some stocks. When he finished his story I said: "So, you think you are a jackass? May I comfort you by saying you never did a wiser thing. You will have plenty of opportunities and you will never regret steering an ethical course in your personal activities."

December 24, 1931.

. . . Last night I was at the Secretary's Office discussing the agricultural credits program of the Administration when Hall brought in a mimeographed statement which he said [John R.] Fleming[25] was presenting as his Christmas gift to the Secretary. The Secretary read it and he fairly jumped out of his chair and dramatically extended his arms to the heavens and let out a peal of thanks. I asked him what had happened. He said, "Would you

25. A special agricultural writer in the Office of Information of the Department of Agriculture.

believe it, the War Department engineers have issued a public statement that the Columbia River Basin project is unsound from an engineering, economic and agricultural point of view." He looked at me and said, "Do you get that—army engineers, and where do they get their interest in agriculture? Do you suppose that a certain gentleman has given this matter further thought and has concluded this is his way out of the dilemma?" I said, "It is interesting and I would love to know just as much as you." Fleming was called in and he told us he had been working over there with the army engineers, had run afoul of the Washington representative of the Columbia River Basin propaganda sentiment and through him had picked up a clue to this action of the army engineers. The mimeographed report bears the date of December 19, but it had not been given any publicity. This man told Jack Fleming that the Electric Bond and Share, the Montana Power and the Washington State Power companies had jointly agreed to get behind the Columbia River Basin project. I believe he was also told by the same man that [Albert] Goss of the Grange had somewhat relented in his opposition. Later on he reported that he looked up Goss and found that he had and that raises another interesting question. Goss, it now seems, did not oppose the proposition on the grounds that the purpose is to develop the power aspects and use the revenues in developing the irrigation aspects, so it would not be subsidized irrigation. Fleming is going to do his best to get, through some of the underlings over there, the real explanation of this action by the Army engineers but it looks like a report staged at the instance of the President. . . .

1 9 3 2

About Saturday, December 26, I was called over late in the evening by the Secretary and as I arrived [Elton L.] Marshall[1] also arrived. The Secretary asked me to bring with me the bills dealing with farm relief, and particularly those bearing on the distribution of Federal Farm Board wheat. When I reached his office he seemed to be quite excited about this bill and it developed that what they had in mind was the measure that Senator [Arthur] Capper[2] just introduced, providing that the Board should turn over to the Red Cross and other relief agencies 40 or 50 million bushels of wheat. The Farm Board had just discovered that they would be left holding the bag, and that on this 40 or 50 million bushels of wheat they had advanced large sums and they would have to take up money advanced by non-government agencies on this same wheat, since these other agencies held the first liens, before it could be turned over to any relief agencies. So, they had just, evidently, awakened to the fact that they were going to be in a very unfavorable position. But, what was more significant was the fact that the President, himself, realized that he would, if the Capper bill passed, be in the position of approving the bill or vetoing substantial relief to the needy. As the Secretary put it, if the bill reached the President in its present form, it would be absolutely deadly. Furthermore there was nothing in the measure to prevent graft in the distribution of the wheat and to guarantee that this wheat would get into the hands of those who actually needed it. Marshall was put to work to draw up amendments to shape the bill up along those lines.

Last week (Wednesday, December 30, 1931) at the time the five rural sociologists were in my office, [W. E.] Grimes[3] called up and told me that the special committee of the Farm Economic Association had ar-

---

1. Solicitor, Department of Agriculture.
2. Senior Senator from Kansas.
3. Professor of agricultural economics at Kansas State University.

ranged to meet the Secretary at 12:45 and wanted me present. . . . I went over to the Secretary's Office and arrived after the Committee of the American Farm Economic Association had gone into his office. I stepped in without saying anything and sat down and listened to them operate on the Secretary. They did a whale of a good job. They were all flashing fire from their eyes and they shoved him into one corner after another, from which he could not extricate himself. They had him where he admitted that he thought interpretation was essential and even price forecasts were essential but this was not the time to make them because no one could do more than sheer guess work. They had not developed the theory enough. There were reactions so when that came up I said, "Now that is a point where I would like these gentlemen to elaborate. They are in better position than we are to know. Is the work we are doing shot through with inaccuracies, even granting that there are some mistakes, to the point where it should not be continued?" To a man they jumped on it vigorously. The Secretary at one point of the discussion said, "Of course, I believe in interpretation but under these conditions I think it better for State people to make the final interpretations and issue them to the public. We can have our men make interpretations and hand them to the State people for interpretation in their localities, can we not Olsen?" I said, "I feel we can do something of that kind but I also feel it would not be a good policy. In the first place there is no self-respecting man in this Bureau or department that will lend himself to that—it will take the heart out of their work to say go to the State institutions [when] they [now] can state with reasonable freedom the conclusion of their findings. Furthermore have you ever seen anything known by a group of people that can be called 'secret'? What would be the effect when it was noised abroad that the Bureau of Agricultural Economics was performing secret services for certain people and they would have us anyway." Someone made a remark that led the Secretary to think they were shooting at me and he said, "Don't jump on Olsen. It has not been a case of his running away from it. It has been a problem of mine, dragging him away from the outlook." I perked up and said: "I thank you, Mr. Secretary." At another point in the discussion several of the boys said the farmers were asking rather pointed questions as to why the Bureau of Agricultural Economics was withholding a service that had been so valuable to them, and what had happened, and if the policy adopted continued what they would have to do, had the Bureau of Agricultural Economics run to cover or something of that kind, and the Secretary concluded they were pointing their shots at me. He said, "Well, don't jump on Olsen he is not to blame for this. If any one is to be blamed on this, jump on me." They pressed him very hard as to the position he would take and said that they must know right soon because if this policy were to be continued they would not send their representatives to the National Outlook Conference and, furthermore, they wanted to advise their following. The Secretary was completely floored. There were some sharp exchanges and yet the whole thing was conducted in a very satisfactory manner.

January 15, 1932.

. . . After my conference with the Secretary Friday night, we rode up to the Mayflower and in the course of that conversation which had, in the first place, revolved around the Columbia River Basin situation the Secretary told me that it was right hard to really understand the President's position. He had, of course, very frankly urged me to use my influence in getting the various farm organizations and various leaders on reclamation to protest vigorously against the Columbia River Basin project and thus support the army engineers. On the basis of this I have been in touch with all of the farm organizations and, as a result, I think all of them will file protests. I met a group of them last Tuesday and placed the matter clearly before them. They were all in fighting mood and were determined to file adverse reports to the project. As a matter of fact, I have people here in the Bureau working with the various farm organizations in the preparation of their reports.

On the way to the Mayflower the Secretary wanted to tell me something very confidential, so he rolled up the window so that the chauffeur would not hear and he said, "The President seems to have a good deal of confidence in me. . . . A member of the Republican National Committee was in to see the President yesterday and commented on me. Hoover countered 'Yes, one fine fellow and I ought to have seven more like him' " (in the Cabinet). This all took place, of course, following Hyde's New York speech where, with Mrs. Hoover at his side, he made a very laudatory speech of Hoover and predicted his reelection, although he had been misconstrued in forecasting Hoover's failure to obtain reelection and had to patch it up with the news boys.

A little later on, as we were riding along, the Secretary said, "The President feels that there are three of us upon whom he can depend to help him in his present troubles—Postmaster General Brown, Pat Hurley and myself—and who have the ability and capacity to really sense the thing to do." "On the other hand," the Secretary went on to add, "he leans on men like Wilbur for guidance in economic matters such as reclamation." That is the inconsistency, as the Secretary pointed out, in the President's position. The Secretary said that of course the President got into this difficulty on reclamation back at the time he was seeking the presidential nomination and when it was important to have the support of these various groups. He could not look ahead and see to what difficulties it would lead in the future. Now that he has already committed himself it is very difficult for him to edge out of it. The Secretary, from what he said, intimated that he rather thought that the Army engineers were reflecting somewhat the influence that had been brought to bear in order to help the President out of his predicament. . . .

Last night (Thursday) I rode up with the Secretary as he was leaving to get ready for the train. The item of unusual interest which developed in our conversation bore on the shift of the Administration in the matter of expenditures. The President had originally, as the Secretary said, stepped out on a huge program of public expenditure to build up purchasing power and demand as a basis for restoring our prosperity. Now it had come to the point where they had practically reversed themselves on that position and were resorting to the most stringent measures to restrict expenditures of all kinds, even those dealing with public building structures. As a matter of fact, the Secretary told me confidentially that the Government short-time three per cent bond issue sold at a number of points below par and that had the effect of forcing the closing of several banks; furthermore that another issue which they had just launched could be sold only with the greatest difficulty and then with the government virtually holding a club over the heads of the bankers. The Secretary said, "What will the situation be when the Government attempts to unload these two billion issue of bonds with which to launch the great Reconstruction Finance Corporation, and what will the situation be when these other great issues of Government bonds, authorized by various pieces of legislation, have been launched upon the market?" The Secretary very properly launched upon a matter which is serious and which may have far-reaching effects upon future financial and industrial recovery. The Secretary used this illustration with me as evidence that it was probably not a bad time to unload some stocks.

January 20, 1932.

Yesterday afternoon the Secretary and I took lunch at the Washington Hotel. We tentatively agreed that the Land Utilization Conference should not be held until some time in February.

The important discussion revolved about the outlook. I told the Secretary I had an administrative program involving about four points, upon which I wished to speak with utmost candor. (1) Our outlook policy; (2) the critical situation in the economic forces; (3) the wet blanket placed upon sending our men to outlook conferences; (4) the general employment situation under which we were prevented from functioning adequately; (5) the expenditure of funds in the way of cooperative projects such as the one we had under consideration with President [W. J.] Kerr[4] of Oregon.

I told the Secretary very frankly that I thought the Administration

4. President of Oregon State Agricultural College.

had made a very bad mistake in the matter of outlook and that the resentment was deep-seated and if they did not watch their step they would have a first-class row on their hands. I told him very frankly that what I thought he should do was to reverse the policy and merely as a face saver eliminate forecasts in terms of price trends. He expressed himself as in harmony with my views but said we could not go the whole distance now. He said, "I have already told you you can interpret but do not put this down in black and white. Make the interpretations available to State Colleges." "Now," I said, "let us clarify that. Do I understand that we are to tell them orally what the data is? If we do that we are going to have them construe our interpretation a dozen different ways. That will never do." The Secretary recognized that difficulty. I said, "Then the thing for us to do is to put out two mimeographed reports— one a report giving the bald facts without any interpretation. That would go to the public as a Department of Agriculture Outlook Report. Second, an interpretative Outlook Report carrying an additional notation, 'Confidential, Bureau of Agricultural Economics. Not to be quoted. For the Use of State Agricultural Colleges.' " He said, "Yes, in the main that would seem to be about the way we would have to handle it now." I pointed out to the Secretary that he was taking a long chance in setting it up in that fashion, because he would certainly then be accused of hiding from farmers information he knew to be good and making it available to outside agencies. In fact it would be construed as a bit of cowardice. The Secretary did not feel any too comfortable under my comments. I said, "All right, I am ready to work under these policies, providing I understand now clearly where we stand."

I then went after the Secretary pretty hard on the Extension situation and also on his vetoing requests made upon our men for outlook assistance in the field. I explained to him that the Extension people had been operating on the basis of temporary men and their time was up and now they were sitting high and dry. I told the Secretary that the policy that had been adopted with reference to the Extension Service and our Bureau was unreasonable on two counts: (1) Why should we curtail these services that were really helpful at a time when farmers needed them? (2) Why should we be curtailed and the Federal Farm Board be allowed to expand as boldly and widely as the spirit moved them? That sort of thing riled and could not obtain. The Secretary said, "Well, I will go with you as far as you are right. In the main I think you are right but I think you are wrong, however, when you state that public reaction will be against us on this. The public wants the public machine cut down 20 to 25 per cent. Nothing would please them more than to have that done." I said, "That may be all true that in a period of extremity the sentiment swings that way but you and I have no reason to permit considerations of that kind to determine our administrative position." I then shoved under his nose the [V. B.] Hart (New York)[5] request for an extension man, the [T. Roy] Reid (Arkansas)[6] request for extension men, the National Potato Institute's request for a man and he said, "Yes, send a man to each of them." . . .

Last night at about 9:45 I went over to see the Secretary a few minutes before he left for the train. At that time I again pinned him down on the outlook and asked him if a statement like this should be put on the confidential report that went to the State Colleges: "Confidential and source not to be quoted. For use of State Colleges of Agriculture only." The Secretary said, "I think you might go further and say: 'This interpretation may be made the basis of your report so long as the Bureau of Agricultural Economics is not directly quoted.' " "Of course," I said, "Hyde, you do not think this is serious but I am telling you that you are letting yourself in for something here but I am not going to harp on that any more." He said, "Come on let us get in the machine and go up to the hotel and we can talk some more." On the way out he said, "I am with you for changing this policy and I am not sure but that we may succeed in getting it changed yet. I just got back from the White House and he (The President) was in good frame of mind and the stage was reasonably well set but there were so many other things I did not get around to bring this up. I am going to try and see him on my return Friday and see if we can not lift the ban completely." . . .

February 8, 1932.

. . . About Thursday of last week (February 4) the Secretary in the late afternoon called me over and told me he had something of a very confidential nature to tell me. He said, "You know I was at the White House reception Tuesday and was in the early part of the line. As I came along the President extended his hand but looked straight ahead and had nothing to say. This disturbed me and I have wondered what it has meant. Do you suppose it represents his reaction to the report I filed with the Army engineers? Of course as far as that is concerned I am ready to pack up and leave any time but I just could not quite figure this out. What do you make of it?" I commented by saying that of course I would be at sea to know just what it all meant but I would not be disposed to attach too much significance to it. The President is now under tremendous strain with the war clouds and other matters hanging over him and there is no doubt but that he is oft time distrait but if it

5. A specialist in agricultural economics and farm management in the New York Agricultural Extension Service.
6. Assistant director of the Agricultural Extension Service in Arkansas.

did mean that he was reacting against the position the Secretary had taken on the Columbia River Basin, I should not worry a bit. As a matter of fact, I told the Secretary I thought he was sitting very pretty with reference to the matter and the President would think twice before he made any moves or permitted him to make any moves in a matter so vital. The Secretary rather agreed that this was probably the case. He said: "Furthermore, you know we were curious regarding the reason why the Army Engineers put out their report. Well, I have the explanation. You know [Samuel R.] McKelvie was in some time back. I told him about the situation but warned him not to speak to the President. He promised that he would not. Later on he told me that he had spoken to Pat Hurley about the whole matter and that Pat Hurley had made the contact with the Army Engineers." I injected the comment that after all then the President's views had been registered with the Army Engineers. "No," he said, "I do not think that is quite a fair impression of the matter. Hurley interpreted the situation and registered accordingly."

Saturday, February 6, the Secretary and I took lunch at the Carlton Hotel. On showing him the article which appeared in the "Washington News" on the Hyde-Wilbur Cabinet row, he laughed and said, "Of course there was nothing to it." Wilbur had said nothing to him about this Army report and he had said nothing to Wilbur. Furthermore the Secretary stated that it had never come up in Cabinet. He said he had his little speech all ready for Wilbur if he brought the matter up, in which he would make it clear that these were his views, that as a representative of agriculture he would have to defend them, that this was in keeping with what he had said, regarding the reduction of production, from the very outset and that his own words would choke him otherwise and that if this policy was not in keeping with that of the Administration, of course he did not want to embarrass the Administration. The Secretary then went on to add that he rather thought he had the President "over a barrel" on the matter and it was rather embarrassing because he did not want to take advantage of him. The Secretary said, for example, the President had received some very complimentary letters of the speeches which he (Hyde) had given in New York City and Detroit, defending the President and the Administration. The letters went on to say that these speeches were the first ray of hope in an otherwise gloomy picture, indicating that the Administration was taking the offensive. As illustrating this same point, the Secretary said that [James F.] Burke of the National Republican Committee had strongly urged him to address an audience at Pittsburgh on Washington's birthday. He had declined to take on the engagement so Burke evidently had gone to the President and the President spoke to Hyde about it. Hyde on that occasion said, "Mr. President, I have the time and energy for only two types of engagements, one dealing with the serious problems of agriculture and the other with the interests of the Republican Party and the Administration. This occasion does not call for my services." The President smiled and said, "Mr. Secretary, I guess perhaps you are right. We will send Wilbur." The Secretary then said that, as a matter of fact he had talked very frankly with some of his good friends, Alex Legge, [Fred S.] Purnell,[7] etc., and placed the position which he was taking with reference to land utilization, reclamation before them and had said these were his convictions as the representative of agriculture and he asked them whether or not he was following the wrong course. They had all agreed that he was following the only tenable course for him to take.

February 10, 1932

Tuesday noon (February 9) after Cabinet meeting I was called by messenger while I was at lunch at the Cornell Restaurant. I postponed my return to the office and the messenger came again, so when I got on the telephone the Secretary said, "Well, if you are a good boy you may publish the outlook in its interpretative form but now this does not mean any wildcatting in price forecasting." I replied that it was awfully good news but I really wanted some more background. He then asked me if I had had my lunch. I said I had but would be willing to keep him company anyway. I met him and we went over to the Washington Hotel and after discussing everything under the sun, I finally asked him what had happened on the outlook and how did the Big Boy react. Hyde then told me that he had a marked copy of the outlook with him and he pointed out specifically the parts that would be eliminated. He said he emphasized the value of these statements to growers and that he thought the issuance of the report in the interpretative form could be of much value to many during these times. He also stressed the fact that there was a good deal of ferment abroad regarding this and in his judgment it would be very good to lift right now the ban on the issuing of the interpretative report and avoid the embarrassment of two widely different reports being issued. The President evidently very briefly remarked, "Very well handle it in that way." . . .

February 15, 1932.

Last night (Sunday) the Secretary telephoned me to come over, having arrived earlier than anticipated and he seemed quite a bit disturbed. . . . He handed me a copy of the message which the President was about to send to Congress. This message dealt with three things: (1)

7. Congressman from Indiana.

Reorganization of Government Departments; (2) Reclamation; (3) Public
Lands.

The Secretary asked me to read the President's message—that is the
two sections on reclamation and public lands. The section on reclamation
in the opening paragraph stated that irrigation of land was not now
logical, since we had an over supply of farm products but then he proceeded at once to say that conservation of water resources was important
and for that reason he advocated the building of storage dams at the
Grand Coulee and various other points. The message went on to say that
power development would be a feature of such projects but in all cases
this power should be leased in advance of the development of the project. In other words, the recommendation goes absolutely counter to the
position which the Secretary has taken. With reference to the Public Domain, the President called attention to the report of the Public Lands
Commission in its recommendations and the legislation which had been
introduced on the basis of those recommendations. He suggested the importance of early legislation on that subject.

The Secretary evidently was flabbergasted and said that he probably
might as well be getting his fishing tackle ready for Florida. He also
looked a little worried. We discussed the political angles of the situation
and I said that it looked to me like a deal made with the Boulder Dam
people which he had to go through on and, furthermore, since the
drainage people were making such effective progress in connection with
their work along that line and it looked like a tie-up with them. Hyde did
not comment at that time but later made the remark that those interests
did not represent the strong political vote in the West and in the South,
to which I agreed. Later on in the evening, after thinking the matter over
I went to the Secretary's Office again and told him that on further reflection, in my judgment there were just two things for him to do—protest
in no uncertain terms to the President immediately and let him understand that his position would virtually mean your elimination from the
Cabinet. I went on to add that I did not think the President was going to
hazard the loss of his support because he was too great an asset to him
politically. In the second place, I told the Secretary that it was very important the Land Use Planning Committee take cognizance of the
reclamation problem and the public domain problem in its first opening
session and that they have something of a concrete, positive, daring
nature to say. To this he agreed and he proceeded to dig up a letter
which he had written to the President before on the Columbia River
Basin, and in the course of this conversation he called me to him confidentially and said that at the dinner in Chicago he was seated next to
Roy West, former Secretary of the Interior, who whispered that they
were seriously considering him for Vice President and Hyde said that
that was his conception of no job at all. Hyde told me this in order to

suggest that the thought possibly had been planted by Wilbur in West's mind, with the idea of lining Hyde up for the position they were taking.

February 19, 1932.

. . . Monday evening [February 15] . . . I had a visit with Secretary Hyde on the progress of the day. I asked him if he had made any headway in killing the President's message. He said he had not taken it up with the President. I told him that I would have no sympathy if the thing went by default, if he did not make any effort to put it off. I urged him to throw down the gauntlet to the President, and that as a matter of fact the President would not dare cross him in this matter to the point where he, Hyde, would resign. He had an appointment with Newton. We went over together and I waited while the Secretary was talking with Newton, about twenty minutes. He stood in Newton's office, waving his hands, visible from the outside and when he came out he told me he had spilled the whole thing to Newton and Newton said it was unbelievable, that he did not understand why the President had taken the position and he did not know just what to do about it. I asked Hyde if Newton had urged him to see the President but Newton had himself registered with the President in a vigorous way and no doubt had made some impression. I think it was Tuesday (February 16) that the Secretary told me that the stage was clear to go ahead in a vigorous way in opposing the Columbia River Basin project. He said the message was going through with some modification in wording but that it appeared the President was doing this to satisfy certain promises made back in 1926 and 1927 but as a matter of fact he would be delighted to have the message scotched. (This of course is a beautiful illustration of double-crossing.) I think it was at that the Secretary indicated that he thought it was all right for the Advisory and Legislative Committee to go ahead vigorously and attack the Columbia River Basin project. . . .

Last night (Thursday, February 18) about 6:30 I had a few minutes with the Secretary. . . . He was enthused about the opportunities of the Land Use Planning Committee to coordinate great forces in the Land Grant Colleges and the Department. In other words he clearly reflected that at least he has seen the vision which we have been trying to plant in his mind, of a great institution made up of the Department of Agriculture and Land Grant Colleges, through which a magnificent economic program can be projected. In commenting upon the resolutions passed by the Advisory and Legislative Committee,[8] he said he thought they were just fine, that with a little change in wording it was all right to

8. The Conference of Land Use planning committee consisting of representatives of farm organizations and the agricultural colleges was meeting in Washington at this time.

have the one on reorganization going out at this time. He said, further-more, that the statements on reorganization were garbled in the Presi-dent's message, but in the main were what he had suggested to the Presi-dent at his request. I asked him about an Assistant Secretary of Agricultural Economics. "Well," he said, "the plan was to get rid of the present Assistant Secretary and the Director of Extension and doing away with the office of Extension Director." Furthermore he had sug-gested an Assistant Secretary of Organization and Service, with a view to bringing all conservation into the Department and he said he had every reason to believe that the Secretary [of the Interior] was looking toward transferring reclamation, parks and other units over to this Department. He said that as far as he was concerned the Bureau of Public Roads and the Weather Bureau did not mean anything to us and he would just as soon see them go. He chuckled when he told me that he and Mrs. Hyde were taking dinner with the President and Mrs. Hoover Friday night. He said, "You know, it is rather amusing the way he is kind of nudging up," and he said, "Again for your own very confidential information I got in touch with Franklin Fort,[9] regarding the Message and told him in no uncertain terms what position I was placed in and that I had just one alternative" (by which he meant resigning from the Cabinet). He con-tinued, "Franklin Fort without my knowledge called the President direct and told him what he was up against and to that the President said: 'If that is to be the result, then there will be no Message.' "

March 21, 1932.

The latter part of last week Dr. A. F. Woods[10] called me and asked that I go over with him to the Mayflower Hotel to see his brother Mark Woods[11] and Burton Peek[12] regarding the wheat situation. I took [O. C.] Stine along and we went to Mark Woods' apartment. It clearly developed that what Mark Woods was here for was to interest Congress in the ex-portation of one hundred million bushels of wheat to China. He said that the Reconstruction Finance Corporation and the Agricultural Credits legislation was helpful but was like heavy dew on a stack of hay. It would take a long time before it would dribble down to the country. He said something had to be done to save the situation and he wanted our judgment of the wheat situation and the effect which the exportation of one hundred million bushels would have on wheat prices.

9. A former congressman from New Jersey and chairman of the newly created Federal Home Loan Bank Board.
10. Director of scientific work in the Department of Agriculture.
11. A banker in Lincoln, Nebraska.
12. A vice-president of the John Deere Company in Moline, Illinois, and brother of George Peek.

In the course of our conversation Mark Woods pointed out that the total deposits of the banks in Lincoln amounted to about 20 million dollars but that practically all these funds were sewed up in commitments already. He said it was practically impossible to get any new credit from any of the banking institutions and that, in his judgment, the only way to relieve the situation was to stimulate wheat prices. The idea was to divert the monies which Senator [Ellison D.] Smith[13] was going to add to the Department seed loans for the exportation of the wheat to China. Mark Woods raised the question as to what agency should handle the funds, adding that the Federal Farm Board was so hopelessly discredited that it would not be possible to give it the funds. I told him that the Reconstruction Finance Corporation should handle it rather than the Department, but he countered by saying that most people were friendly to the Department of Agriculture.

There is now a good deal of concern also regarding the proposed investigation of the stock exchange. Secretary Hyde has told me, confidentially, that a great deal of pressure is being brought to bear to stop that investigation. The "bears" who are especially under fire have evidently made it clear that they would be unsparing in laying bare the facts, that they would explain why they had taken the short side and that in this they have been fully justified, and that furthermore such stocks still were selling at far higher levels than warranted by earnings and economic conditions. In short, it now develops that Hoover's attack upon the gamblers and short selling is reaping in a whirlwind, and that he is moving heaven and earth to stop an investigation, which he glibly advocated earlier in the season.

The undercurrent on the sales tax is also significant. [R. W.] Dunlap called me into his office Friday, saying he had just returned from a conference with Secretary [Ogden] Mills[14] and other Republicans. Mills had frankly admitted that the politically expedient thing was to oppose the sales tax. The financial situation, however, imperatively demanded its passage, that the budget had to be balanced and if the sales tax was not passed it would create an almost impossible financial situation. Dunlap was much exercised about the attitude taken by the farm organizations and asked for material with which to combat their position.

May 5, 1932.

Yesterday when I was out with the Secretary at lunch, among other things he told me he had discussed the Labor Department's bill for shoving the unemployed out on the land with the President and the

13. Chairman of the Senate Committee on Agriculture and Forestry.
14. Secretary of the Treasury.

President had told him, and this he said was very confidential, to put in an adverse report on the bill. He also said he thought he would receive clearance to write a land utilization plank in the Republican platform, and suggest that I be thinking about that. . . .

May 20, 1932.

. . . Under date of May 16 when I was called over to the Secretary's Office with the statement on livestock and wheat for the President, Carl Williams and Jim Stone and [J. E.] Wells of the Farm Board were visiting with the Secretary. I broke in with my material and they abruptly stopped the discussion of another matter. It was apparent to me that they had been seeking the Secretary's ear. After leaving the Federal Farm Board people at their building he and I went up to the Mayflower together and I then asked him what was "eating" Jim Stone and Carl Williams and he said, "They are in trouble again." The Secretary went on to explain that the forty million bushels which had been set aside for Red Cross purposes had gotten them into trouble. They had been compelled to take up about $50,000,000 in loans that outside agencies had on this wheat and, in addition, substantial carrying charges. They were evidently in the situation where they were running into a shortage and they had come to the Secretary to get him to use his good offices in inducing the Reconstruction Finance Corporation to help them. The Secretary proceeded to tell me that he thought they were in a pretty tight place and so far as he was concerned he did not see that there was anything he could do, or any good reason why he should get his fingers into the mess. In the course of our comments he stated that he felt sorry for Stone because he thought he was the one man who represented creditably both the Farm Board and himself and, as a matter of fact, carried the entire burden. He said the same was true when Legge was Chairman, but at that time Legge had the help of both Jim Stone and Charlie Teague in carrying the burden. He said that so far as Carl Williams was concerned he did not have any confidence in him and in fact did not think he had a sense of loyalty and could not be depended upon.

As we proceeded toward the hotel we got into a discussion of the recent political moves. He admitted that Al Smith's radio speech[15] was a political document of the first importance. He said that, in the main, he agreed with the position Mr. Smith took on all issues with the exception of beer and the building program. He said it was not only good economics but awfully good politics and he intimated very definitely that that was what Hoover lacked. As a result of a little urging he made the

15. Smith in a radio address on May 16, 1932, outlined his economic program in which, it was noted, his views did not markedly differ from those of President Hoover.

very significant statement that the trouble with Hoover was the lack of political sense and political principles, that he failed to recognize there was a body of principles operating in the political field that were as inexorable as some of the economic laws about which we were prating but he said that Hoover failed to sense them and did not operate in keeping with them. He went on to say, however, that he thought the Republicans would win the next election because the Democrats have messed matters so much and also because he thought some slight improvement in the conditions would change sentiment materially.

June 24, 1932.

Last Monday immediately following the Secretary's return from the National Republican Convention, he called me over and we had a brief chat regarding some official matters and then we got at once into the question of the agricultural plank. The Secretary seemed to be quite elated about the matter and particularly since he had had to overcome some opposition. [James R.] Garfield had shown his teeth somewhat on the proposal regarding land acquisition, but [Ray Lyman] Wilbur had come to the Secretary's support and said that land acquisition was closely related to land conservation and, of course, Garfield is an old conservation advocate. The Secretary rather intimated that Wilbur had received his instructions regarding this matter before going to the convention. A more heated controversy developed over the allotment plan. Support for the allotment plan appeared in rather vigorous form evidently and created quite a little discussion in the large committee. In that discussion Sam McKelvie and Charles Teague[16] and Mr. Darling (Ding, the cartoonist) took a very strong position for a radical relief proposal. A sub-committee was appointed, composed of those three gentlemen and the Secretary, as I recall, and in that Committee both McKelvie and Teague took a very vigorous position for the allotment plan. Hyde explained that as growing out of Alex Legge's support of that plan and his influence upon both Teague and McKelvie. Ding, the cartoonist, was even more rabid. He was in favor of accepting debenture, allotment or anything in order to satisfy the farm organizations and in order, evidently, to win the election. The committee did not come to any agreement, so they went back to the large committee again, and the simple type of plank, such as actually appeared in the platform, and of which Hyde was the author, was laid upon the sheaf of notes which Garfield, the Chairman, had before him. When the large committee resumed its deliberations, Garfield took up one item after another. The item regarding the agricultural plank was misplaced or passed over and

16. A former member of the Federal Farm Board who had resumed his affiliation with the California Fruit Growers Exchange.

not passed upon; then later when Ding returned to the committee he asked what had become of the agricultural plank. Some one told him it was disposed of. He became fairly livid with rage and accused Hyde of doublecrossing. Hyde responded in vigorous form and said that no one could accuse him of that, and he forthwith took Ding to the Chairman. It was then explained that the item had been passed over and nothing done about it. Ding was very apologetic but it indicates, of course, his state of mind, as well as that of the committee, over the agricultural plank. Sam McKelvie and the Committee as a whole made a very impassioned plea for the allotment plan. He was given support by Teague and Ding. Hyde then got up and said he did not know that any one knew just what the allotment plan was. It was a relatively new thing, it was undergoing revision daily and he thought it was precarious for the committee to adopt a plank of that nature. He said, however, that he had drawn a plank that left it possible to consider that or any other measure that would, as he put it, "be mechanically sound, administratively feasible and avoiding undue bureaucracy." Sam McKelvie jumped up and said, "That is exactly the idea I have in mind," and he withdrew his objection to the plank, and so Hyde's version went through. Hyde went on to say he could not understand why Sam McKelvie took the position he did, unless he was again playing a selfish political game, seeking personal aggrandizement and seeking to cater particularly to certain rural sentiment. Hyde explained Teague's attitude as growing out of the friendship for Alex Legge.

Tuesday evening (June 21) the Secretary gave me a rush call and told me to have a report on the Rainey allotment plan[17] prepared at once. [Eric] Englund was asked to do this and sent his statement over in the morning, and I did not see it in advance of it going to the Secretary. Later on in the afternoon the Secretary asked me to join him and Jim Stone in considering the plan right away. I told him I was tied up then as Chairman of the Land Use Planning Committee but could meet them in the evening. So, we arranged to meet that evening at eight o'clock in the Secretary's Office. Meanwhile I prepared myself for discussion of the plan.

The discussions brought out very clearly that both Hyde and Stone are somewhat uncertain as to the position they should take with reference to this measure. Stone made it clear that he thought the so-called Wilson plan[18] was very good. He thought Rainey's plan had serious defects. Hyde has not committed himself on either the Rainey or the Wilson plan but, evidently, on the one hand, feels he has to give it careful considera-

17. Congressman Henry T. Rainey of Illinois introduced a bill containing a modified version of the domestic allotment plan. It was an emergency measure effective for only one year. It contained a processing tax and called for benefit payment to farmers.

18. M. L. Wilson had brought to Albany his domestic allotment proposal limiting production but depending on elected county committees for enforcement. Governor Franklin D. Roosevelt responded favorably to it.

tion since such men as Earl Smith (whom he regards as an outstanding agricultural leader) is in favor of it. On the other hand he thinks the bills as they are nothing but sop and a bonus and it is the type of thing the Administration should veto if passed. Evidently there is some real possibility of the bill passing. We did not arrive at any positive conclusions, but the arguments that were advanced brought out quite uniformly the weaknesses in the measure. The Secretary had to leave about 9 o'clock, as he called over to the White House. Stone continued with us and as the Secretary left he asked me if I would not come over to his apartment and stay with him over night. I told him that if I could get hold of my night shirt I would. We spent the night together and in the course of the evening he told me of the President's elation over the convention as a whole and expressed his special appreciation of what he, Hyde, had done in that connection. Hyde said that he was not the one responsible for what had taken place and that so long as everything was going along so beautifully he thought it was wise for him to keep in the background. One of the things to which the Secretary had special reference was the wet plank and Hyde said that he thought it was admirably handled by [Ogden] Mills and no better man could so adequately handle it, since Mills came from a wet state and was rather inclined to lean toward the wet cause, and the position which he took could not be charged with partisanship, such as would have been directed at him, Hyde, had he stepped out in that same capacity. Hyde expressed high appreciation of Mr. Mills' ability and the manner in which he handled the episode.

In the course of the evening we had a considerable discussion about political matters and I was quite surprised to hear him say that the toughest man for the Republicans to defeat would be Al Smith. [John N.] Garner[19] was absolutely impossible and [Franklin D.] Roosevelt could not carry conviction and he admitted that Newton Baker[20] had a lot of ability but he did not think he would be nominated. The apparent defection of men like [William E.] Borah is evidently giving them some concern but Hyde is advising the President to forget them and let them go their own way and not quibble to their fulminations.

The Secretary commented upon the visit he had with the President Wednesday evening when we left with Jim Stone. He said he could not make up his mind what the President did want. He seemed to be talking around on all these hot matters that had come up and which, of course, were disturbing him. He rather concluded that what he wanted was the comfort of his presence and the relief that comes from conversing with your friends when you are in difficulty. The Secretary admitted that he was having his share of difficulties.

19. Speaker of the House of Representatives.
20. Secretary of War, second Wilson Administration; a "dark horse" candidate.

June 25, 1932.

The Secretary called me at the Cairo Hotel about six o'clock last evening and asked me if I would be down at the Department later. . . . I returned to the office in the evening and after spending an hour there telephoned the Secretary but he had left. I contacted him at his hotel. I went over there to his apartment again and remained over night with him. In the course of our visit he brought out the startling fact that a run had been underway for two days on the First National Bank of Chicago ([Melvin A.] Traylor's bank) and the Continental Trust and Savings Company but not a word had appeared in the Chicago papers regarding it. In other words the Chicago papers had shown an unusual patriotic attitude in withholding publication of this fact. Evidently it was a very substantial run because the queues of people extended for two or more blocks. The run had gotten to the point in the case of the First National Bank where small depositors were calling for their time deposits. Under the banking laws and regulations a bank has thirty days in which to make good on these deposits. So, the officials of the bank called [Ogden] Mills of the Treasury and asked him what they should do about the time deposits and he said, "Pay them as fast as they are demanded." In other words he told the Chicago bank dealers that the Treasury would be prepared to come to their assistance to the full extent of their need. The situation is now causing a great deal of concern and evidently the financial world is again sitting on a volcano. It is merely a culmination of a situation with which we have been familiar and which it was feared would break. It looks as if Charles Dawes resigned his position with the Reconstruction Finance Corporation in order to safeguard his banking interests in Chicago. . . .

July 6, 1932.

Sunday, July 3, the White House was telephoning around town to locate me in order to get me in telephonic communication with Secretary Hyde. That evening we finally got together and it then developed that Hyde was desirous of having immediate information that he could use in spearing Roosevelt in the forestry part of his acceptance speech. He asked me to call him back that evening or early next day. July 4 I had [C. F.] Clayton of the Division of Land Economics working with me at the office and early that afternoon word came from the White House asking me to meet Hyde at the Mayflower at 7:30 p.m. I met him at that time. He had drafted a statement which was very ironical and harpooned the reforestation idea in a very unacceptable way. It left him open to the counter that he was unfriendly to reforestation as a part of the program, so we spent an hour together going over the event in preparation for a conference which he attended at the White House at nine o'clock. He insisted on giving me his keys to the apartment and to my staying overnight. So, I went back to the Mayflower while he attended a conference at the White House. On his return at 10:30 it appeared that it was a very important conference on the wet-dry issue and nothing was said about reforestation. The balance of the night and the early hours of the morning were spent in working over the forestry statement and it was apparent from our discussion throughout that the administration forces were quite gleeful about the selection of Roosevelt as the Democratic nominee. The next morning he had [R. Y.] Stuart and me in his office to pass on certain items of his statement and Stuart put up some resistance to the issuance of the statement on the grounds that it would give a black-eye to reforestation. The Secretary had very substantially broadened the statement to protect him on that score and I told Major Stuart that with the exception of a few changes we should not oppose the Secretary issuing the statement. The Major evidently was fearful that the Forest Service would be drawn into the scrap and be quoted as an authority for the facts which the Secretary used. This is confirmed to a degree at least by the issuance of a statement by Ovid Butler[21] criticizing the Secretary's attack on Roosevelt, Butler of course being very close to Major Stuart and the Forest Service. . . .

While I was in the office yesterday afternoon Earl Smith was there and I stumbled on him. He pictured the tremendous demonstration, as he put it, of the farmers on July 4. . . . Hyde last night told me he too had a visit with Earl Smith and of course these meetings were nothing but a staging to accumulate support for the Rainey bill of which he is the author. In the course of the conference he said he would like to come over and get my confidential, first-hand judgment of the bill. In due course Earl Smith came over and he touched around first by discussing the hog outlook. He finally got down to his question on the Rainey bill. In opening the subject he stressed the state of mind of the farmers and the desperate situation in which the Republicans were placed in the Middle West. He went on so far as to assert if something was not done, Illinois, Iowa, Kansas, and Nebraska would go Democratic and of course he was friendly to Hoover and wanted to help him in every way he could. I sensed the situation and capitalized on his opening remarks by saying that, of course, the problem could be approached from the strictly economic viewpoint and from the political point of view. From the point of view of relieving immediate distress and aiding the Republican cause I would grant that the bill had merit. From the economic point of view, however, it had very serious defects and I personally could not approve it, stating in that connection that a purely temporary ephemeral bit of assistance would not carry us very far on the road to prosperity, and so far as I was concerned I was not going to support that type. . . . In the course of my conversation with Earl Smith this quite significant comment

21. Editor of *American Forests,* a magazine published by the American Forestry Association.

was made by him. We had occasion to comment upon his equalization fee, debenture and other plans and their practicability at this time, he asserting that he was still an equalization fee man and I commented by saying that he was not optimistic enough to think that the equalization fee plan would work under these conditions, which he admitted. He then laughed at the Hydra-headed monster, as he called it, as a piece of stupid business on the part of farm organization leaders. . . . In walking downtown Earl Smith, in commenting upon Roosevelt's speech,[22] stated that he agreed that it was demagogic but that it would carry quite a little weight. In commenting on what he meant by "demagogic" he mentioned Roosevelt's reference to farm organizations as inspiration for farm relief suggestions. Earl Smith said, "That is purest rot because no one knows the farm organization leaders better than I do and there is precious little sanity and sound leadership in them." In that connection he added, "and it will be sweet for you too if the Democrats come in. I know of three men already who say they are going to be the next Secretary of Agriculture—[John A.] Simpson[23] says he is going to be, and so does your friend [Senator Ellison D.] Smith of South Carolina." He did not indicate who the third candidate was.

August 10, 1932.

Last night M. L. Wilson laughingly admitted, when I pressed him by indirection regarding the authorship of the Senate Resolution 280-281,[24] that he had handed them to Senator [Peter] Norbeck. I chided him a bit for not discussing the resolution with us before he turned the material over to the Senator. His counter was, laughingly, that if he had done that we would take out what they wanted in the resolution. . . . I asked Wilson how he happened to pick hogs and his counter was that the corn belt was in a bad way and that any plan that was put across would have to help the hog producers. "Yes," I said, "that is true but on the other hand it is singling out one of the most difficult commodities on which to appraise the effect of any of these plans." I then asked if [Mordecai] Ezekiel[25] had not been responsible for that suggestion. He laughed but made no reply. I have still to get definite verbal evidence from him or

22. Roosevelt on July 2, 1932, in Chicago accepted the Democratic nomination for the presidency, pledging himself to "a New Deal for the American People." Some of his remarks were devoted to a discussion of the depressing plight of agriculture.

23. President of the Farmer's Union and a leading critic of the Federal Farm Board.

24. Senate Resolution 280 called for an investigation of the restrictions now existing upon international trade in agricultural products. Senate Resolution 281 called for an investigation of the economic situation of hog producers. Both resolutions were considered, modified, and agreed to on July 16, 1932.

25. An economist with the Federal Farm Board who, along with Wilson (a professor at Montana State College), was a leading advocate of production control as presented in the domestic allotment proposal.

any other source that Ezekiel and some other Farm Board people actually wrote the resolutions, although I am convinced they did.[26]

I rather sensed from my conversation with Wilson that the strategy is about as follows. Our report on trade barriers and the adverse reaction to dumping and all that sort of thing will show up the impossibility of the equalization fee and debenture plans and that will leave the field free for the domestic allotment plan to which, . . . as Wilson assumes, there are not the same objections on dumping grounds. I spent a good deal of time with Wilson Tuesday night discussing this whole idea of planning and I think I brought him down to earth a good deal. I made him understand that analysis and planning on the basis of analysis were the life blood of my own thinking and the life blood of this institution, and I believed that in any program of planning for this country we should preserve the individual collective initiative to the utmost and should inject Government agencies as strong-arm controlling factors only in so far as it proved necessary. On comparing notes I think we could agree on a good many planks in the planning program. He said he had noticed my failure to agree to the domestic allotment plan and control measures of that kind. He took some exception to my emphasis on the international approach as a vital one in the picture, on the ground that nothing could be done to break down the protection which tariff groups had already been able to acquire. He evidently does not have too much faith in the Planning Committee but is counting on the Christgau bill[27] as the organization that must be created.

The strategy as it now looms up in my mind from our point of view is about as follows: Wilson, [Howard R.] Tolley[28] and perhaps H.C.T.[29] and others are interested in the general approach of jacking up agricultural prices. In order to do that they are thinking of devices that will make the tariff protective. It is an artificial program which will inevitably break down in some place or another. Taylor I think approaches the problem in making the tariff distinctly odious and accomplishing other worthwhile objectives. Wilson and Tolley are looking forward to saving hard-pressed farmers even though it means subsidy or bonus, or what not. This program of artificially subsidizing, controlling and regulating the tariff groups is contrasted with the other program which

26. William D. Rowley in *M. L. Wilson and the Campaign for the Domestic Allotment* (Lincoln, 1970), p. 143, notes that the scheme for applying the domestic allotment proposal to hogs was developed by W. R. Ronald, editor of *The Mitchell Republican* of Mitchell, South Dakota.

27. Introduced by Minnesota congressman Victor Christgau, the bill called for local and regional agricultural planning with the purpose of readjusting production in line with prevailing demands.

28. Formerly an Assistant Chief of the Bureau of Agricultural Economics who departed in 1930 for California to direct the Gianinni Foundation in agricultural economics at Berkeley.

29. Henry Charles Taylor, before becoming the first Chief of the Bureau of Agricultural Economics in 1921, was an influential professor at the University of Wisconsin. Leaving the Bureau in 1925 he returned to teaching and remained active in agricultural affairs.

recognizes the need of planning on the part of the industry both in the field of production and marketing but which recognizes that the industry operates within the great international framework and that its fortunes are in considerable measure determined by our ability to keep open the channels of trade and permit this country of ours, with its wonderful resources, to expand in keeping with those resources. Wilson would crawl behind the tariff barriers, build them higher and adjust to purely domestic situations. I would revolt against that procedure and say let us be reasonable in the matter of our own market and in turn hold substantial part of other markets adjusting our whole industry to the broad international base. The present Administration leans strongly to the higher protection, domestic basis. At the same time there are elements in it that realize the absurdity of taking this extreme position. The Democratic party in the main leans toward the international approach. On the other hand there are grave inconsistencies in their thinking as witnessed in the Roosevelt acceptance speech with its approval of the domestic allotment plan and almost the domestic basis theory. Whether Democrats or Republicans go in in November, efforts should be made to obtain a more favorable policy toward our international relations and obligations. Undoubtedly the idea of economic planning, placed possibly in the hands of a national economic council set up outside of the Government and representing the great interests of this country, will receive substantial support in the near future. I think it has a place in the picture. . . .

August 12, 1932.

Last night when I returned from the doing over at Constitution Hall I found the Secretary's card with a note that he would like to have me come over to his apartment and spend the night with him.

In the course of our visit he asked me my impression of the President's acceptance speech. I told him the delivery was rotten, that I had great difficulty in hearing any part of it even though I was seated advantageously in one of the boxes. I stated that I got only faintly what he had to say regarding agriculture but I thought he failed to say the right thing. The Secretary then countered by saying that he rather rued that he had not been here while the President was putting the finishing touches on the acceptance speech as he thought he might have prevented some things from going into it. The Secretary then picked up a printed copy of the President's speech and read Section 13, page 9, and then pointed out that the President went out of his way to admit the failure of the Federal Farm Board particularly as relates to its stabilization activities. The Secretary said, in this connection, that he was getting quite a number of letters that were critical of him by reason of his relation to and defense of the Federal Farm Board and that the situation tended to make it rather difficult for him. I told the Secretary, on this point, that I thought the administration if it continued another four years would have to reckon frankly with the failure of the Federal Farm Board in many important respects and take the matter in hand in a very businesslike way in the next session of Congress. . . .

I did not at this time take occasion to comment on the President's failure to recognize the international situation in a very definite way. He took a very definite position as to protective barriers and no suggestions, so far as I could sense, were made as to the need for tariff readjustments. His flat statement that debts should not be cancelled or tampered with raises the question in my mind as to how far he at heart is disposed to go along on a program of international adjustment. The speech in general provides rather significant background against which to project our future thinking on an agricultural program. I had occasion to comment on the President's lack of personality, charm, magnetism and the qualities that count on an occasion of this kind. The Secretary snapped up the thought at once and said, "Give me that speech," and he picked out a paragraph and said the difficulty does not lie in the language. Then he proceeded to read in his own forceful way a paragraph. Then he said, "Of course the President failed to capitalize on his opportunities throughout the entire speech." I asked the Secretary point blank last night whether he was going to promise now for good to accept the Secretary portfolio in case of the reelection of the Republicans. He smiled and adroitly shifted the conversation to something else. My hunch is that he is not through politically at all but that perhaps another portfolio may provide a better stepping stone to what he has in mind.

August 29, 1932.

Thursday evening the Secretary and I had dinner at the University Club and [Walter H.] Newton of the White House joined us. In the course of the conversation the election prospects were discussed and Newton raised the question as to whether or not it would be worthwhile to put some effort in on Florida. Hyde thought it might. Then Newton complained that he had not been able to influence the Reconstruction Finance Corporation in its loans to the State of Florida, that as a matter of fact if they were made at this time they would probably all go into the hands of Democrats, whereas if they were postponed they could be used in such a way to influence the vote. He further complained that the Reconstruction Finance Corporation had been very difficult and that they did not have a good working contract over there. For a while it was thought that [Charles A.] Miller[30] would be approachable but he, Newton said, "seems to lack political sense." A little later on Secretary Hyde commented that Mr. Newton was about as hardboiled a man as he had ever seen to his girls. He said the commands rang out sharply on very little provocation. The girls in his office were evidently of the right type to stand the gaff and were talked to in kind. My own feeling is that

30. President of Reconstruction Finance Corporation.

this is pretty symptomatic of the attitude that obtains in the White House circles from the President down. . . .

September 14, 1932.

Monday night I stayed over night with the Secretary at his request and in the course of the conversation we made reference to credit as an instrument in correcting the present economic situation and particulary the efforts of the Reconstruction Finance Corporation and the Federal Farm Board in that connection. He then made this statement—he said, as usual, that he would deny it if I repeated it—that he had virtually come to the conclusion that the situation could not be corrected through a credit program of any kind, that after all such rotten conditions had developed in various segments of our economic structure that lending merely postponed the day of adjustment and settlement. In any event, it would merely be passing it on from individuals to the Government. . . .

December 6, 1932.

Yesterday morning M. L. Wilson called me on the telephone and asked if I could see him right away. I told him I was in a jam and that later in the afternoon would suit me better. He said that the "three blind mice" were in town and wanted to come in and pay their respects, and they were H. A. Wallace and Professor [Rexford Guy] Tugwell and himself. They came over and Wilson was fairly bubbling over with good cheer and elation.

A little reference was made to their activities both in the South and elsewhere and then inquiry was made regarding the status of the report on domestic allotment. I parried effectively enough and told them it was well in the making, that I had just received copy and had not even managed a complete reading of it. We bantered back and forth regarding the valuableness of the report and I did not give them any satisfaction on that score.

H. A. Wallace seemed to be in a rather serious frame of mind and then he asked me if I could not supply him the part of the report that dealt with the elasticity of demand in pork and pork products. I told him it was not available now but if I could get anything into his hands in Chicago, where he was going to meet the American Farm Bureau Federation people Thursday of this week [I would do so].

Tugwell privately commented to Mr. [Eric] Englund that the stage was all set for the domestic allotment to go through and we would have to handle it. In other words, Englund thought he was trying to convey to him that we might as well reconcile ourselves to the medicine. The significance was rather apparent. I fail to see how it could be construed as anything but as evidence of an attempt to influence our point of view.

Another bit of poor strategy. There was also some bantering back and forth regarding the next Secretary of Agriculture, both H.A., and M.L. toying with the idea but conveying the impression they were not in the running. My own judgment is they are not.

December 9, 1932.

Mr. Ray Tucker[31]. . . called on me to get my personal opinion regarding H. A. Wallace as a prospective Secretary of Agriculture. He told me that Wallace was quite far up in the list and that he was going South to Warm Springs and wanted some advance information regarding Wallace. He said he realized I was personally well acquainted with him and he would like very much to have my confidential appraisal of him for such an assignment. I told him I thought I knew Wallace very well, had great admiration for him, was a close personal friend and was interested in knowing that he was being considered so seriously for this assignment. I told Tucker a little something of my relation with Wallace's father. In my appraisal of him I said I thought Wallace had a very keen mind and thought much more deeply and broadly on the agricultural problem than most men in his position, that he would bring a fearlessness to the assignment that would be refreshing and wholesome and that he should made a relatively good secretary. On the other hand I did state I thought when he felt quite keenly on the issue and took a position he was quite vigorous in the defense of it and that he might be tempted to go off on rather specific tangents without considering amply enough other approaches, and I was not sure whether or not in his relations with the public he would be altogether fortunate. In that connection I expressed the importance of the Secretary of Agriculture being something of a politician and a diplomat in handling the farm problems that were thrown in his lap. I also stated that I had the impression that he was not particularly fond of administrative work and that as an administrator of a Department such as Agriculture, I was not sure just how he would function. Tucker in reply said that my statement very closely coincided with what he had obtained elsewhere. He was in a talkative state of mind and we got in on a number of very interesting subjects.

Tucker has an intense antipathy for Hoover and said that his attitude was, to quite a degree, that of the press in general. As illustrations of this attitude he referred to a number of episodes. For example, he referred to the inability of Hoover to take defeat on anything. He said the election was undoubtedly crushing to him. As an illustration of that he referred to the secret service which was guarding the President. A secret service man (whose name I have forgotten) assigned as the President's close bodyguard on his trip back to Washington from Palo Alto, said that at various stopping places the President shook hands with

31. A prominent Washington correspondent and author of the widely noticed *Sons of the Wild Jackass* (Boston, 1932).

people and he was so absent minded that he did not realize he had shaken hands with his own body guard three times on the same occasion. When he was about to shake hands with him the fourth time, the bodyguard said, "Mr. President." The President then looked up and realized he had been shaking hands with the secret service man. The secret service man put his hand on the President's shoulder and told him he was mighty sorry for what had happened and cheered him up, and that with probably a lot of other influences sort of mellowed him and when he arrived at Washington he seemed more human than ever before. Tucker also told me about the picture taking episode at Palo Alto at the time of the President's nomination when Mrs. Hoover, who thinks she is an artist in the photographic field, stepped out and tried to tell the camera boys that their perspective was not right and that the group was not as it should be, and so forth and so on until the President finally lost his temper and said, "That will do. You may go into the house." The press men's antipathy seems to have gone out against Mrs. Hoover too. As an illustration of that they have realized that she is uncomfortable about the spread between her front teeth and whenever she poses for a photograph she has her mouth shut but the boys fool her by clicking their camera and then she smiles and they then take the picture, spread and all. He also told me that when Mrs. Hoover began learning to ride horseback, instructions had gone out saying that no photographs should be taken until she had learned to ride her horse. The boys then concealed themselves in the bushes around the White House and when she was not looking, they got their photographs. . . .

December 16, 1932.

The early part of this week I had a visit with the Secretary in his office and at which time our discussions ran us in to some of the philosophical considerations in life. He frankly told me that he rather hated to go back to Missouri at this time, not because he relished life here or wished to continue his present work, but because of the attitude that had developed as the result of a man's activities. . . .

The Secretary then went on to develop in some detail his past experience. . . . He told me when he became Governor of Missouri he had a fire insurance situation in the State which was intolerable. The insurance companies had the State by the throat, were asking ungodly rates, were not giving policy holders allowances for balance and the same policies that were being adopted in the case of life insurance companies were not being followed in the case of the fire insurance companies. So, he made his brother the commissioner and it resulted in a battle royal. They fought tooth and nail and at one time they went to the Supreme Court and had decisions in the lower courts, imposing upon his brother commitments to refunds that amounted to over $150,000, as I recall. But, the Secretary said, "we fought it through and we won and we made the fire insurance company bow to a fair deal for the masses. But, what is the price my brother paid—he is paralyzed today, he does not talk, and he limps,'' and the Secretary got up and walked as his brother, with his left shoulder down and his arm dangling at his side. He said, "My brother has not talked since that day. He paid a terrible price for his efforts, but groups like these are never satisfied. You may or may not know that I was, unbeknown to me, virtually slated to be the Vice Presidential candidate. I did not want it then and do not want it now, but the plain facts are that word of this got around to the fire insurance companies, that I was to be nominated Vice President, and the entire organization threw in their forces and of course I was not selected.'' I asked the Secretary why he was reluctant to go back to the State of Missouri. I told him I thought with the increased prominence he had obtained, the influence he could bring to bear upon the activities of the State, politically and otherwise, would be great sport. He got up and walked around and then said, "You know I have not been altogether inactive even as Secretary of Agriculture. In the West end of the State we have the great packing industry. Under the Packers and Stockyards Act I have uncovered the skullduggery going on there and have made myself obnoxious to that part. In the eastern part of the State we have the great grain interests centered at St. Louis and I have their enmity because of the various moves I have made affecting their interests. Anything I attempt to do will be fought by these great groups and what chance does a man have against odds like that?'' I told the Secretary I realized that he might have substantial opposition to overcome but I told him that was life and I believed it possible to stand for what was right despite the attitude of interests such as he had been relating. The general remark he made, however, indicated very definitely that the battle was pretty much of a losing one and in that connection he said something which, if he had analyzed it, would indicate that he was quite inconsistent in his statement. In the first place he started out by saying he was Rooseveltian in his thinking, a strong supporter of him [T. R.] and was for the rights of the people as illustrated by the initiative, referendum and direct primary, but he said now that he thought the direct primary was one of the greatest banes of the nation and T. R. instead of being a benefactor had been a harmful influence in our life. That statement rather contrasted with the other statement in which he recognized the activities of the intrenched interests as represented by the fire insurance, the grain and the packer interests.

December 16, 1932 [a second entry].

Last Tuesday (December 13) when I stepped out of the meeting of the National Marketing Officials I was met at the door by [Henry] Morgenthau, Jr.,[32] who greeted me in a friendly way and said he would

32. Conservation commissioner of the state of New York and a close friend and advisor of President-elect Franklin D. Roosevelt.

like to have a word with me, and then told me that they were going into
a farm relief meeting at which representatives of the various farm
organizations were to be present. There were rumors that had come to
him that our report (on Senate Res. 281) was not going to be favorable
to the domestic allotment plan and he asked me if I did not think this
farm relief group should not be given our conclusions for their guidance.
I told him that I always believed in making information available and
that I would gladly do it in this case if I felt we were in position to do
so. I stated that the report was not completed and I was being put in the
position of trying to state definite conclusions which we had not as yet
reached and, therefore, I felt it would be improper for me or any one in
the Bureau to state conclusions. He rather agreed that that was a tenable
position and then asked me if I would come to Albany to see the
President-elect. I told him I would be glad to be of any service I could
and also asked if whether or not this could be altogether without any
publicity and merely in a purely personal way. I told him I was put in a
position where I probably had to consider a suggestion of that kind a bit,
and said that I was not sure whether or not it would be proper for me to
speak to the Secretary about going. He countered by saying that he
would rather I did not speak to the Secretary. He said, ''You leave this
to me and think about it and we will discuss it later on.'' He left it with
me and I assumed that he was coming over to see me at the Bureau.
Instead of coming to the office he arranged for a luncheon appointment
and we met at Schneider's on 11th Street. I met him there, with [William
I.] Myers of Cornell, [Joseph B.] Eastman[33] and Professor Tugwell. We
sat down to lunch and Morgenthau who was the bellwether very plainly
and confidently took matters in hand and said they had been eating so
much smoke and listening to so much jabber they were willing to hook
up and let me talk. I asked what they wanted me to talk about. He said
they wanted to know something about the report and what conclusions
we were reaching. I told them I was willing to give them some idea of the
way we were trending, in a confidential way, and then I proceeded to
discuss some of the aspects of this report. Morgenthau seemed to be
quite content to take my statements. Tugwell, in particular, tried to raise
some objections but backed away from them and the upshot was the
whole group seemed to agree with the conclusions we had reached with
reference to hogs. Then Morgenthau asked what was the alternative thing
to do. I was trying to elaborate upon that but did not make much
progress in the brief time at our disposal, but in addition got into several
little arguments with Tugwell. For instance, I made the point that I
thought there need be some adjustment in other prices in order to make
it possible for industrial and economic adjustments and to put wheels
agoing. He very flat-footedly stated he would take issue with me on that.
He did not think it possible and that no progress would be made in that
way, that the readjustment would have to begin in pushing prices up-
ward. I told him that led to utterly impossible potentialities. If that came

33. A member of the Interstate Commerce Commission.

to pass and that if industry was going to keep prices at the present high levels and it was going to be a law to move up agricultural prices, we never would catch up with the procession and would break our backs in the effort. The statement which I had been thinking of making along general lines of attack on the whole problem was not made and Morgenthau said nothing more about my going to Albany.

Perhaps in this same connection it may be as well to report the conference I had with Congressmen [James P.] Buchanan [Texas] and [John N.] Sandlin [Louisiana]. Mr. Buchanan telephoned me and asked if he and Sandlin could come over and see me right away. I told him "yes." It soon developed in our meeting what they wanted. Buchanan said that the farm debt situation was a very serious element in the picture and what he wanted me to do was to prepare a careful statement that would set forth the entire debt-credit situation, in order that he and Sandlin could go to Albany and place it before the President-elect. They wanted to do it very soon and they had expressed confidence in our ability to prepare a statement, and one on short notice. I told him I would be glad to prepare such a statement but I also asked if they did not think it would be helpful if we included in that statement a section dealing with a program of action. They said that they would be delighted to have it and Buchanan said, "Any thing that you prepare we will submit as coming from you and your Bureau."

I asked Buchanan what they were going to do in the matter of farm relief. "Well," he said, "they are working on domestic allotment," that he and Sandlin had nothing to do with that. "Oh," he said, "I do not think we will get anywhere with that," and I got what I wanted. As he went out, Buchanan volunteered the comment that they probably would have to tear down our appropriation somewhat but he went on to add, "If I had my way about it, instead of cutting your appropriations I would increase them, but," he said, "it is in the air to curtail the expenditures and you will have to take some cuts with the rest of them." I told him that I appreciated his fine atittude and hoped they would make the cut as gentle and mild as they could.

1933

March 6, 1933 through March 10, 1933.

Yesterday afternoon I called on the Secretary and Mrs. Wallace at the Willard. Mrs. Wallace was not in and while I was there H.A. called the White House to see if Professor [George F.] Warren[1] had arrived. He had been informed by Dr. [Frank A.] Pearson[2] that Warren was coming. He finally located him at the Cosmos Club and asked me to go over with him. I suggested that he probably wanted to see Warren alone and he said, "Come on along." So I went to the Club with him. Warren was pouring over his charts and books and indicated that he had been asked by Mrs. Roosevelt to come down and he was now waiting for an appointment. He entered upon a discussion of the situation with H.A., in which he pointed out that the events which had taken place were right down their alley, that we were virtually off the gold standard and as he saw the thing it was to embargo the export of gold, to suspend specie payments and for the President to indicate in a general statement that we would revaluate on a lower basis, perhaps one-third to one-half of the present gold content of the dollar and that a compensatory dollar reflecting changes in purchasing power should be ultimately established. In the course of one period in which I was with them, Warren finally got in touch with the White House but could not get an appointment with the President but finally got through and had a talk with Mrs. Roosevelt and Mrs. Roosevelt indicated that Warren's appointment would have to be with Professor [Raymond] Moley[3] and that was arranged for today, Monday, March 6. Warren was disturbed about having to contact Moley and asked certain questions of H.A. regarding Moley's knowledge of the

1. A Cornell professor concerned with farm management and agricultural economics who early influenced the thinking of Roosevelt, Henry Morgenthau, Jr., and M. L. Wilson among others.
2. A professor at Cornell and an old acquaintance of Wallace.
3. A professor of public administration at Columbia University, close adviser of the President and key member of the Brains Trust.

subject and his attitude, etc. Wallace could not give him anything so very definite but they planned on how they should proceed in presenting the matter of recognizing that we were off the gold standard and inflating, the thought being that it was a case of inflating or deflating with people rising up in revolt against the taking of their homes. Warren made the statement that there were not enough soldiers in the country to manage the situation if that process continued. Both H.A. and Warren were in touch with [Beardsley] Ruml[4] of New York in connection with the program of the Committee of the Nation and at that time Warren said he thought the report was an exceedingly good one and he approved it. What impressed me during the conversation was the attitude of reverence that H.A. manifested toward Warren who seemed to accept his every statement as "gospel truth" and conform one hundred per cent to his suggestions.

In due course Mr. Wallace stepped out into the adjoining room and I was left with Warren alone. At that time I went over some of his charts and he brought up the question of domestic allotment. He nodded toward the door and asked if H.A. was still supporting it. I told him my understanding was he had not changed his position on it, which Warren said was too terribly bad, that the whole situation was being messed up and complicated by that silly measure. After a bit Wallace came in and Warren turned to him and said, "What about the domestic allotment? Is that not dead?" Wallace looked rather sheepish, laughed and said, "No, I guess not," and then he shouted at Tugwell to come in. He stepped out and, to my surprise, Tugwell was in the adjoining room and Wallace had stepped out into his room. So, Tugwell came in and after some pleasantries regarding his future position in the Department, Warren said he understood Moley was the man he had to reach and he wanted to know how to reach him. Tugwell described Moley as a political science professor, not particularly versed in the economic field, impatient with charts, who would rather deal with matters in a general way. I do not think he gave Warren anything very helpful in formulating his approach. Warren then asked if an inflationary approach and revaluating the dollar was the way out. Tugwell tried to evade answering and Warren pinned him down and he said, "I will put up my program and you put up yours." Warren set forth his program as I have above stated. Tugwell said he had given a great deal of thought to the various inflationary proposals and he did not see how that would work to inflate. Warren tried to point out how inflation had resulted in Sweden and other countries under the policies they had adopted. Tugwell rather sheepishly evaded certain questions and was not convincing at all in his program but finally made the statement that he was opposed to any inflationary move, that

4. Executive director of the Laura Spelman Rockefeller Memorial Foundation with a long-time interest in agricultural affairs. Through the Committee for the Nation he was championing the domestic allotment plan.

he thought the dollar should remain as it is. To this Warren replied by asking how he was going to take care of the debt structure and the revolt that would evidently follow from liquidation processes. To this Tugwell replied that he thought the liquidation had gone very far already, perhaps one-third. With this Warren did not agree and said it was a case of facilitating the processes of liquidation. Then when Warren pressed Tugwell further as to how it would help agriculture, Tugwell said, "I would not lift the general price level but would lift the prices of agricultural commodities with the domestic allotment plan"—and, that did not make Warren any happier. Through all of this I of course maintained a discreet silence and non-committal position although in the discussion on the financial phases I raised certain questions regarding the stabilization of the banking situation, which seemed to register with both H.A. and Warren.

Another interesting development was the fact that Warren had a dinner engagement with Morgenthau, which he left to meet at around 6:30. In that connection it should be remembered that Morgenthau is a Cornell man and strongly supported by the Cornell group and at heart is opposed to the domestic allotment plan. I should also have added that in the course of the conversation before Tugwell came in Warren asked how long that Columbia bunch would be sticking around and messing up the picture, to which Wallace replied that he thought it would work all right and they probably would be around for some time.

In walking over from the Willard to the Cosmos Club, I told Wallace I thought there were a number of things we should chat on very early, that they were quite warm and urgent and thought I could be helpful in giving him the lowdown. In other words, there was every evidence of his utmost confidence and leaning on me in connection with this whole episode. We adjourned to Tugwell's room and at that time I discussed with them the Smith bill,[5] the International Cotton Conference and some matter in connection with the Reconstruction Finance Corporation, all of which seemed to interest them very much and to which they suggested various proposals. Both Tugwell and H.A. were most friendly and confidential and the only conclusion I could draw was that I would be close to them. At around 7:30 the telephone rang. Tugwell went to it. Ezekiel was on the phone and he told him to come right up and at that time Tugwell explained Ezekiel was going to work over some phases of the domestic allotment plan with him and when he came in I realized that while they were going down to dinner I thought it was best for me to eliminate myself from the party because if they wished to discuss revisions of the domestic allotment there was no reason why I should be there to embarrass them. I could not at that time understand why

5. Senator Ellison D. Smith of South Carolina in the second session of the 72nd Congress introduced two bills, either one of which Olsen could have mentioned. S5122 provided for the purchase and sale of cotton under the supervision of the Secretary of Agriculture; S5026 called for crop production and harvesting loans to farmers.

Tugwell was calling in Ezekiel on the domestic allotment but I understand now quite well. I went on down to the Department, thinking I would see Secretary Hyde. . . . I got in touch with him later on in the evening and he again asked me to spend the night with him, which I did. In the course of that visit he told me the new Secretary and Tugwell had been down at the Department in the morning, that he had bumped into them and found them in conference with Ezekiel and so Hyde concluded that Ezekiel was going to be a high economic adviser and probably domestic allotment was going again to Congress.

This morning Secretary Wallace called me over and when I came in I found Ezekiel standing at his desk. Wallace in a rather embarrassed sort of way said to me, "Meet the new Economic Adviser of the Department," and I turned to Ezekiel and said, "Good morning, delighted to know you as the Economic Adviser," and there was an embarrassing pause as usual and I said, "Well, this is very interesting." Then H.A. laughed again without saying much of anything. I asked then if Ezekiel was to be directly attached to him or to Tugwell, merely with the purpose of finding out the proper channel. H.A. said of course he will be attached to Tugwell's office but we three will work closely together. He said, "Well, Nils, I have asked Ezekiel to rework the domestic allotment bill so that it will be ready for reintroduction. As I told you before I would like to have you help get it in shape on the administrative side. We have decided that we should set up about five committees corresponding to the various commodities and here are some of the names we have been thinking of." He mentioned the hog committee and he had [Charles L.] Harlan[6] especially mentioned and we played around somewhat and he was impatient. "Well," Wallace said, "I was most interested in the hog and corn committees to have Harlan and [Foster F.] Elliott,[7] although Elliott was Ezekiel's suggestion." He then sensed that he was fooling around with a lot of detail and I suggested that it would perhaps be well to leave it to Dr. Ezekiel and me to agree upon the personnel for these committees and that the Secretary could check on them later. Tugwell was floating around in the office and I made my exit. . . .

Yesterday Ezekiel and I met in the forenoon and arranged for the committees on the domestic allotment bill. No mention was made of Englund at all. So, I did not mention it at that time and in the afternoon a memorandum came over from Wallace, instructing me to bring these committees together right away and to expedite action. (I understand that this memorandum was written by Ezekiel and signed by H.A. and it was hardly received over here before Ezekiel was on the phone and asking for a time to be set for the conference.) I called the committee together at

6. In charge of livestock reports in the Crop and Livestock Estimates Division of the Bureau of Agricultural Economics.
7. Senior agricultural economist in the Division of Farm Management and Costs of the Bureau of Agricultural Economics.

3:20 and I gave them a little talk in which I, first of all, read most of the memorandum and told them that in keeping with that expressed desire that the committee had been kept small in order that we might expedite consideration of all phases of this thing as quickly as possible. I said that I understood that our attention should be directed at the administrative problems in the handling of the bill and, furthermore, that we should regard the whole matter as confidential so as not to interfere with the setting of the stage for the introduction of the measure. Then I told them about Mr. Ezekiel's appointment and that he was here to work with us in developing these facts and so I turned the floor over to Ezekiel to explain in detail just what he had in mind. At the opening of the session I called Ezekiel in and told him I thought there would be some advantage in having Englund present because he had given the subject a lot of thought and if there was no objection to his being in I would like to ask him to come to the meeting. Ezekiel said it was all right, although it was my hunch that there was an effort to avoid having men like Englund and [O. C.] Stine and others whose views were rather definitely known as adverse associated with these committees.

Friday afternoon (March 3) while we were in the Secretary's Office bidding him good-bye word came to us through [E. N.] Meador[8] that the new Secretary would like to meet the Bureau Chiefs, and we all agreed that it would perhaps be a good time since we were all together. Wallace and Tugwell came along and we foregathered in the large conference room over there. Strangely enough Hyde rather hesitated in introducing all the men. He came over to me in his office and said, "Olsen, it is up to you to introduce H.A." I said, "No that will never do. You must introduce him. You are the one who can." Later on he called Kitchen over to his side and said, "Say, Kitchen who are some of these men," and he pointed to [James T.] Jardine,[9] and pointing to [S. H.] Mc-Crory[10] asked who he was. He took his pad and listed the names—all of which is a commentary on the Secretary's knowledge of his own Department. In due course H.A. arrived with Tugwell and Secretary [Hyde] brought them into the conference room. We all lined up and went through the handshaking. When we were through with the handshaking there was a little pause but Hyde, with his usual adroitness sensed the situation and made a little speech, stating how happy he was, personally, and how sure he was that the whole Department was happy that Wallace was the new Secretary. He commented on the fact that he, the son, should be standing now in the shadow of his father, and paid his fine respects to the father too. When Hyde was through there was a rather painful pause but H.A. sensed the importance of saying something and in a talk that was anything but adroit in comparison with Hyde's talk,

8. An assistant to Secretary Hyde.
9. Chief of the Office of Experiment Stations.
10. Chief of the Bureau of Agricultural Engineering.

Wallace proceeded to say that he was glad to be here, made some reference to his father and to his acquaintance with the Department, that these were trying, stirring times, some drastic adjustments probably would have to be made and he hoped they could be made as painlessly as possible but the situation called for action and if there had to be pain with it that could not be helped. Incidentally, that was anything but diplomatic in an opening statement—he was virtually telling them they were going to have their heads cut off. He said that the scientific work of the Department had been developed to a high degree of efficiency during all these years and in that connection he made reference to his friends in the Department, Mr. Olsen and Mr. Englund (who was there), and said that we would have a good deal to do to bring the economic research up to the high level of the scientific research and that the economics people would have much to do in helping to formulate a program for agriculture. He meant well but it was a very awkward statement and I have been kidded by Hyde on down to the last person present at the meeting. Hyde afterwards spoke to me about it and said it was quite unfortunate the way he stated several thoughts, but he was sure they were not meant as they sounded. Immediately following the conference with the new secretaries, Hyde called me aside and said the new Secretary wanted to see me and [W. A.] Jump.[11] The various members of the group were standing around and [C. W.] Warburton was hanging around too and as Jump and I stepped out into the outer hall to meet the Secretary, Warburton came along and so Wallace said, "You had better come on too." So, we went into Jump's office and Wallace really gave the impression that he wanted quite immediate action on a number of things. He turned to me and said, "Well, Nils, what do you think we can do to fix up the domestic allotment plan? I would like to have you people get busy and work over the measure with a view to perfecting it administratively." I said, "Well, H.A., you may rest assured we will be glad to do everything we can in that connection." He said, "Of course I have some reservations as to how it will work but that is all right, we will get organized and work on it." We had a little exchange there regarding the operation of the plan and he got into a special point, but stopped shortly and said, "We do not need to discuss any technical questions now." I followed up and said that there were several types of action that I thought should be seriously considered by him for immediate adoption and I referred to the debt situation, the report and bill we prepared. I referred to certain items in the taxation situation. I referred to the farm relief report (Public Document 184), and the report on land utilization. I said that all these activities would lend themselves to splendid planks in his program. "Well," he said, "I am

---

11. Assistant Director and budget officer in the Office of Personnel and Business Administration.

going to count on you heavily for suggestions and I wish you would concentrate on those matters." Wallace then turned to Warburton and said, "What do you think we can do to put some economic extension into the Extension Service?" Warburton said, "We have been developing economic extension for the last several years and of course can do more of it." Wallace asked Warburton if he thought the Extension Service could help to reduce the acreage. Warburton said, "Whatever the plan adopted is we can of course get behind it and put it across. We got into trouble with the Federal Farm Board on their program and there is quite a bit of bad blood throughout the Extension Service on that." Then Jump and Wallace had exchanges regarding the personnel, particularly the local office personnel, and Jump adroitly said he better forget about things of that kind and for the time being ride along with his present force.

. . . Jump sensed that H.A. was getting himself crosswise with his higher personnel and the next morning he evidently spoke to H.A. about it and in less than ten minutes after he had spoken to Wallace, Wallace called me over. I had previously sent over the cabinet material and some other statements and we made a few remarks on them but I realized that in his rather diffident way Wallace was trying to say something. He then said, "Nils, what I really wanted to see you about was the developments that have been taking place. You are a very dear friend of mine and I probably should have told you so that there could be no misunderstanding. I presume that what has taken place must have hurt your pride and even your standing in the Department but I want you to know that it was all intended well and that it probably will be for your good as well as for my own." I told Wallace frankly that I had been a little surprised, if not a wee bit disturbed by some of the developments and I presumed more so because of a reported interview with him in which it had been stated that M. L. Wilson was to be the new Chief of the Bureau of Agricultural Economics. H.A. asked, "Was there such a story?" "Well," he said, "there is absolutely nothing to it," he stated in a rather vigorous way. I said that I just could not imagine a thing of that kind but that I was very glad that he had spoken to me about the matter so that there should not be any possibility of a misunderstanding, that I was anxious to be of the utmost help to him in every way and I hoped that he would regard me as a true friend that he could count on always. Wallace said, "Now I would like to have you go out to lunch with me." I said, "All right, let me know the time." So they called me and when I got over there I found Tugwell, Ezekiel and [John R.] Fleming[12] were also in the party. Naturally we did not get in on any personal matters but Wallace was very friendly and deferential to me in seeking reactions in connection

---

12. Speech writer for the Secretary who served as assistant director of the Office of Information.

with our discussions. At that time Mrs. Wallace was over there and a most cordial exchange between us took place.

I do not recall what took place Wednesday, but Wednesday evening about 11:45 it so happened that I had been working late and my telephone rang and H.A. was on the phone. He said, "I have been trying to get you all day." I said, "I have been around the Department, but perhaps I was out at the time you called." At that time he asked me about my reaction on the calling of the farm groups together and a number of matters that I do not remember in detail now, on which I gave my reactions. . . . The next morning to my surprise about seven o'clock the telephone rang again. I was just rolling out of bed and he asked if I was through with my breakfast. He said, "I thought I would take a walk and I would like to walk over to your apartment if that is all right with you." I said, "Sure I will be all set by the time you arrive." In due course he arrived in the lobby and in due course we walked back to the Hotel Wardman Park, where we were picked up by his car. In the course of the conversation we discussed various matters pertaining to his immediate personnel and I had occasion to comment on [Ernest] Hall[13] and some other people at his specific request who were in his outer office. It was a type of matter that concerned him very intimately, the personnel in his immediate office. When we got down to the office about 8:15, Tugwell breezed in and shortly afterward Ezekiel. Tugwell, H.A. and I had a nice little discussion and among other things I got into the foreign situation and urged a very clean-cut decisive move to give congressional authorization to the Chief Executive to operate on the tariffs and other trade barriers. I found that I was a little counter to H.A.'s ideas and 100 per cent square with Tugwell, and H.A. swung around and agreed that it probably was a very wise move to make. As I was going out of his office yesterday morning he said, "Nils, how would you like to meet me at the Wardman Park Hotel about 7:15 and walk down to the Department?" He said that would give us an opportunity to visit about the various matters that it is hard for us to get together on and it would probably be a rather convenient way of handling this thing and I said, "It is jake with me and that will be the schedule until further notice." The Secretary said, "Fine." (I sensed very definitely that Wallace, because of his presumed close friendship with me, has wanted to avoid giving any impression that this was a closed show matter between us. I think that is at the bottom of the maneuvers that have taken place and he said to me, "You may feel rather peculiar about Tugwell's appointment, but when I get around some time to tell you the story I think you will agree with me that it is all to the good," but I sensed that in this early morning hour arrangement the Secretary wished to avoid the appearance of drawing heavily upon me for advice.)

13. An assistant to Secretary Hyde who remained briefly as an assistant to Wallace.

Yesterday around noon the Secretary got me on the phone and said he was going to give a radio talk that noon and asked if he could not read his speech to me. I said I had better come over. I rushed over and Meador gave me a copy of the speech. I glanced through it and at once saw he was playing into the hands of the domestic "alloters" and had gotten himself out on a limb. Fleming came around and saw what I was reading and said, "Have you got that?" and I said, "Yes." He said, "It is well done is it not?" and I said, "Yes, with three or four bad spots." Fleming, in other words, had been swung right over to the extreme view on domestic allotment, so I went in and talked to Wallace and we had our first real frank exchange on domestic allotment. I explained to him that I understood that we were apart on our views with reference to that measure but I said, "You are getting yourself out on a limb. You have taken a very forward position with reference to international markets and other phases of this situation and you are going to get this into a jack pot." We argued the question of lifting some acreage out of the agricultural plant just as an emergency matter and I said that as a long-time point of view I would lift out our marginal area, that was at the heart of the national resources situation from a long-time point of view but as an emergency matter that would not stand the gaff. I said, "Furthermore, Wallace, you have a monstrosity in this domestic allotment measure and I fear it is going to sink you and I am interested in your not getting into the mess," and he said that he had the same feeling. I said, "Play your cards adroitly and do not implicitly believe the farm leaders, who one time will talk nicely and another time will stab you in the back." He admitted the truth in that. He said, "Olsen, I have got to stand for this program." I said, "Well, stand for it but do not close your avenues of escape. Play this thing with adroitness and furthermore, you are making a mistake when you do not hop on to a number of other elements in the picture. Why not take a good old wallop at the debt and tax situation?" He said, "Well, what changes would you make in this radio speech?" I suggested the kind of changes I would make. Wallace said, "Can you do that right away?" I said I could bring in Fleming as it was a thing he could do more quickly. He demurred some and I said, "Why don't you let me make some changes and then you can use them or not, as you please." So I brought the statement back to the office and made the changes . . . and he took them 100 per cent and said they were fine. He said, "I wish you would get in touch with Fleming and have him work them into the statement." I put Fleming through a good schooling by telling him he would have to play somewhat more adroitly and realize that he could not talk to everybody about these matters. If he were not careful he would be playing Wallace against Tugwell and Tugwell against Ezekiel, both of whom were set on getting this thing shoved down the throat of Wallace and Congress, and that might not be the wise thing. Fleming got the point and promised to watch his step. . . .

This morning Secretary Wallace and I met as agreed and walked the entire distance to the office. The particular matter on his mind was the conference he would open this morning with the farm and cooperative leaders and how he should handle it. I told him I thought he had handled the meeting with the group (Smith bill group) the other day very well, that he gave them an opportunity to present their views, had shown a sympathetic interest, leading them on but did not commit himself. This was the advice I had given on our way back from the luncheon Tuesday and ran counter to the advice Tugwell and Ezekiel gave, when the matter of the Smith bill came up, that he should step out hard.

March 14, 1933.

Last night when I returned the clerk at the desk of the Kennedy-Warren told me that Secretary Wallace had called at the apartment to see me. So, I called H.A. at the Wardman and told him I was sorry not to be in when he arrived. The Secretary then remarked that the Mrs. was out and he thought he would like to come over and visit with me a bit and he said what he had in mind, among other things, to discuss with me was to ask how he should proceed in case this emergency relief legislation was passed, particularly how he should handle the processers. I asked him if he wanted me to come over. He said, "No, it is so late now that would not be necessary," but that he would like me to give serious thought to it, and we could discuss the matter in the morning when we walked down.

M. L. Wilson had also called me and I called him back last night. He said he wanted to come out and see me and I told him he might arrange to take dinner with me this evening, so that is still pending. . . .

This morning as usual I met Wallace at 7:15 a.m. pronto and we were on our way down. He told me that he was arranging to meet a small group of processers this morning under his own arrangements and he asked me how I thought he might best proceed. I told him I thought he had handled the meeting with the cooperative group on the Smith bill in an admirable way passing the burden of the decision to them and putting himself in the position of drawing them out. I said I thought he might tell them that the agricultural interests had indicated their desire to approach the problem in a way that was not stated in the press, giving him broad authority to handle the matter and that he is desirous of working with the various groups who were concerned in the handling of these products, and for him to put up to them the suggesting of various approaches and see what reaction he would get from them. He agreed that that was probably a pretty practical sort of approach and the conversation on that point stopped.

On one of the previous mornings (and we have walked down to the Department every morning since we first began the habit) the Secretary asked me how I thought he should handle the entire assignment if it came his way. I told him I thought he would have the problem of reacting on the proposals ultimately himself but that he should unload as much of the actual administrative burden of ascertaining the various approaches that groups have in mind, possibly upon a unit that he would create directly under him. I said that I thought it would be very desirable that he draw in the various groups and give them ample opportunity to express their views in order that it could not be said that he had not consulted them. I told him I was quite sure he would have his hands more than full in meeting various attacks from every angle and he could expect that they would be absolutely ruthless in their attacks upon him. With this he fully agreed. . . .

But, to continue the conversation of this morning (March 14), I asked the Secretary about calling on Morgenthau. He hesitated a bit and then I explained to him how Morgenthau had been in touch with me before Inauguration and had suggested that I see the President-elect and how I had probably spoiled my chance by my excessive honesty. Wallace then said, "Well, Morgenthau likes to be shown deference—I think it would be a rather good thing for you to call on him." . . .

I then spoke to H.A. about the reorganization activities of the committee of which McCrory was chairman. I told him that I was notified yesterday to appear before them and that I spent last evening with them in a discussion of reductions in our appropriations. I told Wallace I did not think there should be a dollar's reduction of economic research funds—if anything they should be increased. I then told him that I gained the impression that they were confusing the elimination of useless political stations that had been established all over the country with basic research done by the Washington staff. I also told him that I objected strenuously to the idea that in sending any of our men to the field it was field research and should be lopped off. The Secretary was surprised and said that was not what they asked the committee to do, that they had been given the job to look over sub-stations and see how they could eliminate them. He agreed with me that there should be no reduction in the economic funds and said he probably should get in touch with Tugwell. Meanwhile Kitchen and I got in touch with the division leaders of the Bureau asking how they could absorb a 5 or 10 percent cut. As we went over these memoranda my criticism of the whole approach was intensified and I had made up my mind that I was going to tell that committee that we could not operate this way, that if they wanted to cut 5%, 10% or 15%, the thing to do was to tell us the amount and we would proceed to cut our cloth accordingly, but that it was a backward step and I was totally out of sympathy with it. I then called up McCrory and word came back that the conference scheduled at two o'clock this afternoon (March 14) would be unnecessary as they had decided to handle the matter in another way. I may be wrong but I believe Wallace got in touch with Tugwell and told that committee to lay off economic research and curtailment of funds for that purpose. . . .

This morning (March 14) Wallace got me on the telephone and asked me about getting a current daily service in shape for him which we, in general, agreed upon and then in the course of the conversation I said there were various hot matters he probably would want to know about very promptly. He commented by saying, "When anything shows up I will be glad to have you call me." I said I would be glad to do that but if he could have a direct connection working out 'of his office, whereby he could pick up his phone and call me on the inside phone it would be better. He agreed and we think we can work out such an arrangement.

March 20, 1933.

Senator McNary called Mr. [Eric] Englund this morning and asked him if he had studied the new farm relief bill. Englund said he had looked at it some but had not studied it. The Senator asked him to come up in the afternoon and talk to him confidentially about the measure. In accordance with my instructions Mr. Englund told him that this was a matter regarding which probably the Chief of the Bureau should be consulted. McNary said he would be glad to have him discuss it with me. I talked to H.A. this afternoon regarding the episode and told him that this kind of a development would tend to put us both in an impossible situation, to which he agreed. I told him that of course there was every disposition on my part on the part of the Bureau to work with him but, of course, he understood the inherent difficulties in the picture. I told him that I expected to call Senator McNary and tell him that the Secretary was handling farm relief and was speaking for the Department and that his inquiry should be directed to him. The Secretary agreed that probably was the only thing to do and, furthermore, I told him that in case we were called upon to appear before the committee in executive session I would refuse to go on the same ground, that the Secretary was representing the Department in this matter.

My own feeling is that the situation is becoming rather critical and unfortunate. It is very apparent that the opposition to the measure of the Administration is terrific. The bill of course had colossal weaknesses and imposes a burden upon the Department that is just unthinkable. Such men as [Lloyd S.] Tenny,[14] [George] Livingston,[15] representatives of the packers and others are flooding the town. When I tried to arrange for a conference for Tenny with Ezekiel Saturday afternoon he reported back that he was completely upset nervously and did not hardly see how he could meet Tenny. However, he consented to see him a little while and Tenny reported to me that Ezekiel is in bad shape and a report has come to me since that he was given pretty rough handling in the committee. The load that he is assuming is absolutely preposterous. To assume that a "boy of his tender years" cannot only analyze the critical questions involved in the farm relief bill but can also assume the administrative burden of setting up an organization in the Secretary's office is just ridiculous. What I am afraid of is that the Secretary will permit himself to be bogged down with this measure and allow Morgenthau and others to run away with the real worthwhile bacon. I am sorely tempted to unburden myself fully to him. . . .

March 24, 1933.

I, of course, have had my usual morning visit with the Secretary, since writing my last notes, in which I have had an opportunity to edge in on reorganization, farm relief and a good many other matters. . . .

I also took occasion this morning to pay my respects to Ezekiel. I introduced the subject [to Wallace] by saying that Dr. [C. L.] Holmes[16] had told me that Ezekiel had called upon him to turn over certain members of his staff to handle certain matters and there was real doubt about it on two grounds. First of all, I figured that it was really good administrative procedure to work through the Chief of any Bureau and, secondly, if it was the intention to make a raid on the personnel of the Bureau in that fashion it would wreck the work of the Bureau. Wallace countered that that was not the intention at all. He went on to say that Ezekiel had so logical a mind, that he admired it very much but probably it was too logical and not sufficiently practical. I told him, frankly, that I thought Ezekiel was lacking in administrative sense and capacity and that was the point on which he had better watch his step.

This morning I also took occasion to again raise the question of Morgenthau with whom he had had a visit and discussed the farm relief bill. I raised the question very frankly as to where Morgenthau stood. He said, "Of course Morgenthau was a personal friend of the President and he wanted to reward him," and just like any good Semitic gentleman he

14. Olsen's predecessor as Chief of the Bureau of Agricultural Economics and business manager of the Chicago Mercantile Exchange.

15. A consulting marketing specialist headquartered in Minneapolis who also served as executive vice-president of the Millers National Federation.

16. Chief of the Division of Farm Management and Costs in the Bureau of Agricultural Economics.

was naturally looking out for his own fences. He said with reference to credit agencies he was agreeable to Morgenthau handling them. I countered by saying that as far as the farm debt situation was concerned, he (Wallace) was expected to take leadership and Congress would undoubtedly want to vest it in the Department. This morning I intimated rather strongly that it probably behooved him to keep a pretty close eye on the gentleman, to which he did not take exception.

The situation is a pretty one. Wallace undoubtedly has the support of most of the farm organizations, although the Farmers Union will fight him aggressively on his bill and the Grange will not support him. Tugwell, of course, represents the Columbia influence with the President. Morgenthau, on the other hand, represents the Cornell interest and of course the Cornell crowd supported him for Secretary. The Cornell crowd, in turn, are friendly to Wallace but they thoroughly hate the Columbia crowd. They would like to have Wallace adopt their deflation plan but they are deaf on his domestic allotment ideas. Wallace, himself, is none too enthusiastic, in my judgment, about his domestic allotment affiliations but he is having a hard time breaking that little romance. . . .

March 28, 1933.

Following up my understanding with the Secretary I easily induced Congressman Buchanan to introduce the resolution concerning farm mortgage debts and the refinancing thereof. It was immediately passed under unanimous consent March 22 and on the 27th our report went up, constituting, I believe, a record in delivery. Yesterday morning when delivering the report I followed Wallace to the Hill where I found that he had roamed from Senator [George W.] Norris' office over to Senator [Joseph T.] Robinson's office and I parked myself there until he was through with his conference. We overheard Robinson's conversation with the White House, which dealt with the laying of the strategy for certain moves in connection with the farm relief and the unemployment acts.

In due course Wallace came out of Robinson's office, and shortly thereafter George Peek[18] came out. George came over smiling and greeted me and turned to Wallace and said, "Remember the McNary-Haugen crowd were responsible for mobilizing the support behind this proposition." He did not state what the proposition was but it was clear that he was calling the Secretary's attention to the fact that he was indebted to the McNary-Haugen crowd. Wallace, Kitchen and I then

17. A former executive of Deere and Co. (manufacturers of agricultural machinery in Moline, Illinois) and leader in the fight for farm parity in the 1920s. His concern was with marketing, particularly overseas, the agricultural surplus more than with curtailing production. For an excellent study of Peek, see Gilbert Fite, *George N. Peek and the Fight for Farm Parity* (Norman, 1954).

adjourned to Robinson's office and Wallace took time to glance hurriedly through the measure. He thumbed through hurriedly, reading some parts and then made the remark, "This thing looks as though it is chucked full of economics. What we ought to do is to cut all debts by 25%." . . . He read further and then said, "Really there are some good things in this measure." I said, "Sure it is just shot through with good ideas and there is room for lots of action by the Secretary of Agriculture. We have put in your hands a vehicle with which to mobilize public opinion on the farm creditors of the Nation and what more do you want, particularly when we have supplemented that power with facilities with which to refinance such loans as should be taken care of." As a result of the conversation he pulled out his pen and signed the letter. I then proceeded to Buchanan's office and the report was filed, much to the pleasure of Mr. Buchanan. That same evening the *New York Times* representative and other news people got hold of [C. E.] Gapen[18] and obtained copy of the report from him. The next morning the summary of the report appeared on the inside page of the *New York Times* parallel with the President's order consolidating the credit agencies. A little later on in the morning Mr. [Frank] Ridgway[19] of the Federal Farm Board called Mr. [J. Clyde] Marquis[20] and asked for copy of the report, stating that he had heard that we had made recommendations covering debt adjustments. I arranged to have a copy sent over in a couple of hours, after I had seen Tugwell. In the course of the discussion with Tugwell I raised the question as to whether or not it would be desirable for me to drop the Governor (Morgenthau) a note enclosing copy of the report. Tugwell rather felt that I should probably transmit it to be handled by subordinates. To which I agreed. Tugwell throughout seemed to manifest quite a little satisfaction over developments. In the course of that visit at the Secretary's Office Mr. [Paul H.] Appleby[21] told me, confidently, that Morgenthau had called the Secretary and suggested they walk down to work the following morning. So, the next morning Tugwell and I walked down together and Wallace walked down with Morgenthau. A bit later on the Secretary called me and told me that he thought it would be a good idea for me to get in touch with W. I. Myers (Federal Farm Board)[22] and give such explanations as I deemed proper. I called Mr. Myers but he was in conference and he called me back around noon and I was tied up and we arranged to meet late in the afternoon, if convenient to both. I had been up with Mr. Buchanan arranging for some action on the bill and when I called in the evening Myers had gone. The

18. Chief of the press service in the Office of Information of the Department of Agriculture.
19. Director of Information of the soon-to-be-abolished Federal Farm Board.
20. In charge of economic information in the Bureau of Agricultural Economics.
21. Chief assistant in the Office of the Secretary.
22. Myers was close to Morgenthau and soon would be associated with him in the Farm Credit Administration.

next morning we arranged for a luncheon hour but meanwhile I had had a visit with the Secretary in the morning, in which we discussed the matter a bit. The Secretary then told me that he had thought we should avoid any breach with the other people and I told him that that was what I had in mind but that I thought it would be well for us to make clear that we had been in the credit field and what we were doing was merely carrying out the mandates of Congress. At that time H.A. seemed to be quite agreeable to that approach.

I had my luncheon engagement with Professor Myers and we both seemed to be sparring a bit and Myers was throwing out occasional little digs on cooperation. So, finally, I said, "Now as far as this report is concerned," and I narrated how the Secretary had walked down with Morgenthau and suggested that I get in touch with him. Myers said, "Yes, I think it is too bad that we do not have better cooperation in the Government. It should not be necessary for us to get information through the press such as in this instance," and I intimated that cooperation worked both ways. . . .

The following morning I visited with the Secretary and told him about the conference. Tugwell was with me at the time and I impressed the fact that cooperation worked both ways and that I did not see that they had anything about which to complain, and both Wallace and Tugwell seemed to be reasonably well satisfied with the results of that conference.

The next development in the picture was Saturday afternoon when the Secretary got me on the phone from the White House and asked me if I would not get some material ready on debt situation that he could use in his speech that night. He said on the phone that it had been decided that he should change his radio talk and include the reforestation, unemployment, farm mortgage and debt situation and Morgenthau was sending over a statement presenting the facts on the bill itself. I had [Albert B.] Genung[23] prepare the statement and the Secretary tacked on the memorandum that came over from Morgenthau without any change, except the introduction which was quite essential in making the transition. The significant thing about the memorandum was that it wound up with a statement that the President and Mr. Morgenthau had given a great deal of thought to this subject and formulated a plan for handling the farm debt situation. Genung showed some curiosity as to how these matters were going to be handled and raised the question if [John R.] Fleming was going to do all the writing for the Secretary and if we were to be called on for such services we should have a direct contact running to the Secretary, the inference being that he, Genung, should have direct contact with the Secretary. I told him that Fleming was going to handle the writing for the Secretary. Incidentally, it is interesting to observe the

23. Now a senior agricultural economist in the Division of Economic Information.

widespread disposition on the part of various members of the Bureau's staff to establish direct contact with the Secretary by memoranda or otherwise. . . .

April 4, 1933.

Yesterday morning the Secretary asked me to have on his desk by 12:15 three memoranda, one dealing with the transfer of the credit section of the Bureau to the Farm Credit Administration; (2) one setting forth our criticisms and suggestions regarding the farm debt adjustment bill and a third on central agricultural banks in Europe. I told him I did not know about the third memorandum and then he rather hesitated and said he guessed he had asked Mr. [D. L.] Wickens[24] to prepare a memorandum. I said it was the first I had heard of it but would get in touch with Mr. Wickens and see what the situation was. I called Mr. Wickens, and he said he had already sent it over to the Secretary. . . . The original did not come to this office for any member of the administrative force to see, but was sent direct by Wickens to the Secretary.

This morning . . . I suggested that we had some suggestions that might prove helpful to the Administration in connection with the credit program and it might be well to send such comments over to Morgenthau. He jumped at the idea and said that might be a good thing to do and he asked me to prepare a statement. I think it was the same morning . . . that the Secretary said, "Well, Nils, I have something else to shock you. Morgenthau would like to have your credit division. How do you feel about that?" Of course I gave him a song and dance. In the course of the conversation he made the statement that he thought the price analysis men would be more valuable to the Department than the credit men. I said we needed both in our work. He asked me to prepare a statement, which I did and it was later on, according to the Secretary's statement, given to Morgenthau. I gained the impression that H.A. realizes that he is in a hot spot on more matters than one. . . .

April 4, 1933 [a second entry].

Yesterday morning, Rex Tugwell, Wallace and I had breakfast together again, after walking downtown, and Rex uncovered this on the famous statement in the *New York Times* regarding the drastic curtailment of the Government establishments. There were some knowing exchanges between Rex and Wallace and I gained the impression that the

24. Served in the Agricultural Finance Division, Bureau of Agricultural Economics.

press representative had been in touch with them but had gotten his story from [Lewis] Douglas.[25] In other words, Douglas had turned this statement loose as a trial balloon. . . .

This morning the subject came up for discussion between Rex and myself. Wallace had slipped off with James S. Milloy (Minneapolis Tribune) who now meets him virtually every morning for a chat. This contact with Milloy strikes me as being rather unusual since Milloy is of course the confidential agent of [Frederick E.] Murphy of the "Minneapolis Tribune" whose party interests, as I understand it, are with the Republicans. Wallace, of course, impresses me as representing a complex of crusading convictions with a certain ultra frankness and simplemindedness in his contacts in Washington. The latter quality may grow out of his utter frankness, which does command respect and which I have understood, but which also exposes him to the attack of the enemy.

[Oeveste] Granducci of the Kiplinger Agency, in his last visit with me came in chuckling and said he had a very choice bit that tickled him whenever he thought of it. I said, "Let's hear it." "Well," he said, "do you know that the present farm relief bill was written by a news man who was half shot at the time he wrote it?" I said, "That is interesting, was it written here in a hotel room or was it written on a train coming into Washington." He said, "Perhaps the latter is true. Evidently you know something about it," and I did not comment. The fact is that Dante Pierce[26] told me the day of the conference that he, Dan Wallace[27] and, I think it was Milloy, who had sat up practically all night the night before on the train and had drafted the general thought that was included in the measure giving the Secretary of Agriculture almost dictatorial powers. Congress had just granted the President dictatorial powers with reference to the railroads and they concluded it would be a splendid thing to give the Secretary fully as great powers with reference to agriculture. . . .

April 18, 1933.

The picture, to me, seems to be as confused as ever. On the one hand I get reports of the Administration leaning toward one streak and on the other hand I am impressed with all the moves made toward socializing our economic activities. Today's "Herald" says that the President, through Miss [Frances] Perkins,[28] has presented an amendment to the thirty hour week bill providing for planning and controlling industrial production. This morning, as I visited with Tugwell at breakfast, I asked him about it and his counter was that he thought it probably did not go

25. Director of the Budget.
26. Publisher of *The Iowa Homestead* and *Wisconsin Farmer*.
27. Editor of *The Farmer* at St. Paul, Minnesota; no relation to the Secretary.
28. Secretary of Labor and the first woman cabinet member.

far enough, what he would like to see done would be to see the domestic allotment plan applied to industry. He also said he thought there should be a tax levied on those who did not go into the planning scheme of things. He did seem to have the idea that considerable voluntary planning should be engaged upon by the industries themselves, organized in groups, but that certain penalties would be applied in case they did not plan and control.

In my discussion with Tugwell this morning I asked him, bluntly, if he had finally reached the conclusion that we had to adopt the isolation approach and that there was no hope in reorganizing foreign markets. He squirmed a bit and said he would always be strong for the move to open our trade relations to Canada, Mexico and South America but did not think there was a basis on which it could be done with Europe. I told him I thought it would be a slow process but that it would inevitably come and that it would be too bad if we did not stake our sights with that objective in mind. Tugwell rather agreed that it would be the ultimate outcome but so far as the present outlook was concerned he did not see any possibility. That, of course, explains the enormous emphasis that is being placed upon a program of curtailing production in agriculture and in all other fields.

The Secretary seems, to me, to be more or less bewildered and while I have walked down with him several mornings, I find that his theoretical leanings are mostly toward drastic lines of action, with strong emphasis on social justice, and the like.

Last Saturday morning after his two days visit in New York, I stumbled on the Secretary in Childs restaurant and I told him I had just seen in the paper the item regarding the transfer of the Forest Service to the Department of the Interior. I said I could not believe there was anything serious intended in that suggestion but probably it was nothing but a bit of maneuvering. Wallace said, "Well, perhaps under the new leadership that would not be such a bad move to combine Forestry with public lands and public parks." I said, "H.A., you do not mean that. That harks back to the old battle that your Dad had over the same issue. You know as well as I do that the Department of the Interior is shot through with the exploitationist viewpoint and all the expansionists and grafters rally around that Department." The Secretary said Yes, he presumed that was true. I went on to say that I thought the time was not far away when it would be pretty opportune for him to get out and shout his belief. To which he did not give any reply. I have quite a little difficulty in sensing what are the impulses dominating him. I think he probably finds himself in a position with the President which makes it very ticklish for him to assert himself. In that connection I also stressed the emphasis upon the countryward movement by the President and how that would ultimately give us a new agricultural policy but certainly rather counter to what we had all been advocating. He admitted that that was in the air and that the President was taking a position that was hard to square with the views that we had been developing.

I was told that last night Secretary Wallace's appearance before the D.A.R. convention was anything but a favorable showing. He started out by saying that he did not think that he should accept the invitation to address them because of the pressure upon him to bring relief to agriculture. As a matter of fact the engagement had slipped his mind until about six o'clock and he had not made any preparation to speak. He did not have notes and talked for about five minutes in a very halting, diffident sort of way.

April 25, 1933.

Chester Davis[29] evidently is in a complete fog also as to developments. He told me last week that he was to have attended a dinner with Peek and H. A. Wallace, ostensibly for the purpose of being peacemaker between the two, but the very afternoon before the evening of the dinner somebody had intervened and had arranged to have the dinner called off. I gained from Chester the impression that Wallace is not satisfied that Peek is the man to head up the [Agricultural Adjustment] Administration and Peek, in turn, insists on having a clear-cut program and understanding before he accepts the responsibility. Peek, of course, represents the strong-arm business man approach in handling the farm relief program with particular emphasis upon bringing the processing and distributing groups under agreements for price-fixing purposes. Chester tells me that if Peek is made Chief, Ezekiel can hardly last over night because Peek has no use for him and can not stand him. Chester evidently has very high regard for Peek and thinks he would make a good man to head up this show. I think he rather favors the Peek approach. On the other hand both Peek and Davis do not understand how the production control program can effectively work. In that connection Chester told me about a conference that was held about Friday of last week at which all of these commodities committees which have been set up with Bureau [of Agricultural Economics] men were present, Ezekiel and all the other men now connected with the organization, and then George Peek, Chester Davis, H. C. Taylor, M. L. Wilson and [Charles J.] Brand[30] all came in, and Warburton remarked to Brand afterwards that it looked like a

29. One of the authors of the domestic allotment proposal being considered by Congress who was to become one of the key officials in the AAA (Agricultural Adjustment Administration) in charge of the Division of Production.

30. Secretary of the National Fertilizer Association who drafted the first McNary-Haugen bill when he served in the Department of Agriculture.

McNary-Haugen party, commenting particularly upon H. C. Taylor coming in. Brand replied, "Yes" that he was for the McNary-Haugen bill and said so—that was the difference between him and Taylor. Taylor was for it and did not dare say so. At this meeting they were discussing various programs for industry control and also the program for agricultural production control. Chester said he, Peek and Earl Smith were amazed at the plans that were being evolved and said if these were known to the public and aired in Congress it would mean utter defeat of the bill. The significant thing is that the farm leaders who brought Wallace in on the program are speaking that way now on the program that is being evolved. My personal fear is that quite a little bit of the responsibility for these plans may be saddled on the Bureau because of the activities of these committees. In view of that fact it is probably wise that I and the Assistant Chiefs be kept completely out of the picture. . . .

April 26, 1933.

Last night Chester Davis was giving me a statement which was of unusual significance but which he did not complete but as far as it went it was about as follows: I asked him point blank where he was fitting into this picture. He said, "To make out that Peek was opposed to having the Act administered by the Department of Agriculture. That is not true. What Peek was objecting to was an arrangement that he would serve as an Administrator with various individuals thrown between him and the Secretary. He insisted that if he was to be in charge his contacts should run immediately to the Secretary and there should be nothing intervening. What he evidently had in mind was Ezekiel and the group of men that are contacting the Secretary direct and to whom he objects." Davis also pointed out that Peek was opposed to the production control program and he thought much could be gained under the marketing agreement section of the bill. He said Peek was an internationalist in his viewpoint and believed greater effort should be made to open up foreign markets rather than to run to cover in our own market. Chester went on to point out that in this respect he thought his views did not check with those of Tugwell, Ezekiel and Wilson. He, himself, while somewhat cautious clearly leaned toward the Peek viewpoint. He said he was having a meeting last night with the Secretary and Peek, with the purpose of ironing out any differences. I think Chester sincerely feels the farm bill is loaded with dynamite and the Secretary is in a very difficult position.

July 20, 1933.

Last night the following group met at Dr. Tugwell's residence to discuss with him the foreign service work of the Bureau—Messrs. [P. O.] Tyhus, [J. B.] Gibbs, [L. R.] Edminster, [L. D.] Mallory, [P. K.] Norris and myself.[31] We had a very satisfactory session. After some preliminaries we got into a discussion of the foreign service and I presented the highlights and the activities at the present time, stressing the fact that to quite a degree we had concentrated on current crop market reporting activities but had also initiated several studies the purpose of which was to analyze the factors affecting long time trends in competition and demand. Tugwell was especially interested in the work which Norris had done on cotton, as illustrative of this type of thing. I also put considerable stress on the work we had done on trade barriers, pointing out that further analysis by countries was necessary, dealing with agriculture in its relation to the entire economic life and national policy of the country, to arrive at a conclusion as to the possibility of increased trade relations between us and such countries.

Tugwell expressed keen interest in the activities of the foreign service and reiterated what he had told me in private conversation before, that he was interested in developing the Latin American markets and that we should have several men stationed in South American countries, including Mexico. He has also been interested in the reopening of Russia and the establishment of an office there. In general he has made a statement that as soon as recognition of Russia takes place we should immediately send a man to that post.

I think Tugwell is also optimistic about increasing our market in the Orient. To a great extent Tugwell's reactions were along very general vague lines but he manifested an interest in the foreign service, which is in marked contrast to the position which he initially took with reference to the service. I am merely noting at this time that when we received our first statement on the budget cuts both market news and the foreign service were eliminated. I then protested to the Secretary vigorously and the foreign service was restored. It is really quite amusing to observe how his position has shifted completely in this matter.

Yesterday afternoon I had occasion to visit with the Secretary about the market news and told him very directly and bluntly that I thought he was making a serious mistake by continuing his present uncertain policy, the market news was being undermined, we were losing our good men, a lot of ill-will was being built up and it was not doing him or the Department any good. I asked the Secretary if he had read the memorandum I

31. All were associated with the Foreign Agricultural Service which was located in the Bureau of Agricultural Economics. Edminster was in charge of research; the others were foreign representatives home on leave.

sent over requesting $1,020,000 with which to operate the market news. He said he thought he had and he called in [W. A.] Jump. When Jump came in the Secretary said, "Nils wants $1,020,000 to restore the market news" and asked what could be done about it. Jump was very uncomfortable and said he did not know what he could do, that the $150,000 they had set up over the $575,000 was a balance carried over that they had developed in the adjustment of the budget. The only way he saw to give us $150,000 over that program was to take it from barberry or blister rust investigations. Jump then pointed out that if the request which the Department was making for public works funds to handle blister rust and barberry eradication were allowed, he said he thought the approval of the President would enable them to take care of the market news as I had requested.

In the course of the conversation while Jump was there, I had occasion to make reference to the fact that the market news project had demonstrated its value and that ought to be apparent from the reactions that came in from all sections of the country and while it was too bad that other projects should suffer, I could not see how they could operate the market news to good advantage without restoration of the funds requested. Wallace made the remark then that Tugwell did not have that view to begin with and that he was responsible for the complete elimination of the market news. I countered by saying that I thought probably Tugwell had had occasion to change his views on that subject too. I also added at that time that it was my recollection that Tugwell had marked the Foreign Service also for complete elimination.

This morning I told him, the Secretary, that it had been reported to me that Senator [Harry F.] Byrd[32] had had a visit with [Lewis] Douglas and that Douglas in his presence had dictated a note to him, the Secretary of Agriculture, requesting him to make $900,000, or as much of the appropriation available to the Bureau as was necessary to restore the service. The Secretary, kiddingly, remarked to Milloy (Minneapolis Tribune) who was with us, that now that both Nils and Douglas were trying to force the market news issue. I countered by reminding him of what he told me about Douglas' request to him that he make $900,000 or more available to restore the market news in order to take the pressure off the President.

August 12, 1933.

The morning Council meetings are enlightening from many points of view. For one thing, I am impressed with the fact that there is still confusion of thought and very inadequate coordination of effort. Peek measures everything in terms of parity prices and the effect upon

32. Former Governor and newly appointed senator from Virginia.

agriculture of any move that is made in the whole recovery program. As an illustration, he with Tugwell had urged that the benefit payments be made to farmers even though they are very heavily indebted to the Government for seed loans and other advances. One case was brought up yesterday where the man was getting $60,000 in benefits under the cotton program and was owing the Government $80,000. That was such a glaring case that they admitted that it would hardly seem right to make a payment to the farmer and not reimburse the Government for at least part of the previous advance. But, the general disposition was to pay everything out to the farmer and ignore the interests of the Government.

In one of the recent sessions the question of the effect of the labor codes on agriculture was up for consideration. On this particular occasion some were urging the application of the labor code to agriculture and labor, and Wayne Taylor[33] read a telegram from a Georgia farmer . . . setting forth the view that the farmers should advance their wages in keeping with the advance in agricultural prices and, in short, come under the labor code program. Tugwell spoke up and said he thought that farmers had a very fine appreciation of the situation and stated a sound view point. There was division of opinion, however, in the group. Peek, I think, urging that it was not the practical thing to do. I was asked in regard to it and I told them that I thought it would impose an additional burden upon farmers that was unwarranted, that it would be practically impossible to carry through on a labor code because of conditions and, in general, too adverse a position. I was asked to have a statement prepared on this and yesterday morning I gave the highlights in that situation. The reaction was very favorable. Tugwell was not there. I do not know what his reaction would have been. I further made the statement that I thought the labor code applied to some of the processing and affiliated industries under the agreements would tend to increase the cost to agriculture and, in short, take additional income out of their pockets. They asked that I follow up on that and make a further report.

Perhaps growing out of my attendance at the sessions during the past two weeks, when I was asked by Mr. Peek to sit in and at which, from time to time, I have had something to say, General [William I.] Westervelt[34] had evidently taken quite a shine to me. He asked me if I would not drop in to his office yesterday morning and all he wished to tell me was that he was very anxious to have a real heart to heart talk with me on various matters and he referred to some of the things I have said in various sessions, stating that evidently our thinking was running along somewhat parallel lines.

Granducci was in to see me yesterday evening and made reference to his visit with General Westervelt and said that gentleman had taken a

33. Executive assistant to George Peek, AAA administrator, and later became an Assistant Secretary of the Treasury.
34. Director of the Division of Processing and Marketing in the AAA; formerly an executive officer of Sears, Roebuck, & Co.

real shine to me and had said the National Recovery people may have their Alexander Sachs,[35] but we have our Olsen.

[Jerome N.] Frank,[36] the irrepressible Jew, is in evidence at all the meetings. You would gain the impression that a very large part of the job of administering the Act is of a legal nature and I suspect that is a very important angle of the work, but he is pressing for enlargement of his staff continually and is very sore because his appointments have been held up. At a meeting one or two mornings ago, he took a good vigorous crack at [Charles J.] Brand[37] and as much as said that he was the one who was preventing the appointment of his men. Also at one of the meetings he reported on the session he had with [James A.] Farley,[38] [Julien K.] Friant[39] and others regarding the matter, at which Farley had taken a very definite stand for the appointment of lawyers with political background. Peek, on that occasion, said he could do nothing with Friant and, in general, I sense that they are in a jam with Farley on the political angle of appointments. Tugwell on one of these occasions, also, made the flat statement that Brand was holding up the work, and I got through Granducci that Brand was getting in increasing Dutch with a good many in the Agricultural Adjustment Administration, in part because of his attitude on appointments and in part because of his views on various matters and his failure to get things through. Granducci said that Brand would not last long. . . .

August 21, 1933.

In the course of our walk this morning Wallace asked if I could not marshall our data on prices paid by farmers in such a way that we could get before him, weekly, just what is taking place. He expressed considerable concern about the widening of the spread between agricultural and non-agricultural prices and he shook his head at developments. Wallace made the statement that he thought we were running into some real difficulties. I told him that had been my fear throughout—that we were stepping up the agricultural price level and that labor was taking an utterly selfish position and that it was going to take an additional amount out of the farmers. He countered by saying that labor had always been that way and he feared very much that we were going to get into trouble. . . .

October 5, 1933.

Yesterday afternoon the Secretary called me into conference at his office with representatives of the Farmers' Union. Senator [Lynn J.]

35. Chief of the Research and Planning Division of the National Recovery Administration.
36. General counsel of the AAA.
37. Now coadministrator of the AAA.
38. Postmaster General and chairman of the Democratic National Committee.
39. A special assistant to the Secretary.

Frazier had a party in tow and Mr. [E. E.] Kennedy[40] was the outspoken spokesman for the group. They presented a gloomy picture of the agricultural situation, made a very severe attack upon the whole administration program, called attention to the inconsistency between the NRA and the AAA programs and particularly stressed this fact that if NRA could fix prices for industry, then AAA could fix prices for agriculture. The Secretary was sort of on the spot and clearly tried to handle the matter in a diplomatic way to avoid arousing them. For that reason I kept out of much of the discussion, except as to the farm debt, foreclosure end of it. Toward the end of the conference they attacked the cost of production figures of the Bureau and the Secretary rather expressed sympathy with their approach in this matter. He stated, however, in fairness to the Bureau that what we sought to do was to present the cost for the past year and what they were trying to do was to present estimates of what costs should be if farmers were getting returns that industrial capital entrepreneurs in industry were getting. I decided that it was well to keep out of the controversy and the Secretary said he would discuss it further with me.

(This morning walking down I brought it up and said that probably we might do something to present this other view. I said we would be glad to work it over and to talk it up with him.)

Referring back to the conference in the Secretary's office—following the cost of production episode, Senator Frazier referred to the revised statement on wheat which we put out and which stepped up the figure somewhat. He said that sort of statement should not be put out. Wallace stepped out and banged his fist down on the desk and said this Department was not going to juggle statistics in order to help the farmer. He banged down time and again and showed quite a bit of anger.

October 5, 1933 [*a second entry*].

I just returned from a delightful conference with Budget Director [Lewis] Douglas and was very favorably impressed with his personality and his whole attitude of mind. He was apologetic for not meeting his appointment and very easily edged into the matter we had under consideration. He launched out by saying he would like to tell me just a little bit of the philosophy he had in mind in the situation and I told him I would be delighted to hear his views. So, he told me that he sensed definitely that the N.R.A. program was probably pushing non-agricultural prices exceedingly high and widening the disparity between agricultural and non-agricultural prices. He said that the problem of raising agricultural prices was an exceedingly difficult one and that another serious element in the problem was wages of labor. He stressed the need of balance between the several segments of our economic life, and in this connection emphasized the importance of reviving the heavy industries as

40. A strong advocate of the "cost of production" approach to resolving the farm problem.

employers of labor and he went on to point out that until the currency factor was stabilized he thought there would be real difficulty in getting those investigations under way. Then, to my surprise, he said that what they should try to do in their negotiations with Great Britain was to arrive at some agreement as to the value of gold and, at any rate, fix the points between which gold prices shall fluctuate as between the two countries. The immediate effect of that he admitted might be depressing to prices and he therefore thought it would be very necessary to parallel this move with an effort to increase agricultural exports to Great Britain and in turn take non-competititve products from Great Britain. This would mean an adjustment in tariffs but, he said, he did not see any hope as to the ultimate solution of this problem unless we were prepared to stabilize the currency factor and make concessions on our tariffs. Intimately associated with this was, of course, the international debt problem but he said he believed it was utterly impossible to collect these debts and he was favoring a policy of cancellation. . . .

In the course of our conversation Douglas asked if the Secretary's views ran along the same line. I told him that I was quite sure that the Secretary was thinking along lines of maintaining foreign markets and making real concessions on international debts. Since Douglas expressed so much interest in obtaining material from us I told him I thought there were various elements in the picture on which we could throw considerable light, and I mentioned the farm mortgage situation. Before I got that out, he said, "I am working on that very situation and would like very much to see what you have." I told him there was an increase in the foreclosures, and before I could finish that statement he said, "Do you know why?" I said, "Yes, in anticipation of any inflation?" "Yes," he said, "in order to get their portfolios in shape for the deposit insurance was another reason," and he expressed keen desire to have such material as I could give him on that.

As I was leaving, Douglas said he appreciated my calling and wanted me to feel free to call again if he could be of service.

October 7, 1933.

Dr. [O. C.] Stine asked me yesterday if I knew how the policy developed with reference to the Government purchase of food and clothing supplies for distribution to the needy. I told him I thought I had some idea regarding it, but asked what he had in mind. He said that at the time the small pig killing program was under way, Mrs. Roosevelt called Chester Davis and raised the question as to destruction of meat supplies when millions of people were starving and she asked if these supplies could not be given to the needy. Action was taken immediately on the basis of that suggestion, and from that the larger program developed.

Stine also said that the Statistical Council,[41] of which he is a member, had been giving some thought to the price fixing program of the NRA and a good deal of skepticism was present in their group in connection with the "loss leader" item, the rather novel suggestions which had been made of letting the industry itself organize itself to buy up supplies that were used as "loss leaders" and thus prevent their depressing effect upon prices. He said that this was quite confidential but that it seemed to receive a good deal of support from various members of their group. . . .

October 12, 1933.

In this morning's walk with the Secretary to my surprise he made a statement quite early in our walk that he was gradually coming to believe that the way out was in weighting down the prices of things farmers buy. This grew out of an exchange of comments we had regarding the dairy agreements. . . . In connection with this same matter he also, to my surprise, remarked that he thought that we were failing to reckon with the competition between commodities, that it was dangerous to get the price of one commodity far out of line with that of another, and that was what we were doing in the case of milk. He said that might, of course, lead to a conclusion that we will do nothing at all if we have to move them all up at some time but to follow the other course would bring us no end of difficulty. This is rather far-reaching recognition on his part of some of the fundamentals that we have stood for and which I have from time to time stressed in conversation with him.

In this same connection the Secretary said, rather bluntly, that he was beginning to think Peek did not have executive capacity to keep things going and he asked me what I thought of it and I told him I had not been close enough to the scene to be entitled to an opinion but I was conscious of the fact that such things as the milk agreement matter had been handled in a rather disappointing way. . . . This comment of the Secretary tallies with my suspicions as to what is developing. There seem to be cleavages in the personnel everywhere. Chester Davis was brought in to coordinate the administration end but Wallace told me this morning that Peek was holding him off. Frederick Lee[42] is, of course, serving as Peek's special attorney and it is said that he is being paid out of Peek's pocket. [Jerome N.] Frank, of course, is thought to be reflecting the Wallace-Tugwell opinion. "Bottleneck" seems to be the favored description applied to spots in the organization where action is choked, such as

41. The Central Statistical Board or Council, established by Executive Order No. 6225 on July 27, 1933, was charged with promoting the coordination and improvement of the statistical services of the federal government involved in carrying out the purposes of the National Industrial Recovery Act.

42. Peek's personal counsel advising him on the controversies besetting the AAA. Peek had little confidence in the general counsel of the AAA, Jerome N. Frank.

Frank and his legal crowd, Dr. [Frederick C.] Howe[43] and his consumer bunch and Wayne Taylor and his associates and finally Mr. [Glenn] McHugh.[44]

The Secretary, of course, gives the impression of being a much harrassed man and what I fear is that he is giving most of his thoughts to the abstract phases of the program, particularly statistical analysis with which he loves to work, and that he is not keeping himself close enough to the actual realities of the situation.

October 24, 1933.

Mr. [F. J.] Hughes[45] tells me this morning that the rumor was floating around very generally in the Agricultural Adjustment Administration, last night, that George Peek is going to resign. We have nothing beyond that mere bit of a rumor. This in a way ties in with certain comments which the Secretary has made in the course of our morning walks.

One morning the Secretary raised the question as to what I thought of Peek as an Administrator, whether or not I thought he was getting things done. I then told him I thought Peek had a great deal of capacity but of course there were a thousand and one things to do and I realized that there was a lack of coordination and failure to get action on such things as, for instance, the dairy agreements. In this connection, also, I recall various clashes of viewpoint that have been nicely staged in the Council meeting. For example, when Peek made the point regarding the fixing of parity prices and Wallace stated he did not think that was quite the right approach to take, that what we needed to do was to move up prices of commodities in such a way that we did not upset the relationship of one to the other. Wallace in this matter is right. . . .

November 3, 1933.

This morning in my walk with the Secretary I had occasion to refer to the conference with the five Governors and the hot situation with which they were confronted.[46] I expressed the assumption that probably what they wanted was an absolute fixing of prices and he agreed that this

43. A distinguished urban reformer who was consumers' counsel in the AAA.

44. A special assistant to George Peek. He left the AAA when Peek did.

45. Business manager of the AAA.

46. On October 25, 1933, Governor Clyde Herring of Iowa called for a conference of midwestern governors to discuss the farm program. Earlier in the month Governor William Langer of North Dakota, because of the drop in wheat prices and the increase in the price of commodities purchased by farmers brought about in part by NRA codes, declared an embargo on any commodity selling below the cost of production. Early in November five midwestern governors came to Washington and called for both immediate inflation and price-fixing.

was the case. I gained from the conversation that the Governors are on a hot spot politically and they are afraid of the Holiday Association and they are really rushing to the Administration to head off the underhand tactics of the Milo Reno crowd.[47] The Administration evidently is disposed to go quite a distance with them since Wallace said they were meeting with the Governors in his office and were going to draft some kind of a plan under which they might agree to fix prices and allocate to individual growers the amount they could sell at those fixed prices. I asked how they were going to force the consumers to buy at those fixed prices. The Secretary smiled rather sillily and said that was a problem that would be dealt with as it arose and I said, "Yes, and meanwhile you will be taking over huge supplies in order to sustain such prices."

November 7, 1933.

At the Council meeting yesterday morning the dairy mess came out again for airing. . . . Peek suggested that the Federal Trade Commission and the Department of Justice be requested to investigate the monopolistic practices of the distributors and it seemed to be generally agreed that would be the procedure. Wallace was there and assented. My impression is that they are not nearer the solution of the milk situation than they were three months ago and seem to be muddling around very badly.

The farm strike[48] has them badly worried and they are almost frantic in their efforts to get out the wheat checks and advance the corn loan program. In connection with the corn loan program I had occasion to state in this morning's meeting that they would undoubtedly find a good many serious violations of the sealing and that, therefore, a reasonably careful inspection should be provided. To this Peek turned to me and said, "Can you provide the supervision?" I stated, "No, sir, we cannot," and the vehemence with which I spoke aroused a chuckle all around and the matter was immediately dropped. . . .

Wallace made the following pertinent comment in connection with the corn program—that it had great possibilities for trouble next year when the Government would find itself holding corn on farms which would have to be sold and when sold would break the market as much as 10¢ to 15¢ a bushel. Mr. Peek countered, "That may all be but at the present time we have a farm strike pending and something has to be done." In this morning's conference Wallace read a wire from Bill

47. Milo Reno of the Farm Holiday Association endorsed the governors' proposals and threatened drastic action unless the Administration responded favorably. Reno blamed Wallace and the AAA for the continuing depression in agriculture because of their refusal to consider "cost of production."

48. The Farm Holiday Association called for a farm strike after the governors' demands were turned down. This situation prompted Wallace on November 11 to leave on a tour of the Midwest to explain the farm program.

Hirth,[49] suggesting the calling of a conference here at Washington of the Committee of Twenty-Two or such farm leaders as he might select, to go over the entire program of the Agricultural Adjustment Administration and formulate what they thought would be the best program. Peek said he thought it would be a good thing. The prairies were on fire and it was important to allay the criticisms. Wallace said he did not agree. So the discussion went around some and they finally said that they could not ignore them and they might meet them in the West and they might meet them here and that it might be better to have a big conference after Congress convenes in order to use it as a medium to influence Congress to accept the legislative program they propose. I finally stepped into the discussion and said, "I would like to suggest that it might be strategic for the Secretary to invite Hirth and possibly a few other leaders to meet him at Des Moines for an informal discussion of the program in general and the ideas they have with reference to a conference and in that way have them feeling good for the time being and lay the groundwork for a possible big conference after the new year." This suggestion met with immediate approval and it was so arranged.

A memorandum had just come over from General [Hugh] Johnson (NRA) which the Secretary brought back with him, remarking that he had a hot one and on reading it, it developed that some representative of the NRA was criticizing the Agricultural Adjustment Administration very seriously for the dilly-dallying in getting the codes through, that that was interfering with the work of the NRA and carried the further suggestion that the President should be asked to retransfer the authority from the AAA back to the NRA to handle these codes dealing with the industries. Johnson added a comment stating that evidently the situation called for some correction. They all sensed that this was a pretty hot one and they all looked at each other and at Wallace, and Wallace asked if it was true that there were so many codes held up. Dr. [Frederic C.] Howe then commented stating that they were making progress, the machinery was all set up and functioning fine, things were going along nicely and there was no undue delay. [William I.] Westervelt looked at Howe squarely and said that he could not agree, that there was basis for the charge of serious delay, all of which was directed at Dr. Howe. So, the squabbles seem to run along merrily.

After the Council meeting the Secretary called me back to his office and I discovered that George Peek and [Frank C.] Walker, the Executive Director of the National Emergency Council,[50] were there. Wallace was discussing a plan of organization encompassing the complete hierarchy

49. Editor of the *Missouri Farmer* and president of the Missouri Farmers' Association.

50. The National Emergency Council was in effect a subcommittee of the Executive Council consisting of those cabinet members and agency administrators most directly involved in combatting the depression crisis. Walker was executive director of the Emergency Council and executive secretary of the Executive Council.

from the President through the Executive Council through a Director of Compliance, Director of Information and Education and then a series of county boards under which there would be various compliance, farm credit, banking and other local committees. The whole conception seemed to be to consolidate the entire organization and great emphasis was placed upon compliance and enforcement. In general I gained the impression that what Walker was thinking of was a more or less permanent well-knit organization that would jam the whole program down the throats of the American people. The discussion went along and both Peek and Wallace threw in favorable comments and did not seem to find much objection to the organization or to any phases, although Peek's disposition was to go easy on tying up everything locally. . . .

November 18, 1933.

. . . Granducci in the course of his conversation with me last week, and which he repeated yesterday afternoon said that [Jerome] Frank in extenuation of the assumption by lawyers to speak on the economic phases of the program referred to Peek as "plain dumb." In the conversation which I had with Granducci yesterday and at which time he laid before me the page which he had written on the situation in the Three As., explaining in response to my inquiry as to where he had gotten his information that he had had an hour's session with Peek and Peek was enraged and furious, pointing out that a bunch of theorists and radicals were holding up the program and were set on upsetting the whole social order. He said Peek went into the whole matter in a great deal of detail and stated that the situation had reached the breaking point and that he was going through with it. In the course of the conversation he, in turn, referred to Frank as a theorist and radical and so on and that invariably whenever any legal opinion came up delivered by Frank he would say, "Let a real lawyer see this," meaning Frederick Lee. . . .

Incidentally, I asked him why he classed Chester Davis with the realists. He said that he felt quite sure that he was on safe ground there because in passing through Peek's office he leaned over to Peek's secretary and asked her where Davis stood and she said, "Davis is with us." Granducci laughingly added, "You know Peek's and Frank's secretaries just cordially hate each other."

December 1, 1933.

. . . Granducci said he had dug out the following facts regarding the appointment of lawyers, that a man in order to qualify for a pivotal position in the Agricultural Adjustment Administration must meet three requirements: (1) He must have written approval of Felix Frankfurter,[51] and Granducci went on to add that a letter of approval from Frankfurter was equivalent to an appointment—a recommendation from the Democratic high command was not. (2) He must be a member of the order of _____ (Mr. Olsen could not remember the name of this organization) and (3) He must be an adherent of the [liberal] social economic school of thought. I raised the question whether there was not another very definite requirement. He smiled and said, "You mean racial?" I said, "Yes." He said, "I suspect that is the case but I cannot prove it." I said, "You know there is intense feeling developing on the racial issue and now I am speaking of sentiment growing up from without." He said, "That is different," but I said, "Do not take my word for it but talk to Peek, McHugh and some of the other men across the way."

Granducci then raised the question as to who would win out in this contest, Peek or Wallace. I told him, "You made the statement a few days ago when you dropped in for a few minutes that Governor [W. I.] Myers[52] told you you were betting on the wrong horse when you were betting on Peek." Granducci then said that Myers had said that he thought Wallace stood well with the President and he thought he would win in the contest. In the conversation it developed that Morgenthau has a most intense hatred for Tugwell and would not have him in his own department, and does not believe he should be in a Government department. . . .

Harking back to the contest between Wallace and Peek, I suggested that the analysis probably had not been carried sufficiently far. If Wallace was permanently and inseparably associated with Tugwell, Frank and Ezekiel and that group there would be some question of his survival. However, if he would rid himself of those barnacles and then take definite command of the whole situation the likelihood was he would win because he still had a strong following in agriculture as a champion of the farmer. That is also true of Peek and the removal of either one would be a rather delicate matter and the disposition undoubtedly would be to hold both of them.

December 4, 1933.

. . . This morning I walked down with the Secretary, as has been the custom since he came. Ever since the early weeks of my walks with him, when I injected various matters of a policy character and met several

51. A professor at the Harvard Law School who recommended to the President, cabinet members, and other New Deal administrators former students for posts in various departments and agencies.

52. Deputy Governor of the Farm Credit Administration; Henry Morgenthau was Governor.

nasty rebuffs, I have refrained from raising any questions that affected his administration of the Department, or of his work, confining myself to specific problems regarding which he had asked me or which had come up in Council meetings. It has been my purpose to assiduously avoid injecting myself into any of his affairs in such a way that he could say that I was concerning myself with things that were his business.

Just by way of reminder of the rebuffs, I recall (1) at the time of my conference with the Secretary when he was in Senator [Joseph T.] Robinson's office, where I submitted a copy of the report on "Farm Mortgage Debt" and at which he glanced hurriedly without any knowledge of its contents, he remarked that he was afraid that it was a "mess of maggots"; (2) the second day of his administration as Secretary of Agriculture, the designation of [Mordecai] Ezekiel as Economic Adviser, calling me in and introducing Ezekiel as his Economic Adviser and naming members of the staff as members of a committee he wanted to work with Ezekiel; (3) designating a committee on reorganization without as much as mentioning it to me and putting [W. F.] Callander and [L. C.] Gray of this Bureau on that committee; (4) the nasty slap that followed publication of the Mortgage Debt report; namely, Morgenthau, Jr., had taken offence at the publication of the report and spoke to Wallace about it. In that connection the Secretary referred to my "competitive spirit" and that he did not want any competition between departments. At that time I pointed out that I had labored with his Father in helping to defend the Bureau and the foreign agricultural service against the encroachments of the Hoover regime and in that he had contributed and that I did not see but that some attention to the interests of the Department was quite in order. I had him on the spot and he did not have any kind of a counter; (5) his remark when I asked for a meeting with him and Tugwell on land utilization with Gray and myself and he expressed indifference, if not reluctance. He said if such a meeting was held he thought Gray should present the matter; (6) a remark he made in some connection which I do not now recall, he stated that he did not like my arguments too much because he did not want to be convinced against his will. It was really a compliment to me but it indicated an attitude of mind that was most surprising; (7) on one occasion when we were walking over the bridge just below the Shoreham Hotel at the time the early inflation move was on, he evidently construed it as an effort on my part to pry into his cabinet information and he merely looked at me as much as to express reproof and I countered by stating that all I was considering was the problem from an economic point of view.

Another thing that has interested me is the Secretary's failure to invite me to his home at any time since his arrival until the tea that was held the other night when the Agricultural Adjustment Administration and his own office was heavily represented and I was the only representative from this Bureau. Such men as [L. H.] Bean, Fleming, Russell Lord, and all his personal friends in the Agricultural Adjustment Administration were present. Mr. and Mrs. Peek were there and Mrs. Peek referred to the fine visit George had at my apartment, how he enjoyed it and whispered that she would like to have me come over to see them, to which I expressed my thanks and desire to come.

I cite these instances in order to illustrate the peculiar relationship that obtains—one of evident friendship and yet acts that could be construed as anything but friendly and then the continued desire to walk with me daily to the Department and to chatter generally in the most friendly way reflecting frequently, as he does, the mental upset under which he is working.

This morning I thought possibly the Secretary might refer to the split between him and Peek, or between Peek and Tugwell and the articles that appeared in the "New York Herald-Tribune" for Monday and Tuesday, as well as [Frank] Kent's article in the "Baltimore Sun," but not a word was said, although it is a situation which strikes at the very foundation of his administration.

Last Friday, December 1, Lord [William Waldorf] Astor[53] and the Hon. R. H. Brand[54] came to my office and in pursuance with an engagement which Lord Astor had made by personal note prior to his sailing, and I took a few moments to find out what their situation was so as to see if I could arrange for a dinner, but found out that they had arranged for a dinner at which they were to have their Virginia relatives present, but they expressed a keen desire to spend part of the evening with me. In fact they asked me to join them at the dinner. I thanked them and explained that under the circumstances it probably would be best to have dinner with their relatives and meet at my apartment at 8:30. I spoke to Wallace about this and he expressed a desire to meet Astor and Brand but suggested that he come after dinner as he had just returned from Warm Springs and thought he should take dinner at home. This was agreeable and I said I would check with him later. I saw George Peek and he was very pleased with the suggestion and was ready to come to dinner, but we arranged for the evening session and I had at my apartment Lord Astor, Mr. Brand, Mr. Langhorne,[55] Wallace and Peek. The conversation was fluid and interesting and dealt considerably with the present farm program. Lord Astor was very clever in putting questions to Peek and Wallace and Peek was really freer in answering. Wallace at one or two times made a rather pointed slap at the policy of Great Britain in

53. Owner of the *Observer* who was long interested in agricultural affairs and had just published a study entitled *The Planning of Agriculture*.
54. Managing director of Messrs. Lazard Brothers Co., merchant bankers and prominent in British international trade circles.
55. A Virginian related to Brand, whose wife was a daughter of Chiswell Dabney Langhorne of Virginia.

adopting a quota program and in breaking away from free trade and the like, but he too enjoyed the discussion.

Early in the evening calls began coming in from various people in the Department, [M. C.] Merrill,[56] Stedman,[57] Frederick Lee and others. Frederick Lee said the liquor agreement and code would have to be signed by the Secretary by eleven o'clock and he said he had arranged to bring it out and he merely wanted to tell me he was coming with the codes. Frederick Lee, [Edward G.] Lowry of the Treasury Department and [Theodore Penfield] Walker, Vice President of Commercial Solvents, came to my apartment with the codes (Walker, by the way, I understand is a cousin, or some degree of relation to President or Mrs. Roosevelt). A table was cleared for action, moved in front of the Secretary, the codes were laid out and after some superficial examination his signatures were affixed, with the rest of us rather silently looking on. As the codes were finished I very discreetly arranged to keep hard liquors out of the picture, but I had hard cider, soft cider, gingerale appear—all of which were legal—and I said, "Gentlemen, here is soft cider just off the press. We drink to the new liquor code." As I sat back and mused upon the quirks of life I concluded this was a rather unusual occasion—a bone-dry Secretary of Agriculture in the presence of a violently dry British Lord, in the domicile of a throat parched Norseman, signing the agreement to import four million gallons of sparkling, luscious liquors—what could be more divinely conceived? . . .

December 6, and December 8, 1933.

Last night General Westervelt took dinner with me. He is a very unusual man, very keen, alert and well-read, personality, with a deep knowledge of the physical sciences, evidently an expert in higher mathematics, widely read in philosophy, very adept in drawing upon his background of knowledge in illustrating the greatest variety of subjects.

We very frankly discussed the present situation. He, of course, is distressed. He likes Wallace but he thinks he is a mystic. He has on walks entered on philosophic discussions of the "New Deal" and has been driven to conclude that there is an element of mysticism which controls his thinking. Westervelt has taken issue with him to break it down and has insisted that after all such a thing as human emotions, ambitions, ideals and close analysis can, in the main, be broken down into interests, senses and activities, mental and physical, of the human being on which you can put your finger. He said Wallace's theory of social justice

56. Chief of Publications in the Office of Information of the Department of Agriculture.
57. Director of Information and Publicity in the AAA.

grows out of this vague concept and undoubtedly has a great bearing on the position that he is taking on the battle that is now impending in the Department. He thought Wallace was in the main in sympathy with Tugwell's thinking. He had, however, expressed the very highest regard for Wallace and he went very far in stating that much could be done to reform the economic and social order. He stated that he was the original technocrat and a real leader of that movement. He was out in the open on the matter in a propaganda way and his activities had been overshadowed and considerably impaired by the wildcatting of such men as [Howard] Scott[58] who got on tangents. . . .

This morning I walked down with the Secretary and we rode a short distance beyond Du Pont Circle and walked the rest of the way. There was then a period of silence in our walk, nothing further was brought up by me and nothing was said by him. He got to Pennsylvania Avenue and he said, "Let us stop. I want to get a copy of the *New York Herald-Tribune* and the *New York Times.*" Of course, his interest in getting them was tied up with the battle waging between him, Peek and other gentry in the department. We walked a little farther and as he was in front of the White House he said, "Did you see that [Drew] Pearson had libelled me?" I said, "No, what did he say?" "He said that I was bone dry but that on occasion I took a drink." I replied, "Well, I think I can testify that that is not in keeping with the facts. What are you going to do about it?" He said he did not know. I said, "Why don't you invite Pearson over and tell him it is not true and if he is a man of honor and possesses the best ethics of his profession he will express regret and make amends in a public statement." Wallace replied, "No, that would not do." I replied, "I do not know how else you can meet it. My disposition would be that as between men a frank and direct way of handling the matter would have some merit."

The purpose of this statement commenting on the morning walk is to illustrate the attitude of the Secretary in his personal relations with me. What would be more natural than for the Secretary to bring up of his own volition the great battle that is now waging in the Department and which affects his personnel forces. If personal friendship and confidence were genuine and real, he should be interested in any information which I might be able to give him and in any reaction I might have when viewed in the light of the various episodes of the past eight months in which he has struggled to maintain a contact and close personal relation-

58. An engineer who is usually cited as the leading figure in the technocracy movement during the Great Depression. Technocrats endorsed a form of politico-industrial organization of society based on advanced technology and automation in which value would be determined by the amount of energy consumed in production and in which "energy certificates," replacing money, would help achieve a more equitable distribution of industrial products. See Henry Elsner, Jr., *The Technocrats: Prophets of Automation* (Syracuse, 1967) for an overall discussion.

ship on the one hand, and a policy of undermining and even, at times, criticizing. I can draw but one conclusion and that is that his affiliations, after all, are definitely associated with Tugwell and the radical group and that somehow he can not see himself conferring with me about these matters that are of such concern to him. Nevertheless, when specific matters are taken up with him and made specific issues, I think I have invariably won my argument and received approval and support.

December 9, 1933.

Granducci was in to see me December 7 at which time he gave me a number of very interesting bits. He said the Secretary was reported to have said that he would not stand for the resignation of [Jerome] Frank. Granducci said [Chester] Davis had done a remarkable job of keeping himself free from entangling alliances. He said, however, that the impression was abroad that Davis leaned to the Tugwell group. He was also quoted by a person who is very close to him, and whose name Granducci did not give me, to the effect that he feared Peek would have to go. . . .

This morning I again walked down with the Secretary, after having called him, reminding him that it was raining and raising the question as to whether he wanted to walk. He said, "I don't think it is raining very much. I would like to walk." I said, "All right I shall be right over"— this, despite the fact that I find it necessary to put in a call every morning in order to get up and be ready for my walk and then despite the further fact that I have to sit down in the lobby of Wardman Park Hotel and, invariably, wait a half hour before he shows up. This morning we got into the car and rode to Du Pont Circle and in that period I at once launched into the International Institute of Agriculture situation, H. C. Taylor and matters of that kind. The Secretary expressed himself very definitely against the continuation of the Committee for the Nation[59] or any maneuvering to give it new direction. He said he did not want to be involved in any mechanizations to upset the present management. This is on the theory that it is more or less unethical and, furthermore, he did not want to take on any more enmities. We walked down to the corner of Pennsylvania Avenue and 17th Street and stopped at the newsstand as we did yesterday morning, but this morning he got a copy only of the *New York Herald-Tribune,* and at once glanced at [Ernest] Lindley's article on the row and that at once confirmed my suspicion that the Lindley articles are inspired by the Wallace-Tugwell group here in the Department.

59. An organization of business and farm leaders seeking to raise prices by adjusting monetary policies in favor of inflation.

This morning I drove on down to the Department and bravely walked through the lobby of the Main Building with the Secretary, in the thought that it might not be too bad to show that I was not altogether on the outside as far as the Secretary was concerned—at least in appearance.

December 13, 1933.

Yesterday afternoon [C. W.] Kitchen and I called on Congressman [James P.] Buchanan and found him in a most delightful frame of mind. He was glad to see us and entered into a most confidential discussion with us on various matters. He expressed grave concern regarding the Administration's program, particularly the NRA phases of it. He did not see anything in the gold price policy. He expressed considerable approval of the Agricultural Adjustment program which had brought money into the South and created a much better state of mind and economic situation. He stated that he was very fearful that the Administration would lose the support of the House even a year from now and the danger was even greater for three years. He expressed the belief that the only thing that could save the Democratic party would be a marked recovery of economic conditions. Buchanan said that right down in the breast of people who have been benefitted is a deep resentment against the bureaucracy that has been built up and the fear that they will be losing their individual rights. He said this appeared after the world war when the Democrats, likewise, had to carry the brunt of the load and it looked as though it was going to be repeated. I asked him if what he was saying was more or less the sentiment of the southern contingent, and he said it was distinctly so. He said however that he and his colleagues felt they had to go along with the program with a view to bringing us out of the depression. He said that he realized that that was the case but he said most of that came from the Middle West where radicals were bred and in that connection he asked about Chester Davis. I told him Chester Davis was a very level-headed man and a good selection. He said he was afraid of anyone who came out of the West. I assured him that this man was liberal but his feet were on the ground. Then I reminded him that a good many radicals—Democrats—came out of the East. "Oh," he said, "they are not Democrats. They have missions—they are different from the rest of us." I said, "You mean such men as Morgenthau, Tugwell?" He said, "Why yes, they are nothing but socialists." I said, "Well, are not many of these projects approved by the President himself?" He replied, "I have a very high regard for the President and he is trying to do a good piece of work but it does disturb me that the President seems to be so heartily in favor of the NRA program." . . .

December 15, 1933.

This morning I was coming down with the Secretary, and some remark was made by him regarding two men on Ickes' staff who had fainted as the result of the pressure under which they were working. I said that was merely indicative of what was going to happen throughout the Government, that people in our Bureau were being crowded to death and now on top of it all they were unloading the Civil Works Projects, some of which necessarily would be half-baked. I pointed out to him some of the facts regarding some of the Civil Works projects we had taken on and then made reference to the land utilization project which had been forced upon us by Ezekiel. I pointed out that when the Civil Works projects first came up I mentioned the possibility to Dr. [L. C.] Gray and he said "thumbs down" because of the new developments in land utilization now planned and the undesirability of launching such a project now. Ezekiel, however, had virtually given him instructions to formulate such a project, which he had asked be sent to him for transmittal direct to the Civil Works Administration. I told the Secretary that when this was brought to my attention I instructed Dr. [Laurence] Hewes' Office, which office he, the Secretary, had created for that purpose and thus to observe regular procedure. I went further and said that while this project had gone to the Civil Works Administration we had grave doubts about it, that I had not had opportunity to examine it and, as a Bureau, had not approved it. "Well," he said, "that is going too far. I wish you would give me a memorandum covering these developments." I said I would, that actions of this kind were getting to the point that I was not disposed to stand for them any longer. The Secretary seemed to be in the right mood and I said, "As a matter of fact, there have been a great many things that have been exceedingly galling and if it had not been for my high regard for you and my desire to cooperate and be helpful in every way, you would have had a major explosion on your hands." The Secretary laughed good naturedly and said that he realized that was the case and perhaps we might call this a "minor explosion." I said, "Yes, I think it would be minor in comparison with the Peek explosion[60] which is now on the front pages." . . .

Then, after a pause in our conversation, walking along he, to my utter surprise, said, "Nils, perhaps you can advise me on this. You know Peek's situation is a little difficult and I would like to see him get busy and complete his work. The President asked him for a report on this foreign trade matter. I am wondering if you could not help bring together the material that is needed in that connection for Mr. Peek." I

60. Peek, after seven months as head of the AAA, resigned on December 15 to become a special adviser to the President on foreign trade.

countered saying, "I certainly will be glad to do everything I can, H.A. I think we can bring some materials together, although it would be a huge job to take all of the data on foreign trade, analyze it and present a very succinct fine report." He said, "Maybe we should set aside a special allotment from the Agricultural Adjustment Administration funds for Mr. Peek to do this work and then terminate his authority in the Department." On this I made no comment. We were just pointing up nicely on this when we reached the Main Building and I said, "As matter of fact, Peek called me in late last night to ask me if I would not bring together this material and in discussing the question I said that I thought there were probably three broad phases that had to be dealt with: (1) a well reasoned statement of national policy with reference to foreign trade; (2) the bringing together of the material and squeezing out of it such basic facts as might be used for action moves in the very near future; and (3) the kind of organization set-up that would be most effective in coordinating the forces of the Government. Mr. Peek asked me if I would not prepare him a memorandum setting forth my views of the entire situation and this I promised to do." I added, "I suppose this is quite all right." The Secretary said, "Oh, yes." I said, "Possibly you would like to have a copy of that memorandum." He said, "Yes." (My problem now is one of determining whether I should speak to Peek about the delivery of a copy of Wallace. I think it is the thing to do.)

1934

January 2, 1934.

Granducci was in late last week and in that connection showed me the statement which he had tentatively prepared for his next letter, commenting on the low morale in the Department, the fear of reorganization, the intense feeling that had developed in the Forest Service and in the Bureau of Plant Industry over the appointment of the new Chiefs for those Bureaus—both, as he mentioned in his letter later, being Tugwell appointees. He said that his evidence was pretty good that Tugwell was figuring on extensive reorganization, probably along three lines headed by an Under Secretary and Assistant Secretaries. "Land Use" would probably be one, "Technical Production" work and then "Economics." However, his information was that probably Chemistry and some other small bureaus might be absorbed in the Land Use unit, but this Bureau would not. I asked him if he had any evidence on which to base this and he said he thought his evidence was pretty good. This noon in chatting with [W. W.] Stockberger[1] on the way back from lunch we elicited from him that certain reorganization matters were under way. He admitted that [A. F.] Woods was going out as Director of Scientific Work and would land in the Bureau of Plant Industry, that the program was undoubtedly to create an Under Secretary of Agriculture and two or three Assistant Secretaries. Just how their functions would be divided he was unable to say.

Granducci said there was a concerted effort now to draw the fire off Tugwell and an influential official friend of his (Morgenthau?). While on the one hand he was very anti-Tugwell, he was nevertheless disposed to indicate that the past scrap was between Peek and Wallace. Granducci said that [Raymond] Moley had also written [W. M.] Kiplinger,[2] himself,

1. Director of Personnel and Business Administration and head of the Division of Drug and Related Plants in the Bureau of Plant Industry.
2. Editor of the news service for which Oeveste Granducci worked.

that the scrap was between Wallace and Peek, and that Kiplinger was barking up the wrong tree. Granducci, Kiplinger and the rest of the boys know very definitely that this is nothing but a maneuver to pull the fire away from Tugwell.

In speaking of Chester Davis,[3] Granducci said he agreed with me that he was a bright, level-headed man and he had a very high regard for him. On the other hand, in the course of the fight Chester had gone out of his way to say that the scrap was not between Peek and Tugwell but was between Peek and the Secretary. Granducci stated that when Davis would say that his stock sank in his (Granducci's) estimation. In that connection he said that no one could tell him that there was not a concerted effort to pull the fire away from Tugwell, that [Milton S.] Eisenhower and [Alfred D.] Stedman spent at least a couple of hours at a time to try and convince him that the fight was between Peek and Wallace. . . .

January 17, 1934.

. . . This morning I met the Secretary as usual but he hesitated a bit and said that Mrs. Wallace would like to see me. So, I returned to the apartment and had a three-quarter hour visit with her and Wallace's Detroit sister.

Late yesterday afternoon I was over to see the Secretary on the apple quota matter and also to get to him a copy of our report on the incidence of the processing taxes. He then asked me about [G. B.] Thorne[4] being with him at the Committee hearing to handle the charts, etc. He asked me if that would not be better than to have [Mordecai] Ezekiel go along, and he smiled rather significantly, and I told him I thought that was a rather good thought and I was sure that Thorne would be glad to be with him and assist him. The Secretary then got up and paced the floor rather nervously, looking haggard, and said he was to have a visit with Morgenthau and Myers regarding the Agricultural Finance Division matter. I did not get the exact phase of it clearly, but I gathered that they were not together. I think it was Myers who said they were not asking for a transfer of insurance and taxation. Morgenthau and Wallace had evidently been in conference with the President regarding the Department's appropriations. The President's reactions were so favorable, indicating as I understood, that it would be agreeable to him if pressure were brought to restore those items, that he decided it would be a good time to raise the question of the Agricultural Finance Division.[5] So he

3. Now administrator of the Agricultural Adjustment Administration.
4. A statistician in the Division of Statistical and Historical Research, Bureau of Agricultural Economics.
5. Agricultural Finance was a general division in the Bureau of Agricultural Economics.

brought up this item and told the President that he thought it should not be transferred. The President rather blandly told him that, "Oh, I think that whole work might just as well be done in the Farm Credit Administration." Evidently the Secretary did not press the issue at all but he told me to play my cards carefully, but to go ahead.

February 13, 1934.

. . . At the White House reception, all of the section heads in the AAA were present, including [Jesse W.] Tapp,[6] [J. B.] Hutson,[7] [H. R.] Tolley[8] and all the rest of them, in contrast with merely the Bureau Chiefs representing the various bureaus of the Department. . . . Mrs. Tapp and I fell in together and Tapp said he had a "choice one." He said that he had been notified that there was a case of noncompliance under the canning code that was coming over from the NRA. He did not have the least idea what it was all about but a sealed letter came over and when he opened it to his surprise he found that the defendants in this case were [Charles Henry] Tugwell[9] and Silverman.[10] It was interesting from two points of view. The question has been raised as to the Jewish lineage of Tugwell and the reports so far have indicated that he was not Jewish. The name of the older Tugwell's partner, however, suggests undoubted Jewish blood there and at any rate a fast association with Jews in a business way. Even more significant, of course, is the fact that [Rexford] Tugwell's father had been cited for non-compliance with the program projected by the Administration.

Campbell (W. G.)[11] also commented again on the unusual relationship between Miss [Grace E.] Falke[12] and Tugwell, stating that he had never seen anything like it in his whole career in the Department. She seems to be sort of an alter ego and is present whenever he is in important sessions and he also refers matters to her for her to handle with administrative heads. Granducci and others are commenting on her as being another "Robbie" (Miss [Frances M.] Robinson of NRA).[13] In this connection it was interesting last Saturday morning (10 o'clock Council Meeting of Bureau Chiefs in Mr. Tugwell's Office) to note Miss Falke there with her notebook, watching with eagle eye any remarks made by

6. Chief of Special Crops, Production, Processing, and Marketing Divisions, AAA.
7. Chief of Tobacco Production, Processing, and Marketing Divisions, AAA.
8. Chief Economist for AAA.
9. An orchard farmer and fruit and vegetable canner in Wilson, New York, north of Buffalo on the southern shore of Lake Ontario. Both his and his wife's families hailed from the southern shores of England and included on his wife's side such families as the Franklins, Rexfords, and Tylers. On his side were Tugwells, Truslers, and Leaverses. See Bernard Sternsher, *Rexford Tugwell and the New Deal* (New Brunswick, 1964), p. 3.
10. I have been unable to further identify Silverman.
11. Chief of the Food and Drug Administration.
12. Tugwell's administrative assistant who later married him.
13. Assistant to National Recovery Administration Administrator Hugh S. Johnson.

Department people and, particularly, by me. Tugwell made an inane statement on the Land Use policy and all he managed to say was that they had in mind the Taylor bill which would provide for regulation of grazing on the Public Domain and the acquisition of more of the Public Domain by the Forest Service for regulated grazing. Wallace remarked, "Well, that probably would mean increased production," and Tugwell seemed to be embarrassed and he addressed himself to [Ferdinand A.] Silcox[14] and Silcox said it probably would mean greater production capacity of livestock, and Miss Falke at that particular moment seemed most intent in observing reflections of Department men. That reflects, of course, the impossible attitude between regular Department administrators and the "wrecking crew" in the Secretary's Office. . . .

March 13 and 17, 1934.

This morning I met the Secretary and Chester Davis as per appointment arranged and was interested to find that [C. W.] Warburton, following my conversation with him last night had also asked permission to sit in on the meeting. The conference grew out of a telephone call from the Secretary yesterday, at which time he asked if I could not approve the transfer of [W. G.] Finn[15] to the Tobacco Section of the Agricultural Adjustment Administration. At that time I told him of the drafts being made on the Bureau, explaining that they were so heavy that I thought it would be very useful for us to consider the question of policy in this connection. . . .

What I stressed was—if the Bureau is to be retained as a research institution then it must not be robbed of its best men continually and kept in a turmoil. If that were agreed to then what we should have is a field day where we would, so to speak, draw the line and determine upon such transfers as should be made and give the Bureau a chance to fill the vacancies and not come up to the end of the fiscal year with unexpended balances. Davis stated that it was not the thought to have the AAA enter upon research, that he did not know that [J. B.] Hutson was planning research in the field of tobacco, that what they needed were men, who had some research background, to serve in these administrative jobs. He put point blank to me the question of whether it was wrong for them to offer men positions of responsibility at an increase in salary. I told him "No" but that I thought they were making it exceedingly difficult for us by offering these men very extraordinary salaries when perhaps their work was not much different from what they were doing in the Bureau. Davis countered by saying that it was thought to enlarge their duties

14. Chief of the Forest Service.
15. An agricultural economist employed in the Statistical and Historical Research Division, Bureau of Agricultural Economics.

which would entail heavy responsibilities and long trying hours, such as the Bureau men did not have to contend with. I assured him that the Bureau men were carrying a very heavy load and were giving long hours to the work, but that there probably were cases where a very substantial increase in salary was warranted. Davis then said, "Instead of having a lot of friction, I would be disposed to put out an order forbidding the AAA to approach any Bureau people with reference to transfer," and that they would henceforth look to the outside for their people. I countered by saying, "I do not think it would be well to lay down a rule of that kind, that invariably there would be cases where such a transfer should be made and that such cases should be taken up by him and me and considered on the basis of the interest of the two institutions." I did add that I thought for administrative work they could well go outside and get good men who would fill the job, whereas we could not replace these men of outstanding research ability and that from the point of view of the Government it did not seem wise to convert good research men into administrators. Wallace made it clear that he expected the Bureau to continue its research, that there would be a certain amount of research required by the AAA and, in general, both Davis and Wallace clearly indicated that they were supporting the Bureau in its research program. They did make the point, however, that sometimes the Bureau's work was not attuned to the needs of the AAA and was not prompt enough. I said that those were matters that could be adjusted to a considerable degree if taken up with us, but that it made it very difficult for me to bring this about when the matters were not brought up directly with me. . . .

March 19, 1934.

Friday night (March 16) [Jesse W.] Tapp spent the evening with me at my apartment and unburdened himself in good shape. Tapp is wholly fed up on all of this "regimentation," and was particularly bitter against Tugwell. Tapp said that one of the most important things around here was to get Tugwell, [Jerome] Frank and [Frederick C.] Howe out of the picture so that revolution was not tied up with recovery. He said that it had become almost impossible for them to function under the provisions of the Agricultural Adjustment Act because, invariably, Tugwell, Frank, and Howe would inject their social reform ideas at some stage of the game. It became clear from what Tapp said that a rift very similar to the one that grew up between Peek, Frank and Tugwell is well under way between Davis and Tugwell and Frank. As a matter of fact there have been occasions when Davis was about to let the thing break. There are two things that, consistently, seem to be urged by Frank and Tugwell. Frank invariably tries to inject the requirement that the books of the industries concerned shall be completely open to the Department for fishing expeditions. Davis, Tapp and [H. R.] Tolley, evidently, have taken the position that that would merely prevent the consummation of their agreements. Another thing these men have tried to inject into the agreements is general compulsory grading of the product, irrespective of whether it is feasible or not. I asked Tapp to what extent the Secretary was conscious of the breach between Tugwell and Davis. He said he did not see how the Secretary could avoid taking cognizance of it. Tapp felt very keenly that something should be done to really put Tugwell on the spot and get him out of the picture. He says why is it not being played up in metropolitan papers that Tugwell's father is violating the agreements and codes and is now in the hands of the N.R.A. Compliance Board at Lockport, New York? As a matter of fact the local Lockport paper has written up the story, but the press generally has not really sensed the significance of it all. Tapp's correspondence with the N.R.A. Compliance Board in New York would no doubt be made available if called for. Tapp also said the attitude of the old gentleman Tugwell had been brought to the attention of Rex and he shrugged his shoulders and said, "Go after him."

April 23, 1934.

Several days last week I had a telephone exchange with Mrs. [Cornelia M.] Pierce, Secretary to Congressman [Walter M.] Pierce of Oregon, regarding the smut conditions in our Pacific Northwest wheat standard. There was a good deal of heat expressed. I managed to keep cool and told her we were giving the matter careful consideration. She told me that the Northwestern congressional delegation was having a meeting with the Secretary on the subject and she wanted all the facts before that meeting and I arranged to place the facts in her hands. . . .

Also last week the Secretary called me and said he had appointed a committee made up of [Edwin G.] Nourse,[16] Black (J. D.)[17] and [Walter P.] Hedden,[18] to consider the relationship between the Bureau and the Agricultural Adjustment Administration. This was the first I had heard of it and I said it was not clear to me what he had in mind. I realized there were certain problems of personnel, etc., we had been discussing from time to time but just what was the significance of the appointment of a committee was not clear to me. I suggested to the Secretary that it might be well for me to come over and have him explain the matter a little further. A little later on I went over and he was smiling as usual, but had an air of diffidence, which is rather a characteristic manifestation

16. Director of the Institute of Economics at the Brookings Institution.
17. At this time a professor of agricultural economics at Harvard.
18. An economist (associated at times with Nourse) who served as Chief of the Bureau of Commerce in the New York Port Authority.

when I come to his office, and he said, "Well, this has greater interest and promise than I originally thought. I just had a meeting with Dr. Nourse and I rather believe now that these men will appraise the whole situation and help determine the direction which the whole Agricultural Adjustment Administration program should take. It seems that it is rather necessary to determine upon the relation between the Bureau and the Agricultural Adjustment Administration, according to Dr. Nourse." I said I thought that was a very desirable thing to do. It was a question whether it should be done at this time, as there were many things in the situation that had disturbed me and others and I thought a thoroughly good appraisal of the situation was quite in order. . . . I spoke pretty frankly on the subject and he understood that I was in no pleasant frame of mind, but, as usual there was no decisiveness about his reaction and I was left without any conception as to just where he stood, except that in general he wishes to maintain the Bureau and its work but he also wishes to honor the Agricultural Adjustment Administration and their plans and so in a vacillating way he does not point up his reactions.

That same day Dr. Nourse called me and said, "Olsen, we are ganging up on you." I replied, "Yes, I hear there is some kind of a ganging up. When do we get together?" He asked, "How about tomorrow morning?" I said that was "jake" and so the three of them came over Monday morning. I greeted them by asking them to put all fire arms on the large table, but that if it came to using machine guns I wanted real action and wanted to make sure there was no jamming of the guns. We got off to a very easy, good start and Nourse seemed a little embarrassed at the outset. He started by saying he would like to have me express myself, and he asked what I knew about the whole matter. I told him about my conference with the Secretary and he wanted to know how I felt about the whole question of relations and I countered by saying that I thought it would be more logical for him to state just what his committee had been asked to do in order that I might then make pertinent comments. We had quite a little discussion in which Dr. Nourse said that he was not clear, himself, just what they were expected to do but it was a question of just how the Bureau should function in relation to the Agricultural Adjustment Administration, etc. I then made quite an extended statement in which I pointed out some of the problems in relationship, in the questions of bailiwick, the question of draft upon personnel and general administrative relations and indicated that there did not seem to be much difficulty in connection with the service work. There was some question as to what the Agricultural Adjustment Administration had in mind in connection with regulatory work, and [a] question in connection with Hutson's maneuvering and that in the matter of research work there were certain things that had developed which raised questions in my mind. I felt that Nourse and Hedden were reasonably friendly and Black was, on the other hand, ostensibly friendly but reflected the grand planning idea,

the new planning organization and the development of which I think
Tolley is primarily repsonsible. The Secretary in connection with his conference on this matter told me that Tolley had presented a very elaborate
extensive program for the Planning Division and that he, the Secretary,
had hesitated to approve it and that was really his reason for appointing
the committee.

April 26, 1934.

. . . There is undoubtedly a move under foot on the part of Tolley,
John D. Black and a number of men to take over the leadership in the
economic research field and the thing to do is to have Granducci point
out how these various planning sections are being organized and planned
by Tolley, in which they are contemplating research of the very nature
we are doing, how they are taking over our men and then have him point
out how the various sections of the Bureau are breaking their backs to
assist the Agricultural Adjustment Administration. Beyond that it should
be brought out that the other bureaus of the Department are seriously
raising the question in their minds as to whether or not they are to
become satellites and agents for the Agricultural Adjustment Administration, that there is new leadership for the Department and their work,
which has been scientific, will be modified to reflect the political situation and, beyond that, to point out that very successful raids have been
made on the Department by other departments, such as the Department
of Interior taking over the Erosion Service of the Bureau of Chemistry
and Soils. My personal feeling is that Tolley is the spearhead of this
effort and that his name should be trotted out as being definitely
associated with it. . . .

June 20, 21 and 26, 1934.

Mr. [George Y.] Harvey, Clarence Cannon's secretary, was in my
office this afternoon in connection with the drouth. He had hot-footed it
over from the Federal Emergency Relief Administration, where Governor
[Wallace] Crossley[19] of Missouri, who is also the State Director of Relief,
and Professor [Henry Andrew] Buehler, a State geologist, were raising
hob because we had not put all of Missouri in the drouth area. He said
that they had expressed themselves forcibly over there and wanted to
come over and put us on the spot. He told them that he wanted to come
over and speak to us and that they (Cannon's Office) could do more
than they on this matter. Harvey told me then, confidentially, that he did

19. Former Lieutenant Governor (1916–20) of Missouri.

not think that the whole of Missouri should be in the drouth area (incidentally Cannon's district is well taken care of) and he knew we were doing a good job, that there might be some counties in the southwestern corner that might be included. Our information shows that that is one of the best sections of the State. I told Harvey that we were making a continuous investigation of the situation and would designate additional counties in Missouri as the facts would warrant. I told him to convey to the two gentlemen that if they also wished to see us, that we would be glad to see them. Mr. Harvey seemed to be anxious to say nice things about us and I told him we were trying to do our duty as we saw it and elaborated somewhat on what was developing here in the way of trying to force us into an expanded drouth relief program beyond what conditions would warrant. I told him it made it very difficult when unreasonable pressure was brought to bear. I also told him that Mr. [Ralph Fulton] Lozier[20] had written a couple of letters that were not the kind that I expected from him in view of our feeling that we were doing an honest job. He agreed one hundred per cent. He said that Lozier had shown him the letter. He had called Lozier and told him of the additions to the drouth area in Missouri and that eight or ten counties in Lozier's district were included. He felt very pleased indeed and he brought out a letter and showed it to Harvey and said, "This is the kind of thing that makes those fellows come across." I assured Mr. Harvey that we proceeded to the designation of additional counties in Missouri and Illinois on the basis of the facts and not because of Mr. Lozier's letter. . . .

June 25, 1934.

Eric Englund told me that M. L. Wilson[21] evidently was quite satisfied to get out of the Department of the Interior that it had become unbearably hot for him. He said that Ickes was very much displeased with the way the Reedsville Project[22] was going and had called Wilson and his staff in and had given M. L. "Hail Columbia" in the presence of his employees. This tallies with Tapp's comment to me that [Hugh] McRae[23] was getting hold of the Subsistence Projects and not only determining the location but the mode of operation of such projects in the

20. A representative from Missouri.
21. Formerly director of Subsistence Homesteads and now Assistant Secretary of Agriculture.
22. The Subsistence Homestead Project at Reedsville, West Virginia, in which Mrs. Roosevelt took an interest, was poorly managed and continuously involved in controversy. For an insight into its troubles see *The Secret Diary of Harold Ickes: The First Thousand Days, 1933–1936* (New York, 1953), pp. 205, 207.
23. McRae in 1934 was president of the Southeastern Council headquartered in Wilmington, North Carolina. See Paul Conkin, *Tomorrow a New World* (Ithaca, N.Y., 1959), pp. 277–84, for a brief discussion of McRae's career and views about farm colonies in the South.

South. It looks as though there was a first rate head on between Ickes and Wallace in the offing as indicated by the passage of the Taylor bill[24] and the fact that there is a feeling, as well as statement, abroad that Ickes wants Forest Service. At the same time it looks very much as if Harry Hopkins[25] is taking over all phases of relief as far as the public is concerned, including drouth relief, and is playing himself up as the man who is handling all of these matters, including the submarginal land program and the whole rehabilitation effort. . . .

June 30, 1934.

A few days ago Granducci was in and told me that the Administration looked upon Tugwell and Frank as serious liabilities. I asked, "Does that mean the White House?" He replied, "It does not mean anything else."

Granducci asked me if his appraisal of administrators in the Administration was a correct one: W. I. Myers (FCA) one; Morgenthau (Treasury) two; Jesse Jones (RFC) three. He said he discussed it with Mr. [Louis H.] Bean[26] and Mr. Bean expressed surprise at the statement he made regarding Wallace and wanted to know what he meant by "good administration." Bean did not upset him in his views and, with my limited background, I told him I thought he had come close to appraising the situation aright. I asked him, point blank, if he was coming in to bid me good-bye July 1 and he said "No." I said, "I do not understand. Some seem to think the whole thing is headed for the bow-wows and that I am scheduled for the junk heap." He laughed and said, "Well, don't worry about that. You are too smart." He went on to say that he had not heard anything at all of that nature and if he did he surely would rush it over. . . .

July 14, 1934.

I had a visit of about one hour and a half Thursday, July 5, with the Secretary at which the discussion was practically entirely on the Land Economics Division matter. The Secretary started out by saying that he had read my memorandum more carefully and had practically concluded that we had better go through with the suggestion that had been made by

24. The Taylor Grazing Act vested in the Secretary of the Interior authority to create grazing districts in areas of the public domain deemed "valuable for grazing and raising forage crops."

25. Federal Emergency Relief administrator and president of the Federal Surplus Relief Corporation.

26. Now economic adviser to the AAA.

the special committee.[27] In a quiet way I stated that I regretted that he had reached that conclusion, that it was my own feeling and that of my associates as we had stated in the memorandum that there would be complications growing out of such an arrangement, that it would tend to undermine the morale of the Bureau still further and lay the ground work for making other inroads on the Bureau's separate identity and that the entire arrangement would not facilitate cooperation beyond what could and would be obtained under the present arrangement. I stated there was very definite disposition on our part to cooperate and utilize our resources and in helping to develop the factual and research basis for the program. The Bureau, as it was, was going very great lengths in that direction, that to take the position that we had to place divisions of the Bureau under the headship of the Agricultural Adjustment Administration was to me a mark of lack of confidence in my willingness and ability to bring about such cooperation and I did not think that he felt that way about it. I reminded him of a position he had taken with me at the outset that we should keep the Bureau separate as a research and service institution. He said there were some who did not feel that way about the relations. I said that we might as well be frank. He stated that there are a number of people who feel that the whole problem would be very much facilitated if there were another head of the Bureau. He said, "[Chester] Davis, [M. L.] Wilson and I do not feel that way about it because of our very real affection for you." He went on to remark that I had very good administrative ability and a singleness of purpose which were my great assets. I asked him if he felt that I was not delivering and if I was in any way being a hindrance to him in his work. "No, no" he said, "that is not the case" but there is a feeling that there is sort of a "separatist" attitude on the part of the Bureau that made it difficult to function, that I and other people in the Bureau had views regarding various things that were being done that did not tally with the views of the Agricultural Adjustment Administration and so on. I picked him up on that and said, "I am sure, H.A., that you would not have me and the group of men working any other way. Surely the time had not come when we can not have our own convictions on the matters that are being undertaken in the field in which we are working." "No" he replied, "that is right." . . .

The Secretary said, "Well, I think Davis, Wilson, you and I had better get together for another session on this at an early date," and he asked me to arrange for a meeting Saturday. . . .

Saturday July 7 the four of us met in the office. The Secretary started out the conversation by saying that I did not feel that this was a suitable arrangement. . . . He went on to say that everything had to be done to make the AAA program a success and that there had been some feeling that there was a "separatist" attitude on the part of the Bureau

27. To share the Division with the AAA.

that made it difficult to function and that there was not the fullest cooperation. Davis spoke up and said that he never had any problem in his relations with me, that as long as we worked together there would be no trouble. He did say, however, that there had been a good many reports coming to him of difficulties in getting the Bureau to function with the AAA and that was all he had to base his feeling on. . . . He said that he thought a mistake was made when the AAA was set up at all. It should have been a Department of Agriculture matter and that all the Bureau should have been drawn in as part and parcel of the AAA program. In other words, we should all be more or less blended together in one mass. The Secretary spoke up in that connection and said he did not arrange it that way for the reason that he had right at the very outset sounded out the possibilities of having the Bureau carry the load. He said that he had set up committees of various kinds but the functioning of those committees clearly showed that the Bureau was dead as far as carrying the action program was concerned. He said he had his feeling probably with reference to the corn-hog program. I spoke up and said I did not recall that the request had at any time been made that the Bureau be requested to handle the action program of the AAA Act. My understanding was that we agreed to service the AAA program as fully as possible. The Secretary very clearly adjusted himself to that and said that was true.

Wilson did not have very much to say but he injected the fact that he had been over to a meeting in the Interior Department and that they had set up machinery there for carrying through on a big land utilization report . . . and that he was made Chairman of the Committee on the Land use part and that [Lewis] Gray was by acclamation selected by the meeting to head up the report on land use and that, he said, put Gray in position to mobilize both forces of the Department on the report and that the arrangement that had been proposed was down that alley. I countered and said that I did not see that the Land Economics division was in any different position than any division of this Bureau and other departments, that the various units would expect to contribute as Gray would indicate. Again the meeting broke up without a decision. Wallace left but before he left it was agreed that Davis should get together a group and discuss the whole question of relations between the Bureau and the AAA. Davis had previously said that he did not feel that he would wish to express himself finally on this until he had seen Tolley. In other words, Tolley was clearly the moving spirit as far as the AAA was concerned in this show.

Re visit with Wilson and Davis—Wallace had said that he discovered that there was considerable fear on the part of various bureaus of the Department that the AAA would tend to disrupt them and, generally, create a difficult situation. . . .

Thursday we had our meeting in Wilson's office—Chester Davis,

M. L. Wilson, Tolley and myself. We met at three and broke up about 4:30. It was an odd meeting. There was a lot of jesting on other things before we got in on this subject and then Wilson said, "Well, we will continue the discussion from where we left off the other day and then he proceeded to elaborate on the organization that had been set up. He was the Chairman, L. C. Gray was the Executive Secretary and had the big job of mobilizing all the forces and as executive secretary he was in position now to levy upon the whole Bureau of Agricultural Economics and all other bureaus. . . . All of this chatter was to build up an atmosphere which would cause me to say, "Go ahead with the arrangement." I let them all talk. Davis said that he did not quite understand my objections to the arrangements. I, with great humility of voice and demeanor explained and in the course of the conversation Tolley then made his contribution. He said that he could not understand the basis for the position we took. He said that he had been out in California where the Extension Service, the whole Department of Agriculture, the Giannini Foundation, etc., were working together under one head and seemed to have no difficulty. Just why it would work there and not here was more than he could understand. He said that he wanted to make clear he had no personal interest in this, there was no attempt on his part to walk off with something he should not have, that there was no jealousy on his part, that he would conserve the Bureau and that was certainly the viewpoint of such men as Nourse, Black and Hedden on the committee. In fact, it was quite apparent from his discussions that he was expressing a personal feeling of which I was conscious and to which I paid no heed in my reply to Tolley that I believed there were complications in the joint set-up and that eveything could be accomplished without incurring those dangers. The discussion took that kind of counter comment without replying to his personal reference. Davis in the course of the conversation made the statement that . . . we should not have dual heads for a great number of divisions on the basis of dual administration. Wilson remarked, "Well, I guess we are not getting very far." I replied, "I am putting forth our position here very sincerely and honestly and I presume it is up to you and to the Secretary to determine what is to be done."

July 20, 1934.

Perhaps about ten days ago [Paul] Appleby[28] telephoned and told me that George Peek[29] had spoken to the Secretary about a special committee on foreign trade, representing important units of the Government, to work with him. Peek emphasized the importance of getting men who

28. An assistant to Secretary Wallace.
29. Now special adviser to the President on foreign trade as well as president of the Export-Import Bank.

had background to judge and decide an administrative position, to assist them in the work. Wallace said, "All right that is agreeable, whom do you want?" and Peek replied that he thought Olsen should be on the committee and to this Wallace agreed. Appleby in conveying this to me said something that intimated that he thought that this was a little something of an honor.

Yesterday a meeting was called by Peek in his office at which were Dr. [Jacob] Viner,[30] [Oscar B.] Ryder of the Tariff Commission, [Alvin H.] Hansen[31] who is now with the Department of State and I from the Department. Dr. [Clandius T.] Murchison, Chief of the Bureau of Foreign and Domestic Commerce, was not present. Peek had a few of his men with him there and presented a balance sheet for Brazil. His purpose evidently was to get the reaction of this group. Viner and Hansen right at the very outset took occasion to display their profound knowledge of foreign trade by criticizing the assumed conclusion that an unfavorable balance in the case of Brazil was unsound or uneconomic, that on the contrary there were both natural and industrial reasons why we bought more from Brazil than she bought from us. Later on in the discussion I had occasion to say that I agreed with them in theory and in principle but that the existing balance whether favorable or unfavorable was nothing that was set and fixed and that the success in breaking down barriers was increasing efficiency on the part of our industry in competing with foreign countries for such a market would probably reduce that unfavorable balance. I sensed that what Peek was doing was trying to get the reaction of these several representatives of the Departments to an analysis which he wished to present to the President.

After the meeting Peek asked me to remain and then he told me that that was the purpose and that furthermore he had selected men from the various important departments who could speak with authority, including Ryder who he said was very close to Pat Harrison[32] but whom he thought rather narrow in his thinking. It seems that Peek is riding pretty high with the President and with Secretary [Cordell] Hull. When Hansen went over to the Department of State, after Peek thought he had virtually engaged him for his own unit, Peek stated that he was quite discouraged and possibly would have been justified in throwing it all up since the establishment of a Division of Statistics over at the Department of State was clearly intended to counter him but he said he made up his mind that anything that was done for Agriculture would not be done by the Department of State and that he had a duty to stay with the farmers. So, he just made up his mind he would organize his own little group, carve out his own little field and keep on pressing and now he has taken up with the overlapping, conflicting or parallel lines and the lack of

30. A special assistant to Secretary of the Treasury Henry Morgenthau, Jr.
31. Chief economic analyst in the Division of Trade Agreements.
32. Senior Senator from Mississippi.

coordinated effort and Peek said he rather expected that something may break when the President returns. As indicative of this he called attention to what the President had done in assigning [Donald] Richberg to coordinate the N.R.A., P.W.A. and a number of other recovery activities. Peek is clearly alive to what the situation is over here in the Department and particularly the problem I have with "the powers that be."

July 21, 1934.

Granducci told me yesterday afternoon that at least four prominent people in Washington had told him that Chester Davis would be out of the AAA if it were not for his desperate need for a salary. Among those four was George Peek who told him that Chester Davis was more than fed up. Granducci also told me that three men were on their way out—[Frederic C.] Howe, [Jerome] Frank and Tugwell. Howe was going to be attacked on the ground of his immigration record and socialistic activities; Tugwell because of his vanity and ridicule was to be the technique used on him. Frank was to be eliminated on the ground that the Secretary had not authority to set up a new legal division since the organic act of the Department requires that all legal work be done by the Solicitor. I rather think the attack on Frank is a weak one. He also told me that the attack was to be made from within and from without. . . .

August 16, 1934.

Shortly before three o'clock yesterday afternoon Mr. [Milton S.] Eisenhower called me on the telephone and said that the Secretary would like to have me say the following in the press release on the drouth report:

> Mr. Olsen commenting on the report said, "It is interesting to note that the Triple A program has not in any way acted to make necessary the reduction in cattle and sheep. As a matter of fact if it had not been for the Triple A program it would have been necessary because of feed shortage to slaughter more cattle and sheep than is now proving to be the case. This has come to pass because the Triple A program has increased the quantity of forage and amount of corn available to other kinds of livestock than hogs.

Eisenhower went on to say that if I did not want to make the statement that the Secretary said he would make it himself. As soon as the statement arrived I went into a huddle with [Eric] Englund[33] and [J. Clyde] Marquis in order to get at the factual basis of it and concluded that it

33. Now assistant Chief of the Bureau of Agricultural Economics.

would require modification in order to square with the facts. I realized that a request such as this, when it came from the Secretary, placed me in a difficult position to refuse but, at the same time, I was determined that I would not put out statements that were not truthful and that I should not be put in the position of propagandizing for the Triple A program. We prepared a statement to which I could subscribe and modified the press release so as to have me comment on other phases of the report as well. This was all done under great pressure since fourteen or fifteen newspaper men were pressing Eisenhower for the release. . . .

When Marquis took the press statement over, one of the girls in the Secretary's Office asked him if he was not going to show it to Dr. [Mordecai] Ezekiel. Marquis replied that he did not understand that he had anything to do with it. "Oh yes," she said, he had written the original statement. That raises the question as to whether the Secretary, himself, inspired the thought and if he actually asked to have it included. The revised statement was rushed to Appleby for approval and he and others in the Secretary's Office said it was a great improvement on the original. . . .

August 24, 1934.

The day before yesterday Congressman [John N.] Sandlin (La.) arrived in town and secured the designation of counties in his district as Emergency Drought Counties. . . . Sandlin evidently made his first contact with [W. A.] Jump and Jump, in turn, put him in touch with [C. W.] Warburton I think in my absence. Sandlin evidently was somewhat diffident about seeing me regarding the matter and that was later verified in what he had to say. Jump, however, came over and saw me regarding the matter and said Sandlin was very anxious about it and he thought it behooved us to go as far as we could in the matter. He emphasized that Sandlin and [Clarence] Cannon and [Edward J.] Hart[34] having the attitude on the Committee they did, it was advisable that we have Sandlin's goodwill. Nevertheless Jump stressed that we should not do what we would not be justified in doing on the basis of the facts. I told him I thought it would be a good thing to have Sandlin come over and have a chat with me and Thursday afternoon he came over and presented a rather direct picture with me of the conditions that existed in the counties. He also in his very frank way stated that he and his family were being hounded to death by everybody in the district and it got to the point that something had to be done about it. On going over the matter we decided that we would first put the counties in the secondary area. Sandlin evidently did not think that this took care of the situation and he contacted Jump and Jump again stated that it would be too bad it we could not do something for Sandlin.

34. Representatives Sandlin, Cannon (Missouri), and Hart (New Jersey) were members of the Appropriations Committee.

In my first conversation with Sandlin—and we had designated the counties in the secondary area before I saw him—I asked him if cattle purchases were in order and he said "No" that he did not think they should sell their cattle. I then said that what we should do was to get the Federal Emergency Relief Administration to extend credit on a liberal basis. Sandlin made the statement that that was what they needed and that they were so badly broken financially, the chances were that the loans would not be repaid and the Government might as well go in with that thought in mind. I then told Sandlin I would like to see what arrangements could be made through [Lawrence] Westbrook[35] and Governor [W. I.] Myers and I called them. Westbrook said that it did not make much difference whether the counties were in the primary or secondary they would function broadly and liberally, but it would help if the Farm Credit Administration would make liberal loans in the territory. I telephoned Governor Myers and he said that to designate these counties for special credit when they were in the secondary area would be breaking their previous policy but that he would discuss it with his people. Yesterday he advised that the situation was as follows: The Federal Emergency Relief Administration was making livestock loans to small livestock owners on the basis of $25 per month, or less. The Farm Credit Administration was handling the large loans. Theirs were mostly to small farmers and owners of livestock who needed the smaller loans, and hence it was a problem for the Federal Emergency Relief Administration. I then queried, "You are not able to handle this situation without Emergency designation?" and he replied, "No, not without violently changing our policies and creating difficulties." I then bluntly asked him if he thought we should put the counties in the emergency area in order to handle the situation and he said he did not like to answer that because he did not have the facts but there was a strong intimation that he thought that should be done.

Fortunately a letter arrived . . . in which [Paul L.] Koenig and [Virgil C.] Childs[36] said that they had passed through northwestern Louisiana and found conditions there fully as serious as the counties in Texas which we had placed in the Emergency area. I called [Mrs. Charles S.] Bouton,[37] Arkansas, on long distance and checked with her on the conditions in counties in Arkansas adjoining Louisiana that had already been included in the drouth area and in checking on another list of counties adjoining Louisiana she said that in their judgment they should now be Emergency counties, with the exception of possibly three counties, on which they would give us a report.

I should have indicated that yesterday Under-Secretary Tugwell

35. An assistant administrator of the Federal Emergency Relief Administration Committee.

36. Koenig and Childs were employed in the Division of Crop and Livestock Estimates of the Bureau of Agricultural Economics.

37. Crop statistician in the Bureau of Crop Estimates in the State Plant Board, Little Rock, Arkansas.

telephoned me regarding the Louisiana situation and asked what could be done. I gave him the facts and told him that we were making a special investigation to see what we could do. I understand also that Congressman Sandlin had a visit with the Secretary but no communications came to me from the Secretary on this subject.

On the basis of Koenig's report and the fact that conditions in this section of Louisiana appear to be as bad if not somewhat worse than they are in the adjoining emergency counties in Texas, Warburton and I agreed we would put in the counties even though [W. F.] Callander[38] and his men were not thoroughly agreeable. They did not express definite opposition but said they were not quite on the same basis with them as other designations that had been made.

I had Sandlin come over late yesterday afternoon and he was most friendly and cordial and chatted about many personal things and when we went over the matter and I finally told him we would put in his counties he was most grateful and when he left he said he appreciated the matter deeply and said, "I'm for you," and he added, very frankly, that he was honestly reporting what he had seen with his own eyes and what he believed to be true and he felt that he did the thing that was justified in asking for the designation and we were justified in making the designation. . . .

August 30, 1934.

About ten days ago I had a visit with Dr. Tugwell on Institute matters[39] following my luncheon hour with [Joseph C.] Green of the Department of State. I told him I understood that he had notified the Department of State that he was not going to Europe and I told him that it was quite important to get the matter definitely decided. He then showed me a letter which he had received from Ambassador [Breckinridge] Long[40] in response to a wire which he had sent him. Confirmation of the wire was imbedded in the letter and stated that Long did not think the meeting was of much account and that it would not be worth his while to come, although he would be very glad to see him. He went on to say in the letter that [Henry C.] Taylor was absent and that he had not conferred with him, also that the representation was mostly made up of diplomats and he did not think there would be much opportunity of getting anything of consequence across. I told Tugwell that I disagreed with Mr. Long and that he evidently did not understand the work of the Institute or what had transpired during the past few years. The fact that we were not returning to the Institute after a prolonged absence and particularly since Taylor had been successful in convincing the Italian authorities and

38. In charge of crop and livestock estimates in the Bureau of Agricultural Economics.
39. The International Institute of Agriculture was scheduled to meet in Rome in October.
40. Ambassador to Italy.

others that the Institute should be revamped, it seemed desirable for us to make a good deal of the meeting. I told him, however, that it was a matter for him to decide.

At the conclusion of my talk Tugwell seemed to waiver considerably and said he evidently made a mistake in wiring Long. He said he wanted to discuss it with H.A. and also with his wife, and he spoke of his "kids" going to school and the need of getting them packed up, etc. . . . Word subsequently came back to me that Tugwell decided not to go. I went in then and had a talk with Wallace and I told him some of the facts regarding the negotiations with Tugwell and that there had been decisions on both sides of the fence until I did not know where we stood. I told him some decision should be made one way or the other. . . .

In the course of a day or so Dr. Tugwell called me and said I evidently had done a good job with Wallace on the Institute and that he had now practically decided to go. . . . He then asked me if I would not consider plans for his trip and he telephoned me today, at which time he told me he was seeing the President at Hyde Park, leaving this afternoon and that he would like to have me check on sailing accommodations, and plans with our offices. This I have done in a conference with him and he very frankly said that he did not know anything about it, that I knew what was the thing to do and he would be guided by my suggestions. We are to have a wire from him after his visit with the President definitely informing us as to his decision.

November 13, 1934.

. . . [Jesse W.] Tapp told me Sunday that M. L. Wilson had gotten himself into a tight situation up in Pennsylvania. He was addressing a group up there and some farmers asked him about the failure to get the corn-hog checks into the county. So, Wilson cheerily promised that the checks would be right there. He reported the matter back to the Agricultural Adjustment Administration and it developed that they were in a tight situation but they put pressure on their force and sent the checks up by automobile, so that they were there the day before or on election day. The newspapers got hold of this and Tapp rather suspected that M.L. and the Administration were not right on the spot. . . .

November 19, 1934.

Mr. Harry H. Schutz[41] a few days ago in my office told me it was most amusing the way the political pressure was put on the cotton people to get out the checks just before election. Evidently a number of con-

41. An agricultural statistician employed in the Division of Crop and Livestock Estimates of the Bureau of Agricultural Economics.

gressmen in Texas, although I am not altogether clear in this now, insisted on having the checks for their districts mailed promptly and special
forces were put to work in the AAA getting out the checks, and the
checks were sent by air mail at a cost of $10 to get them there just before
election.

Mr. Schutz also said that the pressure which individual congressmen
made through appointees which they had in the Auditing Section of the
AAA to get the checks out to their counties interfered very seriously with
the general work of checking the records and issuing the checks generally. The significant fact that he developed was that any number of
employees in the Auditing Section represented individual congressmen
and were very responsive to the pressure which those congressmen put
upon them to facilitate the issuance of checks to people in their districts.

November 28, 1934.

Sunday evening (November 24, 1934) Tapp telephoned and asked if
he could come over and see me and I told him he might. It developed
quite soon that he was disturbed over the situation between the
Agricultural Adjustment Administration and the Secretary's Office. . . . Tapp, of course, expressed the bitterest attitude toward
Tugwell and Appleby whom he regards as insinuating and ruthless in
method, as well as Ezekiel, Bean, Howe, [Gardner] Means[42] and the rest
of the crowd. He also spoke about the desirability of getting our
marketing work well set up so that they could drive Howe out of the picture. Very confidentially he told me that [Chester] Davis was getting
himself set to eliminate Howe. It appears that Howe was at Chicago a
short time ago and gave an address in which he advocated municipal
ownership of milk distributing agencies and the distribution of that commodity by municipalities. Howe had some weeks previously prepared a
similar address which came to [Alfred D.] Stedman but Stedman killed
it. This time Howe did not come to Stedman with his address but proceeded to spill it forthwith. About this same time Davis was in New York
City addressing a group there in which he was encouraging the whole
idea of cooperation between the Government and industry in the
distribution of products, including milk and other products. Tapp, of
course, was right on insisting the situation was intolerable.

I gathered from Tapp that Davis and he at least feel that Wallace is
not doing his duty. Tapp spoke of Wallace as a rotten administrator and
in which I concur. He also discussed Wallace's "bleary-eyed" economics
and mysticism. He recognized that the overwhelming Democratic victory

---

42. A Columbia University economist who was an adviser to the Secretary in 1934.
Along with Adolf A. Berle he was the author of the important study, *The Modern Corporation and Private Property,* published in 1932.

probably strengthened the hands of Tugwell and his group and that it might come to a showdown where Davis and he and others would quit and he went on to say that with Davis quitting they could not put the pieces together. . . .

Monday, November 26, I tried to reach Davis but both of us were so busy that we could not find a mutually advantageous time. Tapp had gotten in Monday morning and told Davis he should by all means see me as soon as I called and Davis had given orders to admit me without delay, but Tuesday morning was as soon as I could call at his office, and I arrived there about 9:30. He was very cordial and friendly and his first remark was: "Well, Nils, I am not seeing much of you. Have you cut Helen and me off your visiting list?" I said I had not but that all of us were so busy, we did not get around much to visit. Davis continued, "Helen spoke to me about it several times and we are expecting to see something of you," and then he gave me his address and blind telephone number and made it very plain that he hoped I would add that to my social register. . . .

Davis then spoke of the Consumers' Counsel situation. He said that had given him a good deal of concern and he tried to find among his papers an illustration of the putrid material appearing in the "Consumers' Guide." This he did not find but he made clear that he was disgusted with the propaganda and misrepresentation that was appearing in that sheet and he said he had been thinking about the possibility of asking me to arrange to have the Bureau [of Agricultural Economics] take over all the research functions of the Consumers' Counsel, and in that way place himself in a good position to abolish the entire unit. He went on to say, very confidentially, that the Federal Emergency Council now had under consideration the consolidation of all of the consumer units throughout the Government with the purpose of assigning to the new consolidated unit the purely information propaganda activities, leaving to regular research agencies the research functions. . . . Davis called for the budget of the Consumers' Counsel. It has a budget of $230,000 and what I suspect is that he will be turning over substantial amounts of that budget under this arrangement to the much maligned "B.A.E."

Davis then made reference to a speech which Howe gave at Chicago and in which he advocated municipal distribution of dairy products. Davis said, "That may be the position to take but it is my feeling that a position like that should be taken after careful analysis and weighing of the facts and mature conclusions reached. Such consideration of the matter had not been given and no such policy has been reached." Then Davis referred to the fact that he, Davis, made a speech in New York where he expressed the hope that greater cooperation between business and the Government might develop, running fully counter to what one of his own employees was saying. He then asked me if such things obtained in the Bureau and if we tolerated it. I did not lose much time in telling him that such a situation in the Bureau would be absolutely intolerable, that the men realized that we had to function as an organization and that questions involving policy were referred to the Chief and while we might have our differences, we finally agreed on a position and that was the position of the Bureau. He then went on to explain that Howe's activity was merely part and parcel of the policy being pursued by one of the three groups with which he had to contend, the membership of which in many cases had been determined before he was placed in charge and whose loyalty, therefore, ran to others rather than to himself. He went on to say that there is of course the Tugwell-Ezekiel-Bean-[Calvin B.] Hoover[43]-Means group, the Howe-[Thomas] Blaisdell,[44] etc., consumer group and then the legal group. He said, "Now let me take you back to the days when Peek had reached the breaking point. When he was either voluntarily eliminating himself or was being requested to eliminate himself from the picture there were three groups and the faction represented by him was the so-called conservative faction; the other extreme being represented by Tugwell and an intermediate group represented by himself, Tolley and some of the other boys. With the elimination of the Peek group the situation was changed so that we had the radical Tugwell group, comprising Howe as well as Frank and the middle group of the old set-up. Now the cleavage is between those two groups and the strivings of the radical group seemed to be to put us on the spot and force us increasingly to the right so as to make it appear that we are all big-business minded and fighting for the interest of some of the big boys. In this fight they can of course play upon the mass emotions which are running very liberal today." And, so, Davis thinks it is a pretty tough position and he said he had come to the conclusion that some of those people, and not least of all, Appleby, are interested in possibly even eliminating Davis and Tolley and Tapp, and others of that kind. "As far as I am concerned I am not worrrying about that," said Davis, "I can very well step out when the right time comes." Davis went on to say that what makes it difficult is the fact that it is hard to know who is Secretary of Agriculture. He commented that it was awfully hard to understand the position that Wallace is taking, but, he said, "One of these bright days he will have made clear that he is the Secretary of Agriculture." . . .

In discussing the machinations of Appleby-Tugwell and that group, Davis said: "You know you have not passed unnoticed. You may recall that at a previous conference I made reference to the attack that had been made upon you and that I had intervened in your behalf." He went on to add that Tugwell had, in a conference with him and the Secretary, said there was just one way to solve that situation and that was to remove the Chief. Both he (Davis) and Wallace had immediately taken

43. Economic adviser in the Consumers' Counsel Division.
44. Employed by the Legal Division of the Department of Agriculture.

issue with Tugwell. I laughed and said I supposed the Under Secretary had a ready substitute for my place, too. Davis hestitated a bit and smiled and said, "He had some ideas." I said, "Perhaps Ezekiel." He replied, "No." "Well," he said, "I do not mind telling you he had Calvin Hoover picked for the job." (That is a very choice bit, when you stop to reflect that from the early days of the new Administration there has been this little coterie of men surrounding Tugwell, brought in as his own trusted advisers, operating as a clique in unhorsing bureau chiefs, putting in their pets, creating dissension and animosities between various parts of the Departments—a situation which is a sad reflection on the administrative acumen of the present Secretary.) . . .

November 28, 1934—Today I went over to see Appleby on the latest move in the cotton investigation. . . . Appleby said that they had trouble with the Cotton Section of the AAA and on so many of the things they wanted to do had been resisted by [Cully A.] Cobb[45] and practically all members of the division. He said, as an illustration of what he had in mind—the question of how the adjustment program and the application of the Bankhead Bill were affecting tenants and croppers was constantly up for consideration. He, Tugwell and others have urged that plans, contracts and policies be formulated with a view to conserving their interests. Appleby went on to say that Cotton Section has seemed to lean in favor of the landlord and has blocked their efforts to protect the interests of the little fellow. As a concrete illustration, Appleby said that they had sent a member of the Cotton Section to one of the southern states to investigate a particular case. He had reported back in favor of the landlord. They put another investigator on it and he came back with the report that the Cotton Section man had wilfully misrepresented the facts in giving a report of the kind indicated. . . . Appleby went on to say that the Secretary was not overly impressed with the charges that subordinates were not loyal to immediate superiors, certainly as within the department, but when it came between this and other departments then he was very meticulous in observing the relations of one official to another and of observing the principles of loyalty. . . .

I also gave Appleby a statement showing our estimate of the effect of the drouth and the reduction program upon the total yield of cotton this year and he said that he needed this material to answer [Colonel J. E.] McDonald[46] "who was plugging for a measure which would permit unencumbered production of cotton and a benefit payment on the domestic allotment." He said the Texas crowd was whooping it up pretty strong for that and Marvin Jones[47] had gone along pretty well but was keeping himself in a comfortable position. . . .

45. Chief of the Cotton Section of the Agricultural Adjustment Administration.
46. Commissioner of the Texas Department of Agriculture.
47. Chairman of the House Committee on Agriculture.

November 28, 1934 [*a second entry*].

[C. T.] Forster[48] within the last few days in discussing the cotton situation has commented on the attitude of Wallace and that of Appleby in the matter of discipline. Forster says that the Secretary just did not like to fire any one. Appleby on the other hand leans strongly in that direction. He added that sometimes he had difficulty in knowing just who is Secretary of Agriculture, H. A. Wallace or Appleby. He said further that it is the most confusing situation you ever saw in the outer office of the Secretary—Appleby, [C. B.] Baldwin and [James D.] LeCron[49]—no one handles a matter clear through but each of them will dabble with it and the net result is that no one knows what is the status of a case and very frequently attention to specific cases calling for action will have been delayed as much as a month. . . .

December 6 and 7, 1934.

This morning I had a visit with the Secretary and at the very outset discussed the special committee designated by the Policy Committee on Cotton and of which the proposal was to make L. A. Wheeler[50] chairman. . . .

I then told the Secretary that Mr. [C. W.] Warburton and I had been carefully considering the activities of the drouth designation committee and we were both of the opinion that it would be very desirable to abolish that committee, that to continue it would be merely to invite pressures to bring in more counties and that would result in putting additional pressure on the various relief agencies. I indicated that certain congressmen and senators had already shown their hand in that direction and Warburton anticipated a very bad drive when Congress reconvened. I also indicated that I discussed the general matter with Chester Davis and while I had not mentioned the abolition of the committee to him, he was in agreement with us regarding the policy of designation. The Secretary stated that seemed logical and proper to him and indicated that it would be quite all right for Warburton and myself to prepare such a memorandum. . . .

As I got up to leave his office, Secretary Wallace said, "I wish you would tell LeCron to arrange for a luncheon meeting with you, [Mordecai] Ezekiel, [Louis H.] Bean and myself Saturday noon, to discuss some projects that you might undertake." He made no mention whatever of Chester Davis and at the spur of the moment it did not oc-

48. Chief investigator in the Office of Personnel, Department of Agriculture.
49. Assistants to the Secretary of Agriculture.
50. Chief of the Foreign Agricultural Service in the Bureau of Agricultural Economics.

cur to me to react. I no sooner got back to my office than I realized this would create another indelicate situation. Hence my conference today.

At four o'clock yesterday Warburton and I went up to see Chester Davis regarding the drouth matter. We laid the subject before him and I indicated how the Secretary stood and Davis approved of our preparing a joint memorandum to him and to the Secretary, jointly, abolishing the committee and preparing a reply which they might sign, and also possibly to prepare a press release closing the county designation matter and abolishing the committee. . . .

Wednesday, December 5, . . . I told the Secretary that we were already making a number of studies, that we were agreeable to making as many as possible bearing on the problems of the Agricultural Adjustment Administration, that the Bureau was in an unusually good position to make objective studies but there was a limit beyond which we could not of course function. The Secretary agreed and said he thought it would be very desirable if the Bureau could be making a number of cool objective studies. He said, "You know the AAA people are engaged to some degree in propaganda and pressure stuff and we need some one to appraise the work and guide us soundly." I replied, "H.A., if you recall that is what I said to you at the very outset of your administration and it has been my daily thought that the Bureau would function in that way." The Secretary then suggested that we might work out some arrangement whereby we could make several studies in the several commodities that would be very helpful along these lines. . . . I went on to add that I thought it would be a splendid thing if there could be an understanding under which I would be giving him, freely and fearlessly, reactions on a great many matters that passed over my desk and through the Bureau in which he might and might not concur, but that would be all right and he at any rate would have the benefit of our objective judgment. I told him some of the proposed memoranda would deal with the way in which the emergency program was affecting the activities of the regular bureaus. The Secretary said, "Well, I do not know that interests me so much." I countered, "H.A., I think it probably should interest you. Just as an illustration—the manner in which you are providing for commodity loans on cotton, taking any and all kinds of nondescript receipts is certainly a type of thing that if pursued will undermine the Federal Warehouse receipt. Surely you do not want something done that will tend to destroy a valuable document like the Federal Warehouse receipt." He replied, "No, I had not thought of it. A memorandum of that kind would be very helpful." The Secretary closed the conference with his remark that he thought it would be a good thing for me to talk to Ezekiel and Bean about the matter and I said I would. He also remarked, "I wish you would talk to Appleby about it. Davis had a pretty warm discussion with him on it and I think it would be well for you to see him too." . . .

December 8, 1934.

This morning at 9:30 I had a visit with Chester Davis. . . . We discussed Appleby and Chester said that he had known Appleby about twenty years or more and had always regarded himself as a close friend of his, but he would bear watching. He said that he had reached the conclusion that Appleby had made up his mind that he wanted to be a "king maker." I asked Chester if Appleby was not also a very close friend of the Secretary and if the Secretary did not regard him with the utmost confidence. Chester said he felt sure that that was the case. Then I asked him if he thought Appleby was operating in the interest of the Secretary. Davis replied, "My gracious, No." But, is he doing this willfully and intentionally? Davis replied, "No, I do not think he is doing it with any thought of injury to the Secretary but he thinks the Secretary should be kept under the Tugwell influence and other influences should be kept out." He went on to remark that the boys of the Secretariat were evidently cooking up various plans for which the Secretary fell. In that connection Davis said that they cooked up the idea that it would be a good move to have Tugwell called to Warm Springs[51] after his return from Europe, to let the country know that Tugwell was not on his way out. Henry A. fell for this plan and cleared it with the President and Tugwell as the real Secretary of Agriculture and Wallace playing second fiddle. We agreed that there were three secretarys now to reckon with, Tugwell No. 1, Appleby, probably No. 2 and, finally, the Secretary proper (Wallace) but a word that is becoming rather common around special circles now is the "Secretariat" of the Secretary. . . .

December 10, 1934.

Saturday noon a luncheon was arranged in the Secretary's Office with Dr. Ezekiel, Dr. Bean and the Secretary and, to my surprise, Chester Davis was there. The luncheon and the conference were a howling success. After we had gotten under way on our salad the Secretary turned to me and asked how the Bureau could use its forces in making an objective analysis of various elements in the program and problems as they arose. I told him I had been glad to have the Bureau render just that type of service, that was the field in which it could in my judgment be of exceedingly great help and I reminded him of the number of studies that we already had projected and on which we had made delivery at least in part and assured him that there would be a great willingness to take on additional work as resources would permit. . . . Some question I think was directed by the Secretary to

51. The Georgia retreat for victims of infantile paralysis where the President had a cottage.

Chester Davis and he then lit out along about the following lines. He said, "I think there is need for clarification and adjustment in the handling of these matters and I am going to suggest that we discuss this matter now in confidence and frankly and openly. I have not been satisfied and pleased with the way things have been handled in connection with our work. There is no effective coordination and utilization of our resources in an orderly way, but it has seemed to me there has rather been a disposition to be fighting on the flanks. As an illustration the question of amendments to the Chicago Milk agreement came up and I had made up my mind that I wanted this time, in that case, to bring in all of the criticisms in order that they might be taken into account in the development of the docket and the preparation of the position and the statement which the Agricultural Adjustment Administration would take. I brought in [Jerome N.] Frank and his legal group, I brought in [Frederick C.] Howe and the Consumers' Counsel group, I gave them copies of the amendments amply in advance of the meeting at which they were present, I made the statement there that I wanted their complete and full reaction, but I did not get much discussion at that time. After the docket had been completed, the statement prepared and a position taken, then along came about a 35 page memorandum from Frank finding fault with this and that, and another hefty document from Howe throwing out objections from the Consumers' Counsel group. I have no objection to criticism—in fact I seek criticisms and suggestions but I think there is an orderly and effective way to handle matters of this kind and that is what I am dissatisfied with. Confidentially, over in the Federal Emergency Council we have been seriously considering the proposition of consolidating the propaganda activities of all of the units dealing with consumer interests in the Federal Government. Altogether there are 27 or 28 of them, as I recall. I have not been satisfied with Dr. Howe's attitude and his propaganda and I am not satisfied to be influenced by that type of thing in the handling of our work. As a matter of fact, propaganda has no real place in the formulation and administration of our policies, although I recognize it has a place when properly handled by the proper unit. It has been my thought that if this was done that Dr. Howe would go with them on the propaganda activities of the Consumers' Counsel unit. There are very important research activities related to the interests of the consumer and these I think should be continued and expanded. I am thinking of the sort of thing that the Bureau of Agricultural Economics group is doing through [Frederick V.] Waugh's[52] group there. That is very satisfactory and I have thought of the possibilities of building around them and expanding it. Of course, as far as I am concerned it would be all right to retain a small group of research people in the Agricultural Adjustment Administration working on the consumer end of the thing." Both Ezekiel

52. In charge of marketing research in the Bureau of Agricultural Economics.

and Bean had a few exchanges with Chester and the point they were trying to make was that Howe and his group were merely trying to bring the consumer aspect of the problem to their attention in order that it would not be overlooked. Davis met all these approaches by saying that as far as he could figure out what the Consumers' Counsel group was attempting to do was not to get money back to the growers so much as to get things to consumers and to point their attack upon middleman margins. Secretary Wallace expressed agreement with the thought that Chester Davis developed. I retained silence on that point but when Bean made the point that there were two kinds of research, one of the more substantial long-time character which clearly fell within the Bureau's domain, the other analyzing from a short-time point of view specific things that arose and needed rather quick solution. On the matter of the latter type of activities he thought it could best be done by the group in the Agricultural Adjustment Administration. To this I countered that we were doing both types of research, that as a matter of fact no small part of the time of our research people was taken up in so-called "service research" done under pressure. It was done, however, by the regular research people and that interfered with their devoting sufficient time to their regular projects. I stated that it was my conclusion that the most effective handling of the short-time emergency types of research was by the specialists who were devoting their time to more substantial studies and almost invariably where an inquiry had been sent to a division that was not doing the research, the handling of it was inadequate. In other words I made the point that both types of research should be done by the Bureau people and in order to do it it would be necessary to strengthen its forces. With this Chester and H.A. expressed agreement. I also commented on Chester's suggestion that it would be all right if the research group were left in the Consumer's counsel to handle consumer research problems. I said that could be done but it seemed to me it would inevitably lead to unnecessary and undesirable duplication and the work in that field could be best done by the group that were collecting the facts and making a great variety of studies on consumers' problems. With this Chester and H.A. agreed, although Bean expressed the idea that duplication was not such a bad thing. To this I agreed, within reasonable limits.

Ezekiel expressed the idea that the Bureau might be working on a number of matters that were of vital importance to the AAA program and the preparation of the annual report. He spoke of the processing taxes study we made and bringing it down to date, he spoke of the monetary policy, and he had a third thing in mind which, however, he did not get around to mention. The Secretary spoke up and said that it frequently happened that the President asked him about this and that, and the other thing about which he wanted to say something and it would be very helpful if he had reports on these various matters. I summarized that phase of the situation by saying that as far as the processing taxes were concerned it would be a relatively easy matter to bring that material down to date and I would be glad to do that through the standing committee I had created. I said that I also had created a committee on the subject of Monetary Policy, that I had made three, if not four preliminary reports . . . and would be in position to deliver a pretty well rounded out report by the middle of January. I called attention to the fact that I had a Cotton Committee, a Fats and Oils Committee, a Social Security Committee, a Direct Marketing Committee, and that I would be prepared to create committees as we developed subjects on which research was imperatively needed. I stated very definitely that I thought the logical procedure was to single out a few very vital subjects for investigation, set up committees, have them give preliminary results if need be and be prepared to round out a report at the strategic moment. If we followed this course of setting up committees to deal with specific problems, one at a time, we would gradually cover the field and we would be able to expand this type of thing as fast as our resources would permit. This seemed to be satisfactory all around and the luncheon closed without anything definite in the way of instructions or conclusions being stated by the Secretary.

As I stepped out, Ezekiel sought a word and said, "Well, that will work out really very nicely. If Howe goes over to the new unit you can take over the research people he has and have them work under Dr. Waugh and have them handle those problems." I replied, "Yes, I think if that is to be done we can work out some basis on which the research that is called for in that direction can be conducted."

(At the Secretary's tea yesterday afternoon, Dec. 9, I was impressed with the fact that it was purely Bureau Chiefs, and only Bureau Chiefs that were present from the regular units of the Department and that every division head of the Agricultural Adjustment Administration and the Secretariat of the Secretary's Office, including Miss [Grace] Falke, were present. . . . At the tea I seemed to sense a demure, stricken attitude on the part of Mrs. [Louis H.] Bean as I shook hands with her as I was going out and Mr. Bean seemed to hold my hand as though he wanted to say something.)

December 15, 1934.

. . . Last night I attended a buffet supper at the Russian Embasy in honor of V. V. Ossinsky, Vice President of the Soviet State Planning Commission. It was informal and representatives of the economist group were particularly in evidence, Brookings [Institte], Commerce, Peek's organization and the Department of Agriculture was heavily represented—Tugwell, Tolley, Stine, Englund, Miss [Mary G.] Lacy,[53]

53. Librarian of the Bureau of Agricultural Economics.

Kitchen and myself and a good representation from the entire Department. The affair was conducted quite informally and I presume there was some conversation between Charge des Affaires Lehmann[54] and Ossinsky but evidently not a great deal. In leaving I had occasion to speak to both. Lehmann speaks good English but the other gentleman did not speak an English word that I heard. What I am trying to record, of course, was the important part of the affair seemed to be the buffet supper which was quite elaborate and the generosity with which liquors were dispensed from the time the supper began until after midnight when I left—vodka, Scotch, champagne, cognac all stand out in my murky mind and my general impression of the affair is that it was intended as a means of appealing to the physical in order to loosen up on the intellectual and the mental as the interests of Russia might dictate.

December 24, 1934.

Last night at the dinner given by Mr. [Walter A.] Wentworth, of Borden & Co., at the Mayflower, Wallace and Mrs. Wallace were present and it developed in my conversation with Wentworth that the friendship goes back to college days at Ames when they were classmates. Wentworth in commenting on Wallace said he was a very hard and good student but he was very much then as he is now—had very little time for playing but was grubbing away all the time. The party was made up of dairy people altogether . . . and it struck me as rather illustrative of technique employed by representatives of the great interests.

The party was purely social and was very well done. I took [Arthur A.] Lauterbach[55] and his wife home and in the course of the conversation Lauterbach remarked that it became very tiresome to be fighting all the time, to feel that you had rather a slippery type of fighting to deal with and that there often was such a lack of appreciation of the reality of the situation. He said he thought the whole thing would shake down to the point where there would not be so much left of the Agricultural Adjustment Administration but that most of the activities would be taken over by the regular bureaus. He said that, as a matter of fact he thought the Secretary, himself, was going to appreciate the value and importance of his regular bureaus and that there was evidence of his leaning more and more on them. In connection with personnel matters Lauterbach said the Secretary was on a tough spot and that he seemed anxious that things should be handled in such a way as to avoid ructions. I remarked that I had sensed that but that sometimes it might be the best thing not to smooth over a situation but go right down the line and have it out. With this Lauterbach was in full accord.

54. I have been unable to further identify Lehmann.
55. Served in the Dairy Section, AAA.

December 29, 1934.

Christmas Day Anna[56] and I made a few calls. . . . Late Christmas evening we called on Chester and Mrs. Davis and even though it was late they were very delighted to see us and, in fact, they had been planning to have me for Christmas dinner and seemed especially pleased that we called. . . . Chester, in the course of the conversation, remarked that it was a trying sort of a situation, that he did not expect anything very bad growing out of the forthcoming Congress, although of course there would be the usual disturbing things; that he did not expect any far-reaching legislation as far as agriculture was concerned, except perhaps some legislation that would definitely put the land policy work on a permanent basis and in the regular bureaus that all these years had been working on the land problem. He went on as compared with himself. He said, of course, we were career men who had been with the Government a long time, left a permanent contribution and left our mark. He was one of those who came in on a particular assignment and did not have the same feelings about continuing and, furthermore, that opportunities on the outside were quite as attractive and that he was giving himself about six months more.

That evening while we were discussing with Chester the various troublesome situations including the wildcatting over here in the Department, Chester hesitated and then said, "I suppose you have heard the latest, have you not? Well, H.A., Rex and M.L. got together and decided upon a division of labor. H.A. is to have the Agricultural Adjustment Administration, Tugwell is to have all the bureaus except" (and Chester stopped and smiled) and I said, "Yes," "except the Bureau of Agricultural Economics and the Extension Service, and M.L. is to have the Bureau of Agricultural Economics and the Extension Service." I said, "Well, that is interesting and as far as I am concerned it is quite agreeable," but I did not follow up with any comments. However, this is very interesting as reflecting the position in which Tugwell, the great economist, finds himself with reference to this Bureau and the Extension Service and how these radicals are driven to work out some division of labor. A division of labor should, of course, be set up on functional lines and it is absurd to think of the Under Secretary assuming a bailiwick where he would have nothing to do with a couple of the Department bureaus.

56. Olsen's sister who was working for General Foods, Inc., in New York and editing cookbooks published by the *New York Herald-Tribune.*

1935

Granducci told me this morning that he had just seen the Secretary and the Secretary had expressed every willingness to see him, although he has held him off for months and months. I asked him "How come?" and he said he was quite sure it grew out of the crack they had in a letter regarding the failure of the Secretary to support Chester Davis. Davis evidently told Granducci that immediately following the issuance of that letter he was called over by the Secretary and his attention called to the item and asked if it reflected his views. Davis was put on the spot and he squirmed somewhat but said he presumed he should say that he inspired the item but that was not true but the thought did coincide with his view. They then had a two hour conference which was quite wholesome and in the course of which Davis suggested that Wallace see Granducci.

Granducci points out that Wallace does not stand high in Administration circles and this time he says that Wallace does not seem to know how to reach decisions and does not stay put on his decisions either on policy or in the administration field. I asked him if he thought Wallace was in any danger and he said no; he thought Wallace could remain Secretary of Agriculture as long as Franklin D. was President.

Granducci again repeated that he thought Davis would not remain very long because he could not afford to. The social demands and the costs of meeting them were too heavy. I asked him what opening he had, if any, on the outside. "Well," he said, "I do not mind telling you that he can go to Sears Roebuck any time and that, of course, is through [William I.] Westervelt.[1] Of course you understand where the tie up is." I said, "I suppose that goes right back to George Peek."

Late Wednesday afternoon (January 15) the Secretary asked me to

1. Brought into the Agricultural Adjustment Administration by George Peek; returned to Sears Roebuck & Co. after Peek's departure from the agency.

come over immediately after his press conference. He was buzzing around a good deal and after a while said, "Yes, it is in connection with the cotton matter. I wish you would push as quickly as possible the report you are making. That is the hottest thing we have in the picture." It appeared from the conversation that he was seriously thinking of the international cotton agreement to control cotton exports and, for the first time, he brought into the picture that in the report we are expected to develop a reference to the cropper and tenancy situation. He said that situation was very bad and admitted that the AAA program probably contributed to the unemployment. He referred to what Calvin [Hoover] had done[2] and also to [Frank] Tannenbaum of the Rosenwald Foundation[3] and asked me if I would not contact Hoover and work out the difficulty with him and work out an attack on that problem. Yesterday afternoon I had a visit with Hoover in my office and he then told me how a committee had been set up to investigate this matter. [D. P.] Trent[4] was chairman, [C. L.] Holmes was brought in, and apparently this was considered a very good line of attack which would actually get the facts. Trent and [Cully] Cobb[5] expressed fear that it would offend the landowners and lead to trouble and gradually weed out of the program all of the early moves, and when it was finally submitted to Hoover for his approval he flatly refused to have anything to do with it. It appeared to me that that probably killed the effort by that committee.

Hoover then told me that a committee had been appointed in the Agricultural Adjustment Administration to handle landlord-tenant relations. It appears that the croppers are getting only 1/9th of the benefit payments. Hoover went on to say there had been a veritable guerilla warfare in the Department which he sensed I knew about—on the one hand the local people, with whom he was in sympathy, were trying to get justice for the cropper and poor tenants, whereas the Cotton Division and others in the AAA were inclined to favor landlords' interests. He said the most recent episode grew out of the so-called Norcross Association of Arkansas. It seems the cropper tenants have organized a union and Norcross had dismissed 20 or 30 of his croppers who joined that union. The legal section of the AAA here in Washington took the position that Norcross had no right to dismiss under the contract. The Cotton Section takes the position that the landlord does not have to retain the same tenant although he must hold the same number of tenants. I

2. In a study of the effects of cotton acreage reduction on tenant farmers in the South.

3. Tannenbaum came to the AAA in December 1934 with the preliminary findings of a study sponsored by the Rosenwald Foundation which he had directed. The study indicated that tenancy was growing rapidly and that only federal relief had prevented mass starvation and rioting in rural areas of the South. See David Eugene Conrad, *The Forgotten Farmers* (Urbana, 1965), pp. 122-23.

4. Assistant director of the Commodities Division, AAA.

5. Chief of the Cotton Production Section, AAA.

merely cite these episodes to illustrate the kind of guerilla warfare that is going on within the ranks of the Department.[6]

February 16, 1935.

. . . The Secretary asked me, however, if I would not get [Frederick D.] Richey[7] and [W. A.] Jump and meet him at nine o'clock in his office. Richey was out of town and so [M. A.] McCall,[8] Jump and I met the Secretary at about 9:30, Feb. 7. The Secretary then told the story and illustrated his move by saying that he told [James P.] Buchanan that there are personnel differences that often arise administratively and they had to be handled, that he had just acted on one in the Agricultural Adjustment Administration and while he had the highest regard for Mr. [Jerome] Frank he had concluded that it was utterly impossible to function with Frank in the organization.[9] He went on to add that he had sought to place Frank in some other part of the Government. Jump spoke up and said he thought that was a good move because the situation was precarious and it would be very serious for the Department. . . .

During the three days of the hearings on the Agricultural Bill (Feb. 6, 7, and 8) Congressman Clarence Cannon (Mo.) was anything but friendly as the record will show and I had the impression that he was to a degree reflecting an arrangement with Buchanan on the matter. At any rate on the very last day, at the close of the hearing, I was told by Jump that Buchanan wanted to see me in his office. I went there and found Senator [Tom] Connally with Mr. W. D. Espy waiting for me. Buchanan at once broke in and, after the exchange of greetings, said that Mr. Espy was an important man in Texas, a friend of his and he wanted me to do everything I could do to find a position for him in the Bureau, that he had passed the examination, etc. I advised him that of course it would be dependent on having a vacancy into which Mr. Espy would fit. Buchanan said he would not write [Arthur W.] Palmer[10] under the circumstances and that he had some doubts about the wisdom of writing

6. For the impact of the Arkansas episode see Conrad (fn. 3), which examines the plight of sharecroppers in the New Deal, and Donald H. Grubbs, *Cry from the Cotton* (Chapel Hill, 1971), which examines the Southern Tenant Farmers Union and the New Deal. Hiram Norcross, a planter in Tyronza, Arkansas, removed all tenants who were members of the Southern Tenant Farmers Union after checking with the county agent as to whether such action would impair his cotton reduction contract with the AAA. He was assured it would not.

7. Chief of the Bureau of Plant Industry.

8. Assistant Chief of the Bureau of Plant Industry.

9. Frank was removed from his post as general counsel of the AAA and was quickly appointed a special counsel to the Reconstruction Finance Corporation. In 1937 he was appointed to the Securities and Exchange Commission. He was never removed from his post as general counsel to the Federal Surplus Relief Corporation, an emergency agency.

10. Chief of the Cotton Division, Bureau of Agricultural Economics.

me because of our differences. I replied that "there should be no reason, Mr. Buchanan, why you should not write me on this or any other matter which deals with mutual interests. I would deal with you in my usual direct, fair way on any matter that you wished to take up with me," and he laughed. Then Senator Connally spoke up and said he had been down to see me three or four days ago and that I was going to check with Palmer, and that Mr. Espy had reported that Mr. Palmer had tried to see me for three days and had been unable to reach me and I said that was the situation, that I had been before the House Appropriations Committee continuously for three days and all of my time was taken up with that. Buchanan laughed and said, "Yes, Congressman Cannon has had Olsen in tow for three days." The meeting broke up by my saying that I would be glad to review the matter personally and see just what the situation was for a possible opening for Mr. Espy. Mr. Espy later called and Senator Connally telephoned and I advised that there was not an opening for which he could be considered at this time. This episode in itself is a beautiful illustration of the high pressure that is brought to bear to force people into our regular bureaus, when the Chairman of the Appropriations Committee (House) at the close of a hot hearing on our appropriations, in cooperation with Senator Connally from the same State, and the candidate himself present, attempts to force the issue— then, I call that first rate pressure. . . .

April 9, 1935.

Friday noon, March 1, 1935, before the Ames, Ia., meeting at which the Land Grant College representatives were to be present to confer with AAA officials regarding a nationwide research project dealing with farm adjustments, M. L. Wilson[11] telephoned me at my apartment and told me he would like very much to have me make the rounds with the group at these four big meetings arranged for in several states. I told him that I had not heard about the meetings, that it was very short notice and much as I would like to join them I did not think it would be possible for me to make the trip. I said I would like to have [Eric] Englund or [C. L.] Holmes represent the Bureau if that was agreeable to him. He countered by saying, "No that would not be the same as having you." I replied that I would think it over and get in touch with him again.

The following morning I spoke to Englund about it and discovered that Englund had taken the initiative regarding these meetings and put M. L. Wilson on the spot for not having brought the Bureau into the picture. Wilson saw the incongruity of the thing and that accounted for his calling me. It was about the time I was planning to go West and I told Wilson I would attend the Ames meeting. I was not, however, a for-

11. Now Assistant Secretary of Agriculture.

mal member of the official party from Washington, that was made up of Wilson, [Howard] Tolley, [F. F.] Elliott,[12] James Jardine and [C. W.] Warburton. As a matter of fact, in order to avoid being drawn into the thing I took an earlier train. I was a little late arriving at the meeting and seated myself in the audience. Jardine and Warburton were up with the rest of the boys. In the course of the session, during an intermission, Wilson got in touch with me and said Warburton and Jardine were to make a brief talk and he would like to have me also speak briefly. I told him I should like to have something to say during the conference but in view of the fact that I was not oriented in this, I preferred my remarks to come later. So, in introducing Warburton and Jardine, Wilson referred to the fact that I was there and would be glad to have something to say later on. The conference was clearly "planted" to play up the AAA as the research agency to handle the farm management problem. Elliott expounded on the farm management material which our Division of Farm Management and Costs has been working on all these years and outlined the plan. In the discussion the State people asked about coordination of the project by some Washington agency and several said, "What about the Bureau of Agricultural Economics," and I was about to speak on such action when others called for the floor, so I postponed any statement until the evening session. At the very conclusion of the evening session they made a special introduction of me and I gave them about a thirty minute talk, in which I commented on the proposals and discussions and clearly indicated that the Bureau had a real contribution to make and that it would be prepared to cooperate in any way that it could, and that seemed desirable, in connection with the project, avoiding any reference to leadership by the Bureau. . . .

The situation at Ames evidently registered with various State people, because Jardine told Eric, on his return, that one of the directors asked if the Bureau and the AAA were not pulling together. On the other hand, Dean [H. W.] Mumford of Illinois, and I think another Dean, came around and said I had said exactly the right thing and that they wanted the Bureau brought right into this matter in a coordinating capacity. At the Salt Lake City meeting the State people stepped right out and said they wanted the Bureau leadership and wanted Bureau men to handle the projects. The same thing was done at the Birmingham meeting and also at the New York meeting. In other words, the plan that was projected of shoving the Bureau out of the picture went by the boards. Following the meeting M. L. Wilson came over to see me regarding three things. He wanted Holmes to serve on the departmental committee on Subsistence Homestead Research. He said that the Reedsville [West Virginia] project was to be the National Experiment Station and that they were going to test out the possibilities on that project. I said that would be quite agreeable and that was disposed of. Then he spoke

12. Now Chief of the Division on Production Planning in the AAA.

of Land Economics and said the Bureau had done a lot of fundamental research work in handling the whole program, that [L. C.] Gray had done fine work in handling the Land Acquisition work but that the fundamental research work had evidently been dropped. This, he said, was serious and he wanted to discuss with me the possibilities of building up the Bureau's research work in land economics. I told him rather frankly that I did not know what was going on in that field now. The dual arrangement had divorced me from knowing what was going on, that I had an appropriation of $90,000 to $95,000 but that I realized that most of that was going to men devoting their time to the action program. I told him I agreed that the Bureau should continue and expand its research program. I said that of course if the funds we now have were put to use for research purposes that would enable us to go quite a little distance and I expressed the thought that the AAA should reimburse us for the money going into the AAA program. Wilson thought we ought to try to bolster up the appropriations and I said I would be glad to consider that.

Then we got into a discussion of this new big farm management project and he talked about the overhead and I shook that down and said I thought we needed a small committee made up of Tolley, Jardine and perhaps Englund, an operating committee made up of Holmes and Elliott and he very frankly said Holmes had a good mind, had written a good book,[13] was ultra-conservative, laissez faire and did not believe in planning. I told him I thought he was wrong in his opinion of Holmes, but we did not finish the conversation because of my meeting and speaking to the Agricultural Editors who were in session in the Department. Later on I went over to Wilson's office and he asked if the arrangements that had been made were satisfactory. I said I had understood that Tolley, Jardine and Englund had worked it out and that it was now set up in such a way as to give the Bureau, the Division and Dr. Holmes the recognition they deserved and should have in the project.

At one of the recent Chiefs' meetings, Wilson, Tolley, Warburton and Jardine reported on the four meetings that were held. The story of what took place, and the fine reactions of the institutions was all developed and the Secretary nodded his head and seemed to give complete acquiescence to the setup of the project. The really striking thing was my presence at the Ames meeting, Englund's presence at the Birmingham and Cornell meetings, and the Bureau's part in the project was not mentioned and no call made on us for any reaction, in fact it was a patent oversight or slip.

Monday morning, April 8, I went up to see Dr. A. G. Black[14] and as I stepped in I said, "Congratulations," and he said, "Congratulations." I said, "A.G., you have a wonderful institution and a wonderful personnel." He said, "I know it, the Bureau has really won for itself a

13. *Economics of Farm Organization and Management* (Boston, 1928).
14. Chief of the Corn and Hog Section of the AAA who succeeded Olsen as chief of the Bureau of Agricultural Economics.

remarkable place," and I picked that up at once and said I had always felt it should be an objective, analytical organization and should not be embroiled with action bodies in such a way as to imperil itself. With this he expressed agreement. He called attention to the direct marketing study as an outstanding contribution of the Bureau's independence and virility of thought for which it stood. I told him that he would have the fine loyalty and support of the personnel and that he would find it a joy to work with it and I said I knew he would find his associates in the Chief's Office exceedingly helpful in every way and while he did not express himself, as I recall it, definitely he did say that he was sure that was the case, that he realized that as a new man he would be under suspicion but he hoped that he would be able to eliminate that.

April 10, 1935.

About two weeks ago (March 26, 1935, at 3:15 p.m.) I asked for an appointment with the Secretary and it was arranged for. As I stepped into his office he was smiling and it was "Hello Nils" and "Hello H.A." and I then said that I had a matter which was of a very personal nature and which I hoped he would regard at present stage in a purely confidential manner, since it appeared that would be the best way of handling. I then told him, bluntly, that I had received an offer from the Equitable Life Assurance Society of the United States, that it looked like a real opportunity to do constructive service that kept me close to agriculture and that I had therefore decided to accept. It was a very brief statement that I made and the response was marked by "silence." He looked at me, did not say anything to begin with and then began to ask questions. "Are there any other advantages that you see in it?" I said I had not really analyzed it carefully to sense all the possibilities but I realized that it was not going to divorce me from research interests which would always be with me and he asked one or two more questions of that kind which I ducked but it was apparent to me that what he was sensing in my going was a reaction against something within the Department and probably more definitely my relations with him. The conversation was exceedingly halting since he seemed to be rather speechless and I was not disposed to say too much. After a rather painful pause I asked him if he had any thoughts as to my successor. "No" he said he did not. He said, "Do you?" I replied, "I naturally have given it some thought because the selection of a successor is so important and because of my deep interest in the Bureau and its work and naturally one would first think of the prospects within the organization and no one could know [C. W.] Kitchen[15] and his work without thinking of him first. I said he was a man of very real ability,

15. An Assistant Chief of the Bureau of Agricultural Economics.

fine judgment, a good administrator, well liked by the organization and he would in my judgment make a very good chief and that the one question that might be raised would be whether or not he stood out as an economist. He of course had no formal training but had done a lot of thinking and reading and I found him exceedingly helpful in appraising the research output of the Bureau. The Secretary remarked that he had heard nothing but the very best things about Kitchen and evidently he was a very able man. I continued, "One would naturally think of [Eric] Englund but Englund in my judgment did not have the qualities of an administrator that Kitchen has." The Secretary spoke up right away and said, "Oh, yes that would not do." Then I said naturally, "You would think of people outside of the Bureau and in that connection the names of [Jesse W.] Tapp and [Howard R.] Tolley occur." Of the two Tapp seemed to me to have most of the qualifications of a good administrator for the Bureau, he had a good mind, good training, had come up through the Bureau under H. C. Taylor,[16] he had devoted a lot of time to marketing and research activities which are so prominent in the Bureau. "He has good personality, appears before groups well, is a good fighter and, all in all, in my judgment would made a very good chief and would be so considered by the Bureau organization." I went on to say that Tolley has a great deal of ability. His interests lay more in the research field. I have not been impressed with the fact that he has the qualities of an outstanding administrator, his personality is not good and he does not make as effective appearance before committees as some men make. So, as between the two, it seemed that Tapp would be the better selection. The Secretary's answer was, "The trouble is with both Tolley and Tapp, they are so vital to Chester Davis and to the AAA program it would be a serious matter to take them out." I said that was true but that the Bureau was one of the greatest considerations and that some sacrifice would seem called for in the situation. The Secretary did not seem disposed to follow the discussion any further and I dried up and said, "Well, H.A., let us just leave this then for a day or two. Think about it and if you wish to see me again I shall be glad to come over and see you some more." He replied, "All right Nils, we will hold this tight," and he let it go at that. Before saying that, he said, "I suppose it will be desirable for me to discuss this with a few and, for example, Rex [Tugwell]."[17] I countered at once and said, "Why, H.A., that is for you to decide but it would seem that it might be better for you to withhold it from Rex and rather discuss it with M. L. Wilson and Chester Davis." He said, "Well, do you have in mind that Rex would be operating on it?" I replied, "I think you know Rex as well as I do and I had understood that Calvin Hoover was slated for consideration as my successor some time ago."

16. First Chief of the Bureau of Agricultural Economics, 1922–25.
17. Now Under Secretary of Agriculture.

Prior to actually breaking the news to the Secretary I had Tapp come over to my apartment and spend an evening with me. I gave him the story. He was disturbed and asked if I could not change my decision. I told him no that the die was cast. Of course he was highly pleased at my suggestion that he be the Chief and he was quite flustered throughout the evening. The question of how to handle it was important. I asked if Tolley should be considered and he said no, Chester [Davis] depended on him so much and if Chester went out, and he thought he would by the end of the year, Tolley would be the natural successor and he was sure Tolley would back him. We worked out the technique that I was to see Chester as he had gone South and after considering the matter we planned to have Tapp call Chester on the long distance phone and tell him but Tapp backed away from that and I backed away too. I thought the thing to do was to tell the Secretary to handle it in his own way without any influence being brought to bear.

I agreed that Tapp should tell Tolley. At one of the early meetings in my office Tapp told me he had done so and that Tolley had indicated that he would do everything that he could. As a matter of fact, Tapp leaked this very significant remark which Tolley made to him that he (Tolley) had told the Secretary six months ago that Tapp was the logical man to succeed me. I was rather dumbfounded and Tapp sensed too that it was a rather ticklish thing but in his fine honesty he let it out as evidence of the fact that Tolley was strongly behind him. That very same evening Tapp called me at the house and in a rather embarrassed way said he had been thinking some more about Tolley's remarks and the only way he could figure it out was when Rex and Appleby returned from the foreign trip they had reached the conclusion that the headship of this Bureau must be changed and had spoken to the Secretary about it and it was in that connection that Tolley had said to the Secretary that Tapp was the logical man to head the Bureau. This, of course, is of a piece with Tolley's attitude for years—in fact, ever since he left the Bureau. I find on going to the conferences at the Secretary's Office when Tolley comes in he assiduously avoids greeting me but I go out of my way to say "Hello Howard" and exchange a few remarks with him.

The Secretary evidently said nothing to Tolley or Wilson about my going but it seems clear that he went ahead on his own individual track and appointed Al Black primarily because he is a close personal friend of his and also because he would be sympathetic with his general policies.

In visiting with Chester Davis yesterday (April 11) at lunch at his invitation, Chester expressed surprise and chagrin at my leaving but stated he thought perhaps I had made a very fine decision and indicated that as far as he was concerned he did not expect to be a slave of the public indefinitely either, but in speaking of my successor he said that Tolley had called him at Memphis about some AAA matters and also told him that

I had resigned and that the question of my successor was up and suggested that Davis meet the Secretary at Chicago. Chester and H.A. evidently talked over the appointment of a Chief and in that connection Chester remarked that Black was a very able man, was sold on the Bureau, and all were of the opinion that the Bureau should be maintained as a fine institution it had been and that he (Black) could be spared because Mr. [Claude] Wickard, his assistant chief, had done a splendid job of backing him up and carrying the load and Jerry Thorne[18] with all of his ability too was there to take over the things. So, they could spare Al. Davis said he knew Tapp had been mentioned but it would be very serious from the AAA point of view to spare Tapp. He said he wondered if I realize all the responsibility that had been placed on Tapp in the reorganization. I told him probably I had not. But Davis' remarks indicated that after all Tapp was cheated out of the Chiefship of the Bureau because of the superior demands of AAA.

April 12, 1935.

The Secretary did not call me back in two or three days as was suggested to discuss further my successor and it was not until last Saturday, April 6, he called me in and then very briefly told me he had picked Al Black as my successor. I of course had known it in advance through other channels. I made no comment but said that I would be glad to help in every way that I could in the transition of Dr. Black. I brought up the question of unused annual leave and he said he thought every effort should be made to arrange to pay me for that period. At that time he called in Dr. [W. W.] Stockberger and [Milton S.] Eisenhower and broke the news and Eisenhower evidently had heard nothing about it, while Stockberger evidently was familiar with the development. The Secretary suggested that Eisenhower, Black and I get together on a release covering the shift and they had in mind putting it out Saturday. I asked if it could not be postponed until the following week because of certain social engagements and the Secretary said that would be all right. The first thing Monday morning, April 8, it developed that a leak on the shift had developed from President [R. M.] Hughes of Ames and the press boys began hounding Eisenhower and, later, myself. I rather urged putting it off until Tuesday in order that I might have my address to the marketing officials out of the way, but in the afternoon of Monday Eisenhower got in touch with Miss [Grace] Leonard and told her the Secretary thought the release should go out right away and then a few minutes later I met the Secretary in the outer room and he thought it very wise to put it out

18. Now Director of the Division of Marketing Agreements and Licenses, AAA.

without delay. Eisenhower had called Miss Leonard before contacting me stating that the Secretary thought the release should go forward, that holding it up was giving the impression that Mr. Olsen was being forced out whereas the fact was that he was accepting a "darn good job." Miss L. asked him to contact me at M. L. Wilson's office before releasing it, which he did.

In my conversation with the Secretary I mentioned postponing the release until Tuesday on account of the Marketing Officials meeting. He said he did not think that would make any difference and he would like to put it out at once. I said, "Fine, put it out." I then returned to my office and called the Division leaders together at 3:15 p.m. I broke the news and of course there was surprise and expressed feeling of concern. The press has been exceedingly fine in that they have not pressed me at all, since the announcement, as to my reason for leaving but in calling on the Secretary in connection with one or two Bureau matters, April 10, he told me that the press was trying to make out that there was a rift between him and myself and that he had stated at the press conference that there was nothing of the kind. That accounts for the letter addressed to me and which was put out as a press release before I got the original copy of the letter from the Secretary. While it is not a letter of particular commendation, it does contrast with the perfectly bland initial announcement that was issued. In reply to the Secretary I merely said, "Well that is interesting. The press has not bothered me at all in connection with the matter. The only time they sought me out was just before the issuance of the original announcement when they wanted to confirm a rumor," and that was all I said. . . .

Eisenhower in coming over to speak to me about the matter said he was not only shocked and surprised but, at the same time, he could not really blame me for accepting an offer of that kind. He went on to add that he, himself, had an offer of a position with one of the large universities as Finance Officer and at one thousand dollars more than he was getting here. He said it tempted him sorely. He spoke to the Secretary about it and his comment was that he questioned whether he would be happy in that work. That contrasts with my procedure in conferring with him and also with the reaction which the Secretary gave when I told him of my decision. There was no expression of regret in either case. The day of the announcement Eisenhower further told me that he rode over to the radio station with the Secretary and the Secretary had made the comment that he liked me personally very much. But Eisenhower went on to remark that the Secretary was a funny fellow. He said that there were times when he really felt so aggrieved that he was disposed to resign and he cited a document which he had prepared at the Secretary's request, at a great deal of pain, and which the Secretary merely glanced over and on which he had no comment to make. Later on the Secretary had occasion to refer to and discuss the document and showed that he had gotten the full significance of the story. This he cited to demonstrate the Secretary's reactions. Eisenhower also commented that the "Department was not what it used to be."

O. E. Reed[19] telephoned me at my home as soon as he heard about the matter and expressed the deepest sorrow and concern. He remarked that it was a pity that a man who had stood out as one who had convictions and dared to express them was leaving the Department when it so sorely needed a leadership of that kind. He said, "I am one of the last three or four of the old fellows and it remains to be seen now what happens. He had previously told me that [Wilber Andrew] Cochel[20] of Kansas City had remarked, following the meeting of the Agricultural Editors here last month, that there was only one man who gave anything substantial, realistic and worthwhile at their meetings and that was Olsen and he had also met an important man, whose name I have forgotten, who said he wanted to meet that man Olsen and discuss with him cotton and other things as evidently he was a man who was thinking about things that were going on and evidently had nerve enough to state his convictions. This man went so far as to ask Reed if he thought there would be any difficulty in getting an appointment with me in order to go over matters. I merely note this as illustrative of how people throughout the country are looking for expressions of independent thinking and backbone here at Washington to offset the flow of one-sided propaganda that has underlaid the whole New Deal program.

Dr. [F. D.] Richey came in yesterday and was quite emotional and right off said that he was terribly sorry, that he had come to realize that I was a man with whom he could work and liked to work in a real daring way. He said he did not blame me for accepting this offer and he went on to comment on the way things were being handled. It was shortly following the announcement of transfer of certain fruit and vegetable utilization work to the Bureau of Chemistry and Soils, he said he was called in an hour before the announcement by Tugwell and told this was a decision in the making. He then got busy and protested vigorously with Tugwell but the stage was set and it went through. . . .

Yesterday (April 11) when I called on Dr. [Henry G.] Knight[21] I had very much the same sort of story. Knight had telephoned me previously and expressed deep concern that I was leaving and that same concern has been expressed by all whom I have met, indicating that there is an undercurrent of concern for the Department and I presume also the positions which individual men hold within the Department. Dr. Knight gave this very interesting comment, that he thought as far as his Bureau was concerned the tide had turned. Shortly after the new Administration came in they proceeded to tear his Bureau apart and he was somewhat disposed

19. Chief of the Bureau of Dairy Industry.
20. A rancher and editor of the weekly *Kansas City Star*.
21. Chief of the Bureau of Chemistry and Soils.

to blame the committee on reorganization which Wallace appointed shortly after he came in. Knight called attention to the fact that Wallace had three friends on that Committee, [C. W.] Warburton, [J. R.] Mohler,[22] and I forget the third. . . . Now, Knight says, the Secretary has realized he has made a mistake and he has set out to rebuild the Bureau of Chemistry and the retransfer of the fruit work and some other things to his Bureau he cited as evidence of that fact.

Miss [Claribel R.] Barnett[23] met me in the halls today and was quite upset about it. She stressed the fact that I had shown such appreciation of library work and she was afraid other chiefs would not sustain that interest. It was an interesting bit in view of her earlier unsuccessful attempt to take the Bureau's library away from us, an effort which she made in cooperation with Tugwell.

The Meeting of the Atlantic States Division of the National Association of Marketing Officials was held last Tuesday at the Harrington Hotel. They were most cordial. I came in while Dr. [F. V.] Waugh was speaking and several of the members came over and bemoaned the fact that I was leaving, that it was putting them in a very difficult position because so many of their services tied in with our work. They said they could work with me and did not feel too optimistic about my successor. I told them not to feel that way, that everything was going to go along fine. In introducing me, Mr. [F. T.] Birdsall made a very cordial statement regarding my work, etc., and after my talk, which was quite vigorous and reasonably daring, a number of them came up to me and said, "We already sense that you are going to be a real influence on the outside, which we need very much." Kitchen told me, afterwards, that they had drafted, contrary to the rules under which they operate, a resolution covering my services and my going.

April 15, 1935.

Mr. George N. Peek joined me at luncheon at the Cosmos Club last Friday, April 12, and we had a very frank talk regarding the situation. He thought I was making a very good move and congratulated me on it. He also said he thought the Company was using very good judgment in acquiring a man like me. I think one of the things that rather pleased him about it was that it would give H.A. a little difficulty. That seemed to be apparent from the discussions we had of the cotton situation and the harassed position in which the Secretary finds himself. On the cotton situation Peek thought the Senate boys, and particularly Senator [Robert R.] Reynolds and Senator [Charles L.] McNary, were going to go the full

22. Chief of the Bureau of Animal Industry.
23. Librarian in the Department of Agriculture.

limit to put the present program on the spot. It is very apparent that Peek is completely out of sympathy with the present program and that he feels the sting of the experience he had with the Secretary a couple of years ago. . . .

[Theodore C.] Alford of the "Kansas City Star" met me on the street and congratulated me on getting out of the Government and into a position of the kind I am to take. He said the prospect looked fine. He went on to say, "The thing that surprises me is that you could stand it as long as you have. Some of my people at Kansas City inquired if the heat from the Direct Marketing report had caused your resignation." I laughed and told him that was one of the greatest parties I had had around here and that I enjoyed it immensely. . . .

INDEX